26

COMIC RELIEF

COMIC RELIEF

The Life and Laughter
of ARTEMUS WARD,
1834–1867

John J. Pullen

ARCHON BOOKS

1983

Printed in the United States of America

Library of Congress Cataloging in Publication Data

Pullen, John J.
    Comic relief.

    Bibliography: p.
    Includes index.
    1. Ward, Artemus, 1834-1867.   2. Authors, American—
19th century—Biography.   3. Humorists, American—
Biography.   I. Title.
PS1143.P84   1983   818'.309[B]   83-10008
ISBN 0-208-02014-4

Excerpts from *Artemus Ward*, by Don C. Seitz,
copyright 1919 by Harper & Row, Publishers, Inc.,
renewed 1947 by Mildred Seitz and Mabel S. Geibel,
reprinted by permission of the publisher.

"The Two Vaults," by Walt Whitman, from *The
Uncollected Poetry and Prose of Walt Whitman,*
edited by Emory Holloway, copyright 1921 by Emory
Holloway. Reprinted by permission of Doubleday &
Company, Inc.

Excerpts from *My Mark Twain* and *Years of My
Youth,* by W. D. Howells, copyrighted in 1910 and
1916 by Harper & Brothers Publishers, renewed by
John Mead Howells and Mildred Howells, reprinted
by permission of William White Howells.

The author thanks the *Saturday Review* for return of
copyright on a portion of this work that appeared in
its February 7, 1976, issue as "Artemus Ward: The
Man Who Made Lincoln Laugh." Another portion of
this book appeared as "Mark Twain and Artemus
Ward: A Bittersweet Friendship Is Born in Nevada"
in the *Nevada Historical Society Quarterly;* it was
copyrighted in the author's name in 1981 with the
Quarterly's appreciated cooperation.

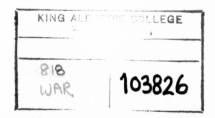

In memory of Jean

Contents

Acknowledgments

Margaret M. Sawyer, of Waterford, Maine, a lifelong Artemus Ward enthusiast, has been an especially good friend of this book, performing research, typing, and a host of other helpful services. Richard Balkin, literary agent and author of that fine book *A Writer's Guide to Book Publishing,* has personally guided *me* with wisdom, encouragement, and endless patience. Others who have helped in ways too numerous and various to detail include the late Flora G. Abbott, Muriel Baker, Ernest W. Chard, Howard L. Davis, Flint O. DuPre, David L. Eynon, John E. Frazer, John W. Garberson, my sister Hope Gillmor, the late Henrietta Gray, Jeffrey S. Harwood, John P. Heffernan, Ruth H. Latamore, the late Ernest C. Marriner, Maj. Gen. S. B. Mason (Ret.), Moria Lockwood Mason, Arthur Monke, my sisters Olive Palmer and Ruth Pullen, Dana, Gary, and Laurence Rounds, Ruth E. Rounds, Dwight E. Sargent, Jeanne Simpson, Lauren K. Soth, George Stevens, and Dwight C. Van Meter. As always, my wife, the late Jean A. Pullen, loyally sustained me through the ups and downs. This book has been under preparation for so long—more than fifteen years, off and on—that I fear there are others of importance I have temporarily forgotten; if so, I deeply regret it and invite them to write and scold me for the lapse. There is one class of people for whom enough can never be said: these are the librarians from coast to coast who always seem ready to help an inquiring author whether she or he lives within their "jurisdiction" or not. To the many librarians who have been of great assistance to me, I am profoundly grateful.

The Man
Who Made Lincoln Laugh

On the morning of September 22, 1862, clouds of depression which had drifted from the battlefield of Antietam were still hanging in the humid air over Washington when members of Abraham Lincoln's cabinet received word that the president wanted to see them at twelve o'clock. Entering a White House meeting-room at noon, they found Lincoln sitting by the table reading a little book; his gaunt, bearded face, which had been somber since the battle, was now relaxed, and the president was chuckling to himself. When the cabinet had assembled, Lincoln looked up and said, "'Gentlemen, have you ever read anything by Artemus Ward?'"

Of course they had. People all over the country were laughing at the letters that Artemus Ward, a semiliterate old man with a traveling sideshow, was writing to the newspapers—letters that had also appeared in New York's *Vanity Fair* and, finally, had been collected in the book Lincoln was reading.

Some of the cabinet members may even have known that the Old Showman was a product of the imagination—that the letters were actually fictions created by a young newspaperman, Charles Farrar Brown, who, while writing a regular column for the *Cleveland Daily Plain Dealer,* had conceived the idea of these misspelled missives describing Artemus Ward's adventures in various towns and cities with his exhibition of "wild beests, snaiks and wax figgers."

But for the president of the United States to be reading a funny book at a time like this!—when only five days previously the dead had lain in dark windrows in the fields along Antietam Creek; and when grief for the killed and wounded was still lying heavy on more than 25,000 homes; and when it now seemed that all this bloodshed had been for nothing, because the battle had been a standoff, and the war was no nearer its longed-for conclusion than it ever had been.

The cabinet members could be pardoned for looking blank. After all, these were tragic times, and presumably the meeting had been called to consider serious business.

"'Let me read you a chapter that is very funny,'" the president said; he then read from *Artemus Ward, His Book* this story, entitled "High Handed Outrage at Utica."

In the Faul of 1856, I showed my show in Utiky, a trooly grate sitty in the State of New York.

The people gave me a cordyal recepshun. The press was loud in her prases.

1 day as I was givin a descripshun of my Beests and Snaiks in my usual flowry stile what was my skorn & disgust to see a big burly feller walk up to the cage containin my wax figgers of the Lord's Last Supper, and cease Judas Iscarrot by the feet and drag him out on the ground. He then commenced fur to pound him as hard as he cood.

"What under the son are you abowt?" cried I.

Sez he, "What did you bring this pussylanermus cuss here fur?" & he hit the wax figger another tremenjis blow on the hed.

Sez I, "You egrejus ass, that air's a wax figger—a representashun of the false 'Postle."

Sez he, "That's all very well fur you to say but I tell you, old man, that Judas Iscarrot can't show hisself in Utiky with impunerty by a darn site!" with which observashun he kaved in Judassis hed. The young man belonged to 1 of the first famerlies in Utiky. I sood him, and the Joory brawt in a verdick of Arson in the 3d degree.

Having finished this yarn the president laughed heartily, and some of his enjoyment seemed to be shared by his cabinet—by all, that is, except Edwin M. Stanton, the secretary of war. Stanton said later that he was angered at what seemed to be pure buffoonery, and he thought for a moment of walking out of the room. But then Lincoln put the book down, sighed deeply, and said, as if in apology, "'Gentlemen . . . with the fearful strain that is upon me night and day, if I did not laugh I should die, and you need this medicine as much as I do.'" Next, proceeding to the business of the meeting, he took up a paper from the table and read it to the cabinet. It was the Emancipation Proclamation.

At this, Stanton's attitude changed. As he remembered it, "'With great enthusiasm I arose, approached the President, extended my hand and said: "Mr. President, if reading the chapters of Artemus Ward is a prelude to a deed such as this, the book should be filed among the archives of the nation and its author should be canonized."[1]

At odd moments, Lincoln continued to derive recreation from the Old Showman. After the disastrous battle of Fredericksburg, Congressman Isaac N. Arnold, of Illinois, calling at the president's office, found him again reading *Artemus Ward, His Book.* Arnold was oppressed by the toll the battle had taken—10,000 or so Northern compared with around 5,000 Southern casualties—and he could not help an expression of shock. Noticing it, Lincoln told him what he had told the cabinet: that if he could not find momentary relief from the crushing burdens of the conflict, his heart would break. He continued to dip into the book throughout the war and was turning to it even when victory approached. As the forces of Grant followed those of Lee toward their final rendezvous at Appomattox, something about the pursuit reminded Lincoln of an Artemus Ward story, and he recited the yarn: a ridiculous tale about a canal boat called the *Sary Jane* that was chased by a pirate craft along the Wabash Canal. (The *Sary Jane* escaped through the stratagem of scattering oats along the canal path; the mules who were hauling the pirate ship stopped to eat the oats while the *Sary Jane* drew ahead and out of danger.)

Lincoln was undoubtedly familiar with Artemus Ward long before he became president. During the 1860 presidential campaign, he may even have been secretly amused by some of the comments made by Artemus Ward's creator, Charles Brown, in his own right. At that time, Brown was city editor of the *Cleveland Daily Plain Dealer,* and the *Plain Dealer,* which claimed to have the largest circulation of any Democratic paper in the country, was supporting Stephen A. Douglas, the Northern Democratic candidate. Lincoln's personal part in this campaign was modest in the extreme. He simply stayed at home in Springfield, Illinois, receiving visitors and writing letters. However, this is not to say that

---

Note: The copy of the book from which Lincoln read, sent to him and autographed by Artemus Ward, reposes not in the National Archives but in the Beinecke Rare Book and Manuscript Library, at Yale.

Republican politicians were not active in his behalf or that political flimflammery was not at its customary height. Republican propaganda portrayed Lincoln as a poor but honest rail-splitter, and there was great traffic in the rails he had supposedly produced. These were carried by marching clubs, displayed at rallies, and used as general campaign symbols. One Republican newspaper described a rail on exhibit in Chicago as one of "The three thousand split by 'honest Old Abe' thirty years ago on the Sangamon River bottoms."[2]

To young Charles Brown, it seemed proper to observe that Lincoln must have been frantically busy to have split all those rails. Brown, in addition to carrying out his editorial duties, wrote a daily column entitled "City Facts and Fancies," and one of the "Fancies" he composed was a story about a trip that the Official Committee, chosen to notify Lincoln of his nomination, made to Springfield. This group had found him splitting rails out in the woods, the story said, and it went on: "There stood Honest Old Abe in his shirt sleeves, a pair of homemade leather suspenders holding up a pair of homemade pantaloons .... 'Mr. Lincoln, Sir, you've been nominated, Sir, for the highest office, Sir,—' 'Oh, don't bother me,' said Honest Old Abe. 'I took a stent this mornin' to split 3 million rails afore night, and I don't want to be pestered with no stuff about no Conventions till I get my stent done."[3]

A few weeks later a letter from Charles Hanks, Lincoln's cousin, appeared in the regular columns of the *Plain Dealer*, probably by Brown's choice. In the letter Hanks said, "I lived within two miles of the Lincoln farm from the time it was settled up to 1857, and during these early times our farms were subject to being wasted by devastating fires, and I know the fence around the Lincoln farm was consumed at least three times. And I know that after the Lincoln family had left the farm... the fence was again burned. ... I think, and I am almost certain, that the rails that are being worshipped all over the North as Lincoln rails, were made by poor Bill Strickland, who is now poor, blind, helpless, and in the Macon County poorhouse. And if these philanthropic Republicans would allow me to make one suggestion, it would be to help poor Bill Strickland, who really did make the rails, and who is as honest as Abe or anybody else."[4]

The *Plain Dealer*, in addition to supporting Stephen A. Douglas in its regular editions, issued a weekly specifically aimed at promoting the Douglas candidacy. It was called the *Campaign Plain Dealer and Popular Sovereignty Advocate*. Brown was also associate editor of this publication, which by July of 1860 was running 40,000 copies a week. It is fairly certain that Brown admired Lincoln as a man, so it is understandable that the *Campaign Plain Dealer* was never particularly hard on the Republican candidate personally. There was nothing much worse than a mention of the Black Hawk War with reference to Lincoln's admitted homeliness: "The Indians, when they came to see his face, gave one whoop and surrendered."[5] Political cartoons were printed, but the cartoonist was so bad that he defeated his own purpose; his caricatures were hardly recognizable as Abraham Lincoln or any other known human being. Rather than attacking Lincoln personally, the *Plain Dealer* concentrated on the unwisdom of electing a man whose inauguration would instantly move the country off the basis of rational discussion, however shaky, that it still maintained, and into the madness and slaughter of war.

In an Artemus Ward letter published in the interim between Lincoln's election and inauguration, the Old Showman tells about a visit to "Old Abe Linkin" at his home in Springfield. Here he finds him being overwhelmed by office seekers who are coming in the doors, through the windows, and down the chimney, one even upsetting Lincoln by crawling between his legs "for the purpuss af applyin for the tollgateship at Milwawky." Artemus drives this troublesome crowd away by threatening to open his cages and let the "wild beests of pray" loose among them—thus winning the friendship of Lincoln and demonstrating his own.[6] It was significant that Brown, who had so firmly opposed Lincoln's election, should so soon send the Old Showman to his support; it was significant also that he should portray kindly a president whose crudities made him the natural butt of so many humorists and would-be humorists. In disposition and intellect, Abraham Lincoln and Charles Brown had much in common. Both had come from a rural or backwoods origin and had experienced early tragedy and hard times. Both were self-educated, but men of considerable intellectual depth. Both were very much part of an era in which American talents were beginning to flourish on the frontier. Of course, Brown had been born in Maine, but he was what his young friend and fellow newspaperman in Ohio, W. D. Howells, once called "a Westernized Yankee." Said Howells, "He added an Ohio way of talking to the Maine way of thinking, and he so became a literary product of a rarer and stranger sort than our literature had otherwise known."[7] In Maine, after his father died, Brown had been put out by his mother at the age of thirteen to be an apprentice printer. After he became a journeyman, he worked his way from printshop to printshop and from type case to editorial desk, and had joined the *Plain Dealer* at the age of twenty-three. In the process he had been knocked around a bit, and while preserving his good nature he had also developed a pronounced wariness toward self-appointed authorities of every kind. At the time, the country was being swept by a wave of intense moralistic effort, and in some of his *Plain Dealer* columns Brown dealt directly with moral dictators. Among the targets of these crusaders were certain books, and not only books but authors who were considered to be "immoral," even though their writings were otherwise unobjectionable. One of the most pathetic victims was Edgar Allan Poe, a hardworking genius whose drinking and other failings led him to a miserable death in Baltimore, where he lay in a grave that remained unmarked for years. Through a continuation of the bad luck that had haunted him through life, Poe's literary executor turned out to be a moralist of the most virulent stripe, the Reverend Rufus W. Griswold. This clergyman saw in Poe's unhappy life and sad end a chance to hold up an example for the multitudes. In order to make the lesson more convincing, he altered certain letters written by or to Poe. He then wrote a newspaper article and a biography portraying Poe as immoral, dishonest, and so on. Taken at face value by other writers, these did immense harm to Poe's reputation.

Brown saw in the *Philadelphia Ledger* a derogatory article about Poe by one of these writers and reacted with blazing indignation in his *Plain Dealer* column of March 6, 1858. In this column he also lambasted Griswold. Although he could not have known about the clergyman's forgeries in handling the Poe correspondence (the full extent of which would only be revealed by twentieth-century scholarship), he branded Griswold's biography of Poe as a production probably unequaled in the history of letters for fiendish malignancy. As for Poe, he wrote, "no stone marks the spot where Poe sleeps and no kindly hand strews flowers upon his grave in summertime; but meantime thousands all over the world will admire his wildly beautiful pages until the end of time."

In his column of November 15, 1858, Brown again criticized a *Ledger* writer. This one had implied that people of good morals were those who read good books, and that ungodliness was principally confined to the uneducated. Brown classed this as "the most exquisite nonsense." On another occasion Brown defended a publication put out by a colony of adherents to the doctrine of free love, then established at nearby Berlin Heights, against censorial attack. "The articles," he said, "are excessively stupid, approximately idiotic, in fact, but they will scarcely damage the morals of any community."

In the *Plain Dealer* of February 3, 1859, Brown even went so far as to discuss the authority of the pulpit. It seems that a Cleveland minister had "hurled powerful and thundering anathemas" against the spiritualists. Brown said that he offered no brief for spiritualism, but he had to point out that anyone whose creed depended on a belief in supernatural events was on very shaky ground when he attacked spiritualists. In the same piece he expressed a doubt that literal interpretations of the Bible are always valid, pointing at their occasional inconsistencies, and going on to declare that "these contradictions are too palpable, and only teach that man, God's own incarnate image, was never meant to trust in Prophets, Priests, Soothsayers, Apostles, nor in Angels even as infallible guides, only as phenomenon and fact harmonize with the Jove within the individual soul. . . . The world is beginning to learn that God does not dwell merely in 'temples made with hands,' at whose altars a few chosen hierophants administer. . . but in every human heart." The real enemy of mankind, as Brown saw it, was plain old humbug, usually preceded by "Thus saith the Lord" or "Thus saith the Expert"—his skepticism was not confined to the pulpit alone—or "Thus saith" something other than one's own God-given intelligence.

Brown's running battle with moral and other tyrants was carried over into his creation of Artemus Ward, the Old Showman, where it was much more effective because Artemus was a work of art—a figure who himself mirrored the follies and foibles of our imperfect society and thus was the vehicle of a criticism that had a humanity, a good-natured acceptance, and an enduring life that no mere expression of editorial opinion could ever achieve. It was also effective because Artemus was directly concerned with another prime target of the moralists, show business. Supreme in this business, for wickedness, was the theater, and all sort of expedients often had to be resorted to in order to stage a theatrical production in some places. Even a menagerie had to present a moral lesson. This could be done in spite of its obvious difficulties, and done well, as it was in an advertisement for Van Amburgh & Company's Mammoth Menagerie, Great Moral Exhibition and Egyptian Caravan. This pointed out that there was nothing like a wild beast show for "yielding innumerable subjects for both moral and religious study. Its chief tendency ought to be to lead us from an admiration of the works to the contemplation of their author, to teach us to look through nature up to nature's God."[8] Thus, entertainments of many kinds were presented not as providing needed recreation but as representating the acts of great and virtuous men, or as elevating the tastes of the republic, or as schooling people in manners and deportment, or as aiding the church, college, and public library as a moral influence—as anything but a means of relaxation and enjoyment.

Artemus Ward's adventures with his tent show, which he was

always careful to describe as "a grate Moral Entertainment," symbolized delightfully this sort of moral tyranny and the timidity with which it was borne in America. Whether or not Brown was referring to unbridled moralists when he termed Ward's wild animals "beests of pray" is anybody's guess. Undoubtedly, however, he had one of these self-appointed clean-up men in mind when he wrote the story about the fellow who smashed up the wax figure of Judas Iscariot and told Artemus to keep it out of Utica. Ridicule like this is gentle but devastating; where it exists, hand-tailored halos of authority soon find their way to the ash can. And although Artemus Ward was created primarily to entertain people, it is clear that Brown was aware of his deeper values, for he once said of humorists in general that "'the truth has found more aid from them than from all the grave polemists and solid writers that have ever spoken or written.'"[9]

Against this background of Brown's mental furniture, by all accounts the creation of Artemus Ward was almost akin to spontaneous combustion. Brown was a person of ever-changing moods, a gaunt, angular young man whose trousers and sleeves never quite seemed to cover his long limbs, and he customarily wore an aspect of soberness, even melancholy. Yet humor bubbled up out of him, one reporter said, "from a placid and almost serious countenance as sudden and as unexpected as lightning from a cloudless sky,"[10] and when—as he sat at his table writing—he had written something that pleased him, he would slap his leg and laugh. Working at his table one January day in 1858, Brown was wondering how he could fill out his "City Facts and Fancies" column, and he thought of inserting a letter from a fictitious correspondent. He began, "Mr. Artemus Ward, proprietor of the well-known side-show, writes us from Pittsburgh as follows."

Brown had no idea what he was starting. "'I wrote the first Ward sketch . . . not supposing I should ever write another,'"[11] he later recalled. Apparently he was not even certain where he got the name of the character. On one occasion he thought he might have borrowed it from the Revolutionary War general Artemas Ward; on another he said he had once known an eccentric old sideshowman whose name, he thought, actually was Artemus Ward. It didn't matter much. Once this antic figure had sprung out of Brown's ink bottle, it took on a life of its own. The first Ward letter, which appeared in the *Plain Dealer* of January 30, 1858, was later revised and improved by Brown for inclusion in *Artemus Ward, His Book*. It is the improved version that follows:

To the Editor of the————

Sir—I'm movin along—slowly along—down tords your place. I want you should rite me a letter, sayin how is the show bizniss in your place. My show at present consists of three moral Bares, a Kangaroo (a amoozin little Raskal—t'would make you larf yerself to deth to see the little cuss jump up and squeal) wax figgers of G. Washington Gen. Tayler John Bunyan Capt. Kidd and Dr. Webster in the act of killin Dr. Parkman, besides several miscellanyus moral wax statoots of celebrated piruts & murderers, &c., ekalled by few & exceld by none. Now Mr. Editor, scratch orf a few lines sayin how is the show bizniss down to your place. I shall hav my hanbills dun at your offiss. Depend upon it. I want you should git my hanbills up in flamin stile. Also git up a tremenjus excitemunt in yr. paper 'bowt my onparaleld Show. We must fetch the public sumhow. We must wurk on their feelins. Cum the moral on 'em strong. If it's a temprance community tell 'em I sined the pledge fifteen minits arter Ise born but on the contery ef your peple take their tods, say Mister Ward is as Jenial a feller as we ever met, full of conwiviality, & the life an sole of the Soshul Bored. Take, don't you? If you say anythin abowt my show say my snaiks is as harmliss as the new born Babe. What a interestin study it is to see a zewological animil like a snaik under perfect subjecshun! My kangaroo is the most larfable little cuss I ever saw. All for 15 cents. I am anxyus to skewer your infloounce. I repeet in regard to them hanbills that I shall git 'em struck orf up to your printin office. My perlitercal sentiments agree with yourn exackly. I know thay do, becawz I never saw a man whoos didn't.

                    Respectively yures,
                    A. WARD
P.S.—You scratch my back & Ile scratch your back. [12]

It has been mentioned that in the Artemus Ward letters parody was not confined to matters of religiously oriented morals. There were also comments on the basic integrity of banks, railroads, and other institutions including the press, even though Brown was a newspaperman himself. A subsequent letter from Artemus Ward reported that in Wheeling, West Virginia, he had been shamefully abused in the columns of a newspaper that he had not favored with his handbill printing business. The editor had called him "a horery heded itinirunt vagabone." Another letter (which, strange to relate, never found its way into any of Brown's collected works) reflected a better reception in Toledo. It went in part

Toledo is a interestin sity. There is probly more promersing and virtuous young men in toledo than there is anywheres. The climit is such that a great many of the mail inhabitants hav to take a gin-cocktale evry mornin afore brekfust. It was hard for them to do it at fust but they take to it quite nateral now. My cangeroo gut out of his cage the other evenin and run off faster nor a lokomotive. The Common Counsil was in session at the time my cangeroo gut out and when thay heerd of the affectin casyualty they unainimersly parsed the follering preambel and resolushuns:

"Wherass, This ere Counsil thinks hily of Artemus Ward; and Whereass, it has pleased Devine Providence to cause his cangeroo to escaip; and Whereass, the resunt escaip of a hyeny in Pauldin county and his terriable doins in a grave yard planely shows the awfulness of allowin beasts of pray to roam through the country—therefore be it

"Resolved, That this Counsil do immediuntly ajurn and assist Mr. Ward for to capter his beast."

Accordinly thay did so. Abowt seving hundred (700) citizuns jined in the pursoot. We chased the little cuss clear up to Tremendusville afore we cawt him. It wood hav made you larf to hearn the little cuss squeal and kick up his legs. On our return to toledo abel and eloqunt speaches was maid by several distingwished citizuns, and awl parsed off in the most pleasant stile.

My snakes is under perfect subjecshun. Among my snakes is a Boy Constructor, the largist in the wurld. It wood make your blud freeze to see the mongster unkoil hisself. If yu put this letter in the papers i wish you wood be more particlar abowt the spellin and punctooation. i dont ploom myself on my learnin. i shall be in Cleveland befour long and my hanbills shall certinly by struck off down to your offis. Set your harts at rest on that pint.
          Very Respectively yours,
          ARTEMUS WARD.'"[13]

A letter from Chicago said, "Chicago is a grate plase. Awl the sitizens think it is a grate plase. They say its futur is brilyunt." And further,

> They say the dume of New York is seeled, becoz it is two far off from Chicago. The only rivuls thay acknollidge is Lundun, Pekin and Tiffin. Thare's a hi breeze prevalin here awl the time, which makes the streets dusty. The Statistick editer of the Demercratic Press told me that he chanes his feet to the floor and wares a small grindstun in his hat when he rites statististicks, to avoyd bein blowd away. Lake Mishigan is lokatid on Chicago. Illinoy is also in Chicago. There aint much muney here. Corner-lots is the principal currency. Fur instance, a sitizun wants a drink, (which he duz quite frequiently) he takes his map, goze to the serloon, gits his beveridge, an then unrols his map. Which seckshun wood yu like a lot in? he sez two the bar tender. The bar tender picks out the lot he duz desire an the papers air made out on the spot. About awl the muney ive taken is in corner-lots, but i spose it is awl rite, partickerly if thay turn that air brilyunt futur loose pritty soon.[14]

Newspapers other than the *Plain Dealer* soon began printing the Showman's letters, a process that was facilitated by the postage-free system of publication "exchanges" of that day, and before long their gentle satire and quaint, exuberant humor were being enjoyed all across America. From occasional revelations in the letters, a picture of Artemus Ward gradually emerged. He came originally from the Pine Tree State. ("I was born in the State of Maine, of parents.") He had been in show business nearly twenty-five years and was a man in his middle fifties, of indeterminate financial means. ("By attendin strickly to bizness I've amarsed a handsum Pittance.") His home, when he *was* home, was in the fictitious village of Baldinsville, Indiana. He was married to a wife named Betsy Jane and had a family. He considered that he had "allers sustained a good moral character," for "I was never a railroad director in my life." Further, "I'm not a politician and my other habits air good."[15] Illustrations usually portrayed him as rotund, flashily dressed, baldheaded—a man of cunning and yet somehow kindly appearance who had obviously learned the ways of the world in a rough-and-tumble school.

Artemus Ward's bad spelling may have amused some people, but mere misspelling was far from being the secret of his humor. This was proved well enough when less talented writers sought (as a few of them did) to counterfeit the Ward letters simply by mangling words and sentences. The invaribale flatness and failure of their productions served to emphasize by contrast a distinctive quality of Artemus Ward: a careful shaping of words into distorted forms that yielded comic images in miniature.

Thus, for "wretched" he often wrote "retchid," conjuring up a picture of a person who is not only miserable but miserably sick, and imprisonment he once described with the phrase "in durans vial," which somehow adds a sense of being bottled up to that of ordinary confinement. His "rain of terror" sounds much more horrible than a "reign of terror," and instead of "frustrated" he once wrote "flustratid," which is more like the real thing. And when he wrote of women, "of all the blessins they're the soothinist," he had accomplished a bit of poetic perfection in the Wardian manner.[16] Often this double-dealing with words was accompanied by a wildly quaint expression of some sort as when Artemus, in parting from the leader of a religious sect noted for its frenzies, said, "Wall, look out for them fits of yourn, and don't catch cold and die in the flour of your youth and beauty."[17]

His sayings were often imbued with that insidious confounding of logic still preserving some indefinable truth which is so frequently the style of British humor. For example, Ward's opinion: "I tell you feller citizens, it would have bin ten dollars in Jeff Davis's pocket if he'd never bin born!" is in somewhat the same class with that of Oscar Wilde on his way to jail, standing on a station platform with other prisoners in the rain and declaring, "'If this is the way Queen Victoria treats her prisoners, she doesn't deserve to have any.'"[18]

It may have been this quality that made the Artemus Ward letters such a sudden success in England when they appeared there in book form. These letters, which the Old Showman sometimes referred to as his "perlite literatoor," were actually so unpolite, so outrageously "uncultured," that few American critics took any notice of them. It was only after the British hailed Artemus that scholarly attention turned toward him. A writer for the *New Quarterly Magazine* of London would say that Brown's conception and delineation came very close to genius, and that setting aside some of the creations of Dickens he doubted if the century had produced any character of greater comic power than Artemus Ward. "His shrewdness and his ignorance, his weaknesses, his vanity, his combination of selfishness and geniality, his own exaggeration of every prevailing national absurdity—all this is brought out by innumerable little touches of quite inimitable art."[19]

The prevailing spirit of Artemus Ward was one of exuberant delight. Thus fraudulence, hypocrisy, greed, and many other human failings were exposed without the intrusion of rancor that is so often associated with personal utterances on such subjects, for the only personality that seemed to be involved was a figure of joy: the Old Showman. That this spirit of joyousness flourished under the dark, doom-laden skies of the War years was remarkable. And that its source could be a man who was himself often afflicted by despondency was, and will always be, part of the miracle of humor.

2

"I Should Think
We Came From Jerusalem"

The *Plain Dealer* building in which Charles Brown worked was at Superior and Vineyard streets, near one of Cleveland's smokier industrial sections along the Cuyahoga River; its location, as one visitor put it, was one "where the traveller in search of the beautiful would not be likely to linger long."[1] The newsroom where Brown performed his editorial duties was dreary and plainly furnished. Brown's "desk" was simply a gashed and ink-stained pine table. His hard, wooden armchair eventually lost one arm. The place was noisy, with steam presses elsewhere in the building rumbling incessantly and a constant stream of people flowing through the open editorial room—politicians, tradesmen, show-business agents, the patent-medicine manufacturers whose advertising was prominent in the *Plain Dealer,* and others intent on using its columns. But when Brown was scratching away with his pen, particularly when he was working on an Artemus Ward letter, he seemed to be off in a world by himself, oblivious of the hubbub and the uninspiring surroundings. A fellow staff member remembered that "he would write away, sometimes laughing to himself, and then slapping the table in the excess of his mirth."[2] James F. Ryder, an early Cleveland photographer, described him: "'He was young, cheerful in manner, tall and slender, not quite up to date in style of dress, yet by no means shabby. His hair was flaxen and very straight; his nose, the prominent feature of his face, was Romanesque. ... His eyes were blue-gray, with a twinkle in them. ... It seemed as though bubbling in him was a lot of happiness which he made no effort to conceal or hold back. When we were introduced he was sitting at his table writing; he gave his leg a smart slap, arose and shook hands with me and said he was glad to meet me. I believed him for he looked glad all the time.'"[3] Another man left a description which was commonly that of the social or public Charles Brown: "His person was tall and thin; his face aquiline; his carriage buoyant; his demeanor joyous and eager."[4]

But those who had an opportunity to observe him more constantly and intimately noticed that his mood went up and down in roller-coaster–like swoops and dives, with spells of high-flying exuberance followed by fits of depression so severe that he was sometimes afraid to be left alone at night. Writing of one of these times in Cleveland, C. C. Ruthrauff said that one night in his room, after walking the floor for hours in a state of utter despondency, Brown cried, "'My God . . . this thing almost makes me wild,'" and the look on his face was unforgettable, seemingly that of a man bereft of reason.[5]

There is much to suggest that some of the disturbances and anxieties that afflicted Charles Brown off and on through his life had roots in his early years. He was born on April 26, 1834, on a farm in Waterford, Maine, a rather heavily wooded town in the southwestern part of the state. His parents were Caroline and Levi Brown. The settlers of Waterford, who included Thaddeus Brown and Calvin Farrar, Charles's grandfathers, and who came mostly from the Massachusetts counties of Worcester, Middlesex, and Essex, were people of almost entirely English extraction who transplanted to Maine a block of New England Congregationalism that remained a very solid structure indeed until the Baptists, Methodists, Universalists, Freethinkers, and other troublemakers started chipping away at it. For the first two decades of the century, Waterford was a Puritan theocracy, with the business of the town and the parish very much the same affair. In fact, only a dozen or so years before Charles's birth, his father, Levi, acting as constable, had marched a group of people to jail because they refused to pay a tax imposed by the town but intended for the support of the Congregational minister. (At the door of the jail, they paid their tax under protest, then sued the town and recovered it.) The names of Brown's people pretty well confirm their Puritan ancestry—for example, that of Bathsheba Farrar, his maternal grandmother; Levi, his father; and Daniel, Jabez, and Malbory Brown, and Calvin and Luther Farrar, his uncles.

Toward his racial and religious antecedents, Brown would betray a peculiar sort of love-hate relationship, a mixture of respect and re-bellion, once he got out into more sophisticated surroundings. He was inclined to be short and satiric on the subject. Once, in response to a friend who asked him about his people, Brown said, "'I should think we came from Jerusalem, for my father's name was Levi, and we had a Nathan and Moses in the family. But my poor brother's name was Cyrus, so perhaps that makes us Persians.'"[6] And once he had Artemus Ward, the Old Showman, declare, "I believe we are descendid from the Puritins, who nobly fled from a land of despitism to a land of freedim, where they could not only enjoy their own religion, but prevent everybody else from enjoyin his."[7]

And yet Brown must have understood the spiritual basis of this attitude. To his Puritan ancestors, being their brother's keeper was not being meanly and arbitrarily dictatorial; it was an aspect of benevolence. It was, in fact, considered to be God's commandment that Christians should prevent their neighbors from falling into vice, sin, and error. If the majority in Waterford could have had its way, there would have been no intemperance, no slavery, no war, no poverty (at least no poverty due to indolence or "vicious indulgence"), no crime, and no dishonesty. People would have studied, worked hard, improved themselves, and paid their debts. Children would have minded their elders. The old and the sick would have been cared for and hospitality would have been extended to strangers. A man who said he had never known better or worthier people than the early residents of Waterford had reasons for his estimate.

Even today the faces of people like them—lean, muscular, earnest, kindly, intelligent even if terribly "set," strict, and determined—looking out at us from the portrait pages of hundreds of histories of such New England towns, strike the same responsive note of respect. Although Charles Brown in later life may have derided them, he could not have failed to value some elements of their good opinion. And he must have realized that his revolt against them was not destined to be a simple business. Maine ancestors with biblical names—particularly if one has known some of them personally—are not to be trifled with; in any accounting with them, decades may go by undisturbedly enough, and yet one cold morning there it is—their invoice on the doorstep along with the milk and the newspaper. Brown's contemporary Nathaniel Hawthorne once wrote about the "gray shadows of his forefathers" and what he imagined they thought about his occupation as a writer of storybooks. *What manner of serving God or man may that be? Why, the degenerate fellow might as well have been a fiddler!* "And yet," Hawthorne wrote, "let them scorn me as they will, strong traits of their nature have intertwined themselves with mine."[8]

Not the least of the traits intertwined with Brown's was the deceptive tenacity Macaulay once noted in the classic Puritan, who, he said, in private might pray with convulsions, groans, and tears, who might be maddened by glorious or terrible illusions, who might awake screaming from dreams of eternal fire—but who, when he took his seat in council or girt on the sword for war, subdued these tempestuous workings of the soul beneath cool judgment and a terrible immutability of purpose. Much of this same brand of determination, which in England had trampled down king, church, and aristocracy and which in New England had subdued the wilderness, was concealed beneath Brown's appearance of physical frailty, his casual attitudes, and the wonderful gravity and calmness with which, most particularly in his lectures, he would seem to be regarding the world.

Certain other aspects of Brown's personality may well have stemmed from the tragedy and deprivations of his early years. As a child he lived in a big white house on the Flat, an area comparable to a village green, in the center of Waterford village. The house had originally been built by Caroline's father, Calvin Farrar. After Calvin's death, Levi obtained title by buying off the heirs who shared its inheritance with Caroline. A large, handsome building on a pleasant lot beside a pond, it was grand enough in its own milieu so that some people called it a "mansion."

Charles had a brother, Cyrus, seven years older than he, and he would have had two sisters had not the little girls died within a couple of weeks of one another in the winter of 1833, the year before he was born, a tragedy that left its shadow upon the family. Caroline, his mother, a chatty woman who always seemed to know everything that was going on all over town (a characteristic that Charles definitely inherited), had a prudence in money matters that did not descend to her son. His father, Levi, a kindly and genial man to whom Charles was devoted, was engaged in many activities including farming, storekeeping, dealing in lands and timber, and running a potash plant. At the age of twelve, Charles was as well situated as any boy would wish to be.

Into this happy and prosperous scene, death came with an unusually devasting effect. Late in the year 1847 Levi Brown became ill, and just before Christmas the gravity of his situation was such that he decided to make his will. Two days later he died. In his will Levi provided that his estate pass for the benefit of Caroline and Charles and left to Cyrus one dollar. Cyrus, who was then around twenty, was perhaps considered able to take care of himself; he had embarked on the career of a newspaperman in a way that was common then, by starting out as a printer.

However, although Levi was a man of several enterprises, he was apparently much more productive alive than solvent dead. The personal estate was declared insufficient to pay outstanding claims and expenses. With the real estate vulnerable to sale, the "mansion" on the Flat must then have begun to assume a certain psychological importance. It may be imagined with what unwillingness Caroline considered giving up the house that had been built by her father, that she and her husband had occupied, and that was the seat of prestige in the community, even though in more modest quarters she and Charles might have been better able to continue a life together.

A complicated series of moves followed. Caroline petitioned the Oxford County probate court for a widow's allowance in addition to her share, representing that she was in poor health and unable to labor for her own and Charles's support, and that she had brought to her husband at time of marriage a $1,000 personal estate of which nothing remained to her. When the petition was granted, she obtained enough out of the liquidation of Levi's estate, real and personal, to purchase the house on the Flat and take title in her own name. The share that would have gone to Charles was thereby practically eliminated. And Charles was put out to be a printer's apprentice at the age of thirteen.

It is uncertain whether he was very much aware of these legal transactions—or whether he cared. He would upon one occasion (in his character of Artemus Ward) speak of a young man who for his sins was punished by the worst calamity anyone could imagine: his aunt died and left him a farm in Oxford County, Maine! One can sense in this remark a realization on Brown's part that Maine was a state to which he was not too well suited, an estimate that is borne out by descriptions of him as a boy in Waterford. A tall, frail lad, he seemed to have no local usefulness whatever; he was not strong enough for lumbering or farming, not adroit enough to operate a shop or mill, not good enough at figures to keep store, not scholarly enough to become a preacher or teacher. The boy's experience as an apprentice printer did nothing to warm his heart toward Maine. He once wrote, "I roamed through the state, setting type a short time in one place, and quietly running away to another."[9] In only one town was he happy for a while. This was Norway, where he worked on the *Norway Advertiser,* a paper in which his brother had acquired a partnership interest. Here Charles was able to attend the Norway Liberal Institute part of the time, when not too busily engaged in the printshop. But both Cyrus and his partner were drinking heavily. In the summer of 1850 the newspaper went broke and was sold; Cyrus and his associate had drunk it under. Cyrus then drifted south to become editor of the New Bedford *Daily Evening Standard,* and with his brother's departure the bottom again dropped out of Charles's world, just when it seemed that he had found a little security.

Brown's eventual departure from his then-uncongenial native state was arranged by an uncle, Calvin Farrar, who had some printing to be done in support of a business enterprise. He took his copy, and Charles, to the publishing firm of Snow & Wilder, in Boston, who somehow got the impression that if they would take the boy they could also have the printing job. They gave Charles employment as a compositor.

Brown never had much to say about his teen-age years in Maine. Seemingly it was a lonesome and loveless period in which there was little he wished to remember. It was also a period that left him a relationship with his mother that does not seem to have been completely fulfilling. Some years later, after he had worked his way from Boston west to Cleveland and settled there, he was on at least one occasion visited by his mother, and of that visit his friend James Ryder recorded a few impressions. The two seemed to be cheerful and pleasant together, Ryder thought, but he made note of one thing that struck him as unusual. Charles called his mother not Mother but Caroline.

Once, Ryder recalled, Charles induced his mother to recite the entire lineage of his known ancestry down to his father. This concluded with her saying, " 'Then your father and I got married, and my father took Levi in partnership, and it was Farrar & Brown.' " Charles told her he remembered as a small child seeing these two names together on a storefront and then asked in mock alarm, " 'Your father and my father—why, what relation does that make *us?*' "[10]

The relationship, it seems, was something less than that of the usual mother and son, or something different from it, although characterized by deep affection on the part of Charles. He would always be writing to Caroline, sending her money (when he had it to send), and giving evidence of concern about her. A fragment of a letter written to a friend in Waterford when well along in his career illustrates his concern. In this letter, the friend is requested to call on Brown's mother and ask her to write to him. "I have written her several times, but haven't received any reply. This makes me very nervous, because I fear my letters may have miscarried."[11]

Whether Charles felt a lack of reciprocal warmth in his mother's feeling toward him or whether he simply had been, through absence and isolation, quantitatively deprived of the emotional security of normal family life and maternal love is difficult to determine. But always it seems plain that he restlessly sought a degree or quality of affection and adulation that was never to be quite satisfied. Charles may even have missed the family in a larger sense that included the two little girls who died just before his birth; such might be the interpretation of his frequent friendships with little girls he met in the families of friends and of his fondness for children generally.

The more Brown's life is examined, the likelier it seems that he felt his early deprivations deeply and permanently. One is tempted to believe that each one of us—sometime before he is fourteen or fifteen—is wound up like one of those little mechanical figures sold by sidewalk vendors and set to walking, destined until the spring runs down to march implacably onward, preset and programmed for an ultimate triumph, disaster, or something in between. To the extent that this may be true, the most important elements of Charles Brown's clockwork were his drives to recoup his psychological losses by becoming successful, loved, and admired; his rational but rather heated rebellion against the strictures of Puritanism; and (this opposing almost everything else, as it happened) a deep-seated and insidiously emotional desire to be "respectable" within the principles of the Puritan ethic.

3

The Years in Boston and Ohio

In Boston, sometime in the summer of 1851, Snow & Wilder put the seventeen-year-old Brown to work setting type for their humorous weekly, the *Carpet-Bag,* and here he encountered several of the influences that shaped his curious art. The editor of the *Carpet-Bag* was Benjamin Penhallow Shillaber, a large, genial man whose Dickensian name was altogether appropriate, for he could have been the model for one of Dickens's more benevolent employers. One of his employees said, "He radiated helpfulness, courtesy and good nature as a hearth fire sends out heat and light."[1] Shillaber was the author of the "Mrs. Partington" stories and sayings, then appearing in the *Carpet-Bag* and shortly afterward published in a book. Although Mrs. Partington, a sort of American Mrs. Malaprop, was immensely popular in her day, there is no reason to believe that she was the progenitor of Artemus Ward. However, the influence of the man Shillaber himself on Charles Brown's humor is readily identifiable. Shillaber saw humor as a "sweet antidote" to afflictions of the mind and body and the natural iniquities of the human heart. Without it, he believed, man would be nothing more than a particularly horrid kind of gloomy-faced hyena. The avowed purpose of the *Carpet-Bag* under his editorship was "to promote cheerfulness."[2]

Humor to promote cheerfulness! It was a simple thought, but an important one, which had not begun to have much importance until the early nineteenth century, and then only in "popular" literature. In standard works, when Charles Brown was a boy, there was very little that could be described as pure humor—fun for the sake of fun alone. Humor there was in abundance, beginning with Chaucer or perhaps before him, but it was usually subservient or applied humor, part of a characterization, satire, burlesque, or something else with an object other than simply making people laugh. In his lecture "The Poetic Principle," delivered in 1849, Edgar Allan Poe advanced the idea that the purpose of poetry was not to set forth a truth or promulgate a moral but to elevate the soul through the contemplation of beauty. In the nineteenth century also, painters began to depart more and more from literal representations of objects, landscapes, people, and events; it was dawning upon them that a painting had a right to exist simply by creating in the beholder an experience of beauty or novelty. It was perhaps in accord with these tendencies that humor began to have a closer relationship with laughter.

Shillaber's philosophy of humor was one that Brown adopted wholeheartedly. A friend wrote of Brown, "To make people laugh was to be his primary endeavor. . . . He believed in laughter as thoroughly wholesome; he had the firmest conviction that fun is healthy and sportiveness the truest sign of sanity."[3]

In Boston, Charles Brown became acquainted with a wide range of American humorists while setting many of their works in type and studying them, perforce, word by word. The *Carpet-Bag* attracted contributors from all over the nation. One article came from Samuel Clemens, then in his teens; it was entitled "The Dandy Frightening the Squatter" and may have been his first published work, although it attracted little attention to the future Mark Twain. Most of the writers hid behind pen names: Peter Snooks, Fred Freequill, Charley Clewline, Enoch Fitzwhistle, and the like. Comic writing was not a respectable form of literary endeavor, and this sort of camouflage was the fashion. Among the real names of the *Carpet-Bag* contributors were Charles G. Halpine, John G. Saxe, John T. Trowbridge, and, most important of all as far as Brown was concerned, George H. Derby, who wrote under the pseudonyms of John Phoenix and John P. Squibob. What Derby excelled in was a completely solemn, horribly funny presentation of utter nonsense. He was one of the writers, Brown said, who influenced him the most. The other was Seba Smith, who was born in a log cabin not far from Brown's hometown of Waterford. Smith created Jack Downing, a backwoods boy from a fictitious Downingville, Maine, who went down to Portland with a load of ax handles, wandered into the state legislature (then meeting in that city), and ostensibly began sending letters home, the first one appearing in the *Portland Courier* in 1830. Later his letters represented him as being in Washington offering advice to President Andrew Jackson. The common sense and audacity with which this rube from Maine took it upon himself to address the president and other high dignitaries on terms of the utmost familiarity delighted readers of that day. The techniques Brown learned from Seba Smith and used in Artemus Ward letters are obvious, but he once admitted that the quaint and exuberant absurdity of George Derby was his greatest inspiration.

After about a year's service as a compositor, Brown himself began contributing to the *Carpet-Bag* while continuing as a printer. Seven of his stories were published over the pseudonym of "Chubb" in 1852 and 1853. When the first one appeared, Brown celebrated by going to the theater and thought, as he recalled, that he was "the greatest man in Boston." The theater fascinated him. A friend recalled that "He studied the plays and courted the society of the actors and actresses. There were few . . . legitimate plays with which he did not become acquainted."[4]

The *Carpet-Bag* ceased publication with the issue of March 26, 1853, and that spring Brown started westward carrying a carpet bag containing his few belongings and the compositor's stick on which he depended for a living. He seldom had more than four or five dollars in his pocket, but always along the way there was a printshop that needed help. Pausing to work here and there as necessity required, riding on public conveyances when he could but often walking when out of funds, Brown was out to see the country. He made his way across Massachusetts, New York, and Pennsylvania and settled for a time in Cincinnati, Ohio. He then turned north, and after working in Dayton and Springfield he brought up on the shore of Lake Erie at Sandusky. Next he walked south along the Sandusky River, and after a thirty-four-mile tramp reached Tiffin. The publisher of Tiffin's *Seneca Advertiser* remembered his arrival. "One day, who should come into the office but a tall, thin-faced, awkward, blue-eyed, light-haired fellow, wearing a straw hat and a long linen duster, who said he was a printer and wanted work, but as my visitor was without money and probably hungry, too, I took him over to the hotel with me to dinner. After dinner my foreman said he would like a vacation and I suggested that young Brown should be tried for a week, which was done."[5] The employment continued, at four dollars a week plus board and lodging, and Brown stayed there something less than a year, setting type and writing. The next jump was to eight dollars a week on the *Toledo Commercial,* where he began as a compositor but soon made the transition to editorial staff, and this was the last place in which he served as a printer. The quality of Brown's writing in Toledo soon made him known in newspaper offices throughout northern Ohio. In the fall of 1857 he was hired by the *Cleveland Daily Plain Dealer* as commercial editor. By January 1858 he had been promoted to city editor, second in command to the proprietor, J. W. Gray. Also in that month, at a convention of Ohio journalists, he was elected co-secretary of the Editors' and Publishers' Association. In April, Gray suffered an eye injury and was laid up for several months, while the paper continued successfully under Brown's leadership. A couple of years later the *Plain Dealer* had reached a circulation of 65,000 in competition with four other dailies in Cleveland—an eminence it would not attain again until many years afterward. It is beyond question that Brown contributed importantly to this success. His competence as a newspaperman and his interest in the business would again be indicated in 1862, when Brown thought for a while of turning from the career of humorist and buying the *Plain Dealer,* at that time made available by Gray's death.

No letters or diary written by Brown during his four-year journey from Boston to Cleveland appear to exist, and there are only a few recorded glimpses of him during this period. One of these, however, is significant; it concerns his continuing interest in shows. Show business of all kinds fascinated him, and during his westward trek he had plenty of opportunity to observe it, for at that time America was supporting an entertainment industry of great noncentralization, mobility, and variety. By the time a settlement was big enough to have a church or town hall, it was also big enough to have a show, and presently one would be along—a "moral" show, of course. The growing nation seemed to have a genius for this sort of thing, and it could turn out showmen almost as fast as it could produce politicians and preachers. There were thousands of traveling enterprises, moving by rail, boat and wagon: circuses, menageries, minstrel shows, Shakespearean companies and readers, dramatic groups, singers, dancers, ventriloquists, and magicians. Brown not only attended these shows, he also went behind the scenes to examine the Madagascar Man Monkeys, Learned Dogs, Mammoth Bears, and other curiosities, and to meet and expand his acquaintance with actors, minstrels, jugglers, acrobats, india-rubber men, trumpet-blowers, bell-ringers, sword-swallowers, giants, dwarfs, bogus savages, fire-eaters, and all the rest. His creation, Artemus Ward, seems to have stemmed directly from this experience. Brown's travels also contributed enormously to the landscape against which this character was portrayed. He was a gregarious young man, and it is easy to imagine him during his perambulations pausing to converse with farmers along a dusty road, resting and swapping talk on the porches of village stores, chatting with

Artemus Ward as a young newspaperman in Cleveland, Ohio, c. 1857. From *Artemus Ward* by Don C. Seitz (1919), courtesy Harper & Row.

other travelers on coaches, trains, and steamboats, constantly conversing with people of all classes, observing a wide slice of mid-century America. Artemus Ward's fictional home was Baldinsville, Indiana. Brown must have passed through a hundred typical Baldinsvilles, and he probably visited many of the places that Artemus visited fictionally with his traveling show.

Brown's years as a printer, at least in Boston and later, also contributed significantly to his education. The series of printshops in which he worked was in itself something of a university; this was true with respect not only to Brown but to Bayard Taylor, Bret Harte, Samuel Clemens, W. D. Howells, and others who started out as printers and later became well-known writers. Howells once wrote that the printing office was "my school from childhood so largely that I could almost say I had no other. . . . My first attempt at literature was not written, but put up in type, and printed off by me."[6] At the typecase Brown had learned the construction of words, sentences, and paragraphs the hard and unforgettable way—by putting them together in metal, bit by bit. At various printshops he was also the beneficiary of the hundreds of newspapers and magazines that arrived postage-free from other publishers. And, particularly while working in Boston, Brown had access to many free libraries. The genesis of such writers as Clemens, Brown, and Howells was almost predictable. A boy went to work as a printer to earn a living, but if he had any sensitivity at all he soon realized that the real materials of his work were not the pieces of metal he plucked from the type case but thoughts, ideas, expressions, uses of the language, and stories, and for these materials he turned to the world immediately around him. And then, in the absence of formal "higher education," which might have made his own surroundings seem unimportant in comparison with those of ancient Greece and Rome or modern Europe, he was likely to come up with something highly indigenous to his own region and experience. Howells said of Brown that he was "the humorist who first gave the world a taste of the humor that characterizes the whole American people,"[7] and further, in recognizing Brown's true ability and intellectual depth, that "it must have been something more than the bad spelling which gave Brown's humor a currency beyond that of any other humorist before his time."[8]

But in 1860, in considering his wide popularity, Brown began to be acutely aware that there was something wrong with his situation. While Artemus Ward was famous, Charles Brown was unknown. Thanks to the exchange system that allowed publishers to swap material free of postage (and free of royalties to authors) his work was being read all over the United States, and yet he was getting only fourteen dollars a week on the *Plain Dealer*. And J. W. Gray, with that benevolence newspaper proprietors have ever shown in protecting their editorial employees from the corrupting influence of wealth, was not inclined to give him a raise.

As a step toward capitalizing on the popularity of Artemus Ward, Brown began tinkering with the idea of giving lectures. What *really* appealed to him was the theater. He would always have a tremendous urge to appear behind the footlights as an actor, but whenever any serious intention of doing so entered his mind it must have encountered the effect of such commonly held opinions as that of Henry Ward Beecher, who termed the theater "'the gate of debauchery, the porch of pollution... the door to all the sinks of iniquity'".[9] It would also summon up the disapproving visages of Brown's father, Levi, his uncles Daniel, Jabez, and Luther, his grandparents Bathsheba and Calvin, and other stern but loved and respected figures who considered that making a show of oneself upon the stage was not a proper business in life.

Puritan antipathy toward the theater had long existed, and for a time had been a legal as well as a moral force. Under the Continental Congress, anyone who acted in, promoted, or even attended a stage play had been barred from holding a national office. In Massachusetts there had been laws on the books prohibiting theatrical entertainments until nearly the end of the eighteenth century, and in Connecticut until the middle of the nineteenth. Even after the anti-stage laws had been repealed, their moral substance was to be reckoned with. In New York, Phineas T. Barnum did not dare call the playacting hall in his American Museum a theater; on the bills it was the "Moral Lecture Room," and the plays were always carefully labeled "Moral Dramas." As one writer said of Barnum, "His patrons being composed of sober-minded young men from the country, and innocent young maidens from the city, it was necessary that everything should be exceedingly proper to please the tastes of youth in search of amusement and ladies desirous of edification."[10]

Pious fraud of this kind was practiced everywhere. Showmen very soon discovered that people who wouldn't go to a theater would go watch a play at a "museum"—a place that was supposed to be educational and therefore respectable. It was a simple matter to fit out a building with one large room containing a stage and with other, smaller rooms exhibiting a few dried-out curiosities from the South Seas, stuffed animals, waxworks, and the like. Artemus Ward's "grate Moral Entertainment" was a parody of this sort of dodge. For many people stage plays were beyond the pale, and actors were ranked accordingly. To Brown's parents and grandparents the idea of a former actor in the White House would have been as astonishing as that of a man on the moon.

For Brown, this was too bad. As critics would later remark, he would have been a superb character actor, but whenever he thought of entering the theater in this capacity, the two sets of mind that existed within him came into conflict. Fond as he was of the society of actors and actresses, he could never quite bring himself to join them professionally. Their easy pattern of friendships and amours, their actual and psychological need to be always in the public eye, and their generally unconventional lives made a milieu into which he would have fitted very naturally and comfortably had these restraints not existed. But as it was, he could never successfully make the leap. On the few occasions when he tried, matters turned out badly. Always the theater would represent a little universe outside of which he fluttered longingly but vainly, like a moth barred from a brilliantly lighted room by the inexplicable glass of a windowpane. He once said that there are three kinds of human beings, "men, women, and the people on the stage."[11] And he could never manage to force himself in among "the people on the stage," great as his affection for them was.

A lecture, however, would allow him to appear on the stage and yet not be called an actor. This was a brilliant solution—a great psychological high-wire act—and an almost perfect example of sublimation as Freud would later define it: the replacement of an original and unacceptable object of desire by another which is not disapproved by self or society. The fact that he was performing a lecture would make all the difference in the world to him and to the stern old spirits who had the top layer of his psyche under surveillance. For not only were the Puritans not against lectures, they were strongly for them. The word *lecture* meant a weekday sermon, a type of Puritan service the established church in England had tried to suppress. Edward Everett Hale, who made a little study of the subject, came to the opinion that half the people who crossed the Atlantic to New England in 1630 came because they wanted to hear lectures, and he was not altogether joking. Hale noted that the more these people had been told by religious authorities in England that they must not go to weekday lectures, the more they had sworn that "as God lived, they would."[12] When Brown thought of being a lecturer, he could have almost heard his ancestors applauding, for this was a revered occupation in New England, made more respectable in recent years by the popular lyceum lectures, featuring such uplifting speakers as Henry Ward Beecher, John B. Gough with his temperance talk, and others who were out to enlighten and elevate the people.

Brown bought a book called *The Western Orator* published in Cleveland in 1860 and "comprising an introductory course of oratorical training with a copious selection of pieces for practice." It was full of excellent guidance on quality, control, and projection of voice; breathing; articulation; enunciation; timing; emphasis; and inflection; and other fundamentals of effective public speaking—and there would later be ample demonstration of the fact that he learned its lessons well.

However, when Brown talked the lecturing idea over with friends on the *Plain Dealer* staff, they discouraged him—in fact, they called him a fool. They could remember a disaster that had taken place at the Franklin Festival. This was a gala affair put on each January by the printers of Cleveland; it included a fancy-dress ball preceded by a banquet at which there was always a long series of toasts and responses. When called upon unexpectedly at the 1859 Festival, Brown had been stricken by a panic and could only remain in his chair, bashfully shaking his head. Next day in the *Plain Dealer* Brown wrote, " 'We scorn the imputation of vanity, but we say our speech was a dignified and striking effort. In answer to a "response" call, we spoke felicitously as follows,' " and the "as follows" was three column-inches of blank space with "immense and prolonged applause" at the bottom.[13]

Nevertheless, he tried again, giving a lecture in Toledo in October 1860, and he continued to jot down notes for what he hoped would be other lectures. Brown also sought to augment his income by making an arrangement with *Vanity Fair* to provide the New York magazine with Artemus Ward letters at ten dollars apiece. Four of Brown's contributions were published in November and December, 1860. One of them was Ward's discourse on "Forts," which went in part:

> Every man has got a Fort. It's sum men's fort to do one thing, and sum other men's fort to do another, while there is numeris shiftliss critters goin round loose whose fort is not to do nothin.
>
> Shakspeer rote good plase, but he wouldn't hav succeeded as a Washington correspondent of a New York daily paper. He lackt the rekesit fancy and imagginashun.
>
> That's so!
>
> Old George Washington's Fort was to not hev eny public man of the present day resemble him to eny alarmin extent. Whare bowts can George's ekal be fownd? I ask, & boldly anser no whares, or eny whare else.

Old man Townsin's Fort was to maik Sassyperiller. "Goy to the world! anuther life saived!" (Cotashun from Townsin's advertisemunt.)

Cyrus Field's Fort is to lay a sub-machine tellegraf under the boundin billers of the Oshun, and then hev it Bust. . . .

My Fort is the grate moral show bizniss & ritin choice famerly literatoor for the noospapers. That's what's the matter with *me*.

Artemus concluded this essay with a little story about something that happened to him in a town in Indiana where, his organ-grinder having died, he attempted to drown his sorrows.

Konsequents was I histid in so much I dident zackly know whare bowts I was. I turned my livin wild beests of Pray loose into the streets and spilt all my wax wurks. I then Bet I cood play hoss. So I hitched myself to a Kanawl bote, there bein two other hosses hitcht on also, one behind and anuther ahead of me. The driver hollerd for us to git up, and we did. But the hosses bein onused to sich a arrangemunt begun to kick & squeal and rair up. Konsequents was I was kickt vilently in the stummuck & back, and presuntly I fownd myself in the Kanawl with the other hosses, kickin & yellin like a tribe of Cusscaroorus savvijis. I was rescood, & as I was bein carrid to the tavern on a hemlock Bored I sed in a feeble voise, "Boys, playin hoss isn't my Fort."

MORUL—Never don't do nothin which isn't your Fort, for ef you do you'll find yourself splashin round in the Kanawl, figgeratively speakin.[14]

Another contribution was "Artemus Ward on His Visit to Abe Lincoln." This was written in the period between Lincoln's election and his inauguration, and Brown had the Old Showman visit the president-elect at his home in Springfield, where Artemus reported that he found Lincoln overwhelmed by office seekers who had filled his dooryard, woodshed, and barn, and were even swarming on the roof.

"Good God!" cride Old Abe, "they cum upon me from the skize—down the chimneys, and from the bowels of the year-th!" He hadn't more'n got them words out of his delikit mouth before two fat offiss-seekers from Wisconsin, in endeverin to crawl atween his legs for the purpuss of appyin for the tollgateship at Milwawky, upsot the President eleck & he would hev gone sprawlin into the fire-place if I hadn't caught him in these arms. But I hadn't morn'n stood him up strate before another man cum crashin down the chimney, his head strikin me vilently agin the inards and prostratin my voluptoòus form onto the floor. "Mr. Linkin," shoutid the infatooated being, "my papers is signed by every clergyman in our town, and likewise the skoolmaster!"

Sez I "you egrejis ass," gittin up & brushin the dust from my eyes, "I'll sign your papers with this bunch of bones, if you don't be a little more keerful how you make my bread basket a depot in the futer. How do you like that air perfumery?" sez I, shuving my fist under his nose. "Them's the kind of papers I'll giv you! Them's the paper's *you* want!"

"But I workt hard for the ticket; I toiled night and day! The patrit should be rewarded!"

"Virtoo," sed I, holdin' the infatooated man by the coat-collar, "virtoo, sir, is its own reward. Look at me!" He did look at me, and qualed be4 my gase. "The fact is," I continued, lookin' round on the hungry crowd. "there is scacely a offiss for every ile lamp carrid round durin' this campane. I wish thare was. I wish thare was furrin missions to be filled on varis lonely Islands where eppydemics rage incessantly, and if I was in Old Abe's place I'd send every mother's son of you to them. What air you here for?" I continnered, warmin up considerable, "can't you giv Abe a minit's peace? Don't you see he's worrid most to death! Go home, you miserable men, go home & till the sile! Go to peddlin tinware—go to choppin wood—go to bilin' sope—stuff sassengers—black boots—git a clerkship on sum respectable manure cart—go round as original Swiss Bell Ringers—becum 'origenal and only' Campbell Minstrels—go to lecturin at 50 dollars a nite—imbark in the peanut bizniss—*write for the Ledger*—saw off your legs and go round givin concerts, with techin appeals to a charitable public, printed on your handbills—anything for a honest living, but don't come round here drivin Old Abe crazy by your outrajis cuttings up! Go home. Stand not upon the order of your goin,' but go to onct! If in five minits from this time," sez I pullin' out my new sixteen dollar huntin cased watch, and brandishin' it before their eyes, "Ef in five minits from this time a single sole of you remains on these here premises, I'll go out to my cage near by, and let my Boy Constructor loose! & ef he gits amung you, you'll think old Solferino has cum again and no mistake!" You ought to hev seen them scamper, Mr. Fair. They run orf as tho Satun hisself was arter them with a red hot ten pronged pitchfork. In five minits the premises was clear.

"How kin I ever repay you, Mr. Ward, for your kindness?" sed Old Abe, advancin and shakin me warmly by the hand. "How kin I ever repay you, sir?"

"By givin the whole country a good, sound administration. By poerin' ile upon the troubled waturs, North and South. By pursooin' a patriotic, firm, and just course, and then if any State wants to secede, let 'em Sesesh!"

"How 'bout my Cabinit, Mister, Ward?" sed Abe.

"Fill it up with Showmen sir! Showmen is devoid of politics. They hain't got any principles! They know how to cater for the public. They know what the public wants, North & South. Showmen, sir, is honest men. Ef you doubt their literary ability, look at their posters, and see small bills! Ef you want a Cabinit as is a Cabinit fill it up with showmen, but don't call on me. The moral wax figger perfeshun musn't be permitted to go down while there's a drop of blood in these vains! A. Linkin, I wish you well! Ef Powers or Walcutt wus to pick out a model for a beautiful man, I scarcely think they'd sculp you; but ef you do the fair thing by your country you'll make as putty a angel as any of us! A. Linkin, use the talents which Nature has put into you judishusly and firmly, and all will be well! A. Linkin, adoo!"

He shook me cordyully by the hand—we exchanged picters, so we could gaze upon each others' liniments when far away from one another—he at the hellum of the ship of State, and I at the hellum of the show bizniss—admittance only 15 cents.[15]

This is one of the pieces that later appeared in *Artemus Ward, His Book,* the book from which Lincoln read "High Handed Outrage at Utica" to his cabinet. (And he may have read this one also. One account has him reading two stories.) Appearing in the nation's leading comic magazine, the four contributions did much to enhance Artemus Ward's popularity, which was already great, as evidenced by the fact that *Vanity Fair* issued an advertisement (published in the *Plain Dealer* among other newspapers) listing "ARTEMUS WARD, the Great American Showman" along with James Russell Lowell, Charles G. Leland, Richard B. Stoddard, and other well-known contributors. The publisher of the *Plain Dealer*, J. W. Gray, of course saw the advertisement, and he also happened to see some notes for a lecture on Brown's desk. Gray was in many ways one of Brown's kindred spirits; he loved humor, made friends easily, and was appreciative of talent. In a sense he had been Brown's discoverer, and he had brought him along to the top of the *Plain Dealer* organization. But he was no man to get into a serious argument with. Although weighing only 125 pounds, he was described by the *Buffalo Courier* as being "pugnacious as a terrier. He rushes into a controversy, as a bull starts on a career, with his eyes shut, regardless of the size or strength of his antagonist."[16] The *Vanity Fair* advertisement and the lecture notes were like red flags to Gray. He called Brown to account for them. Anything Brown wrote, Gray said, ought to be going into the *Plain Dealer*. In reply, Brown asserted that the lecture notes were his property, and so was Artemus Ward, but he would think it over. Finally, Brown made a modest enough proposal; he offered to give the newspaper his entire output for $1,200 a year. Gray refused, and Brown resigned on November 10, 1860, writing for publication that day a note of goodbye and gratitude to his friends, "including every member of the Press of Cleveland." That these friends were many and generous was proved by a farewell banquet where the mayor of Cleveland presented Brown with a $150 diamond pin and these glowing words: "Its brightness is but indicative of the brightest qualities in the mind of the acceptor."[17]

Brown left Cleveland in what was apparently a confused state of mind, and this was one of the very few times in his life when he disregarded the "moral" he had written for Artemus Ward: "Never do nothin which isn't your Fort," than which there has never been a better. Instead of pursuing his opportunity with *Vanity Fair,* which had given him hope of regular employment, he yielded to what was apparently a vague idea of getting into show business (the old temptation). He worked for a time as an advance agent for the singer of comic songs Ossian E. Dodge, under an arrangement whereby Brown would gradually work into appearances on the stage. But by December 21 Brown was fed up with Dodge and, expressing complete revulsion, wrote a friend in Cleveland that "the folly—the madness—of continuing with him grew every day more and more apparent, and I determined to cut loose at all hazards." Leaving Dodge, Brown set out for New York. On the way, the lure of the footlights temporarily got the better of him again. It happened that Brown had a wide acquaintance among minstrel show performers, whom he loved and who loved him for reasons that included his importance as a source of jokes. In Pittsburgh he ran into some of his minstrel friends and was induced to join the show, blacking his face with burnt cork and appearing as an end man in at least one performance. But this was only a brief relapse. He resumed his journey to New York, reaching that city at four o'clock on the morning of January 1, 1861. He took lodging and slept until one o'clock. Then he rose and tried to make a call at the *Vanity Fair* office, only to find it closed. He had forgotten that it was New Year's Day. "Couldn't see anyone and felt blue. Went to bed early," he wrote to his Cleveland friends.

But his report the next day was all sunshine. "Got up this morning and went to the *Vanity Fair* office. Good fellows—glad to see me. Talked ten minutes with them and made a permanent engagement at $20 a week as one of the editors of the paper." Everything had worked out wonderfully. He was to work part of the day at his editorial duties, write whatever he wanted to, and do an Artemus Ward letter when he felt like it. He'd be on the free list for all the plays, circuses, minstrel shows, and concerts in town. Board and room at the Western Hotel would cost him seven dollars a week. "I am certainly a lucky cuss," Brown wrote to his *Plain Dealer* friends. "I don't understand it myself, but it is so. Things are new to me now, and I shall proceed cautiously. But as soon as I get started I will make things whiz, so to speak. I intend to know everybody on Broadway in about six months."[18]

4

Man About Manhattan

Brown's explorations of New York proceeded at a faster pace than even he had expected; they astonished Charles Godfrey Leland, then the editor of *Vanity Fair*. "Quiet as he seemed," Leland wrote in his memoirs, "in three weeks he had found out everything in New York."[1]

One of the places Brown very quickly found his way to was Pfaff's, the restaurant, at 647 Broadway, which was the recognized headquarters of Bohemia in America, a select hangout for writers, actors, artists, and the like. Many of its habitues were *Vanity Fair* writers, but the group was presided over by Henry Clapp, editor of the *New York Saturday Press,* a small, wiry, cynical, bearded, oldish-looking man (he was actually only in his middle forties) with a sharp and shocking wit. For example, he said that Horace Greeley was a "self-made man that worships his creator,'" and that a notoriously vain, out-of-work clergyman was "'waiting for a vacancy in the Trinity.'"[2] His *Saturday Press* was always on the point of going broke, and did go broke in the end, and Clapp died in poverty in 1875, but not before he had helped several people on their way to fame. It was the *Saturday Press* that published Mark Twain's jumping-frog story, and it was Clapp who was one of the earliest and most enthusiastic promoters of Walt Whitman. The poet once said that Clapp "'stepped out from the crowd of hooters'"[3] at a time when help was needed, and his history would not have been the same without Clapp's support. With his eye for talent, Clapp immediately welcomed Brown to the family of Pfaffians. One of them described Brown as he first appeared in the restaurant. "He was an old-fashioned fellow for even those days.... He wore his hair overlong.... On his cravat, over which rolled a small collar, he wore a pin [undoubtedly the farewell gift from his Cleveland friends]. ... His velvet vest was high cut, revealing a tiny stud. His customary garb was a broadcloth frock coat, broadcloth trousers and high boots. He was the incarnation of fun. ..."[4]

The restaurant Artemus Ward found himself in was not imposing. It was in a cellar and was entered by a stairway from the sidewalk. Furnishings were rough—a few chairs and tables, a counter, shelves, some barrels, and the like. At one end of it, beneath the Broadway sidewalk, there was a sort of cave, or vault. Here, in the words of William Winter the drama critic, "after Clapp had assumed the sceptre as Prince of Bohemia, that cave and table were pre-empted by him and his votaries, at certain hours of the day and night, and no stranger ventured to intrude into the magic realm."[5] Walt Whitman, who was one of the regulars at Pfaff's, once started to write this poem about the cave.

The Two Vaults

The vault at Pfaffs where the drinkers and laughers meet to eat and
    drink and carouse,
While on the walk immediately overhead, pass the myriad feet of
    Broadway
As the dead in their graves, are underfoot hidden
And the living pass over them, recking not of them.
Laugh on Laughers!
Drink on Drinkers!
Bandy the jest! Toss the theme from one to another!
Beam up—Brighten up, bright eyes of beautiful young men!
Eat what you, having ordered, are pleased to see placed before you—
    after the work of the day, now, with appetite, eat,
Drink wine—drink beer—raise your voice,
Behold! your friend as he arrives—Welcome him, when, from the
    upper step, he looks down upon you with a cheerful look.

The poem went on for eight lines and a part of another but was not finished. Whitman therefore never arrived at the second of "the two vaults," but the remaining lines of the poem seem to make clear that he was headed toward a comparison with a burial vault, for he wrote of the laughers, drinkers, and jesters at Pfaff's and the throngs on the sidewalk overhead as though they were a passing pageant in a dream: "O You phantoms! oft I pause, yearning to arrest some one of you! Oft I doubt your reality. . . ."[6] Some of the same curious sense of impermanence which seems to have impressed many frequenters of the place was caught by one of the wags of the group who, in order to designate the owner, Charles Pfaff, as the center of the Bohemian world, once chalked on the cellar wall, "C. Pfaff and die."[7]

Unfortunately, the words were prophetic for many. One night Edmund C. Stedman wrote down the names of fourteen people, including Whitman and Artemus Ward, who gathered one evening at Pfaff's for dinner. For some reason he kept the paper and noted on it in 1877, "nine of them now dead,"[8] later observing (in 1890) that he thought no other list of names he could have assembled would have shown a comparable death toll within such a short time. The Civil War and— Stedman believed—the pace, the hard work, and the irregular income of the literary or artistic life in New York at that time, with consequent illnesses and tragedies of various kinds, were among the causes of this mortality.

But while the Pfaffians still met in the cellar restaurant they exerted important influences on Artemus Ward's life and career. His social life, for one thing, was considerably expanded by the literary ladies and actresses who were unconventional enough to visit Pfaff's. One of them, the acknowledged queen of Bohemia, was Ada Clare, a gay, pretty, passionate girl with "pansy-blue" eyes, fair skin, blond hair, and a turned-up nose. Ada had borne an illegitimate son in Paris, but her loyal fellow-Pffafians always defended her before nosy outsiders by insisting that the child was the result of an immaculate conception—a superhuman reputation on which poor Ada would eventually default by dying of a mad dog's bite in 1874. She and Brown were good friends and would later entertain a thought of literary collaboration, but there was never a romance between them.

With another of the Bohemian young ladies, Brown was destined to become more deeply involved. This was Adah Isaacs Menken, a dark-eyed, lovely, curvaceous, and talented Jewish girl a year younger than he. Like Ada Clare, Adah Menken wrote poetry and appeared on the stage, but she was considerably more gifted, and she had a hunger for fame that would lead her to spectacular heights and to a variety of friendships and amours with Walt Whitman, Charles Dickens, Dante Gabriel Rossetti, the elder Dumas, Algernon Swinburne, and others. Adah was learned as well as beautiful. She had studied the classics, and knew French, Hebrew, German, and Spanish. She had, however, one particular problem when Brown first met her, and if he looked upon her with eyes of longing and of love, this difficulty was among the reasons why matters between them did not proceed further at this time.

Adah's marital status was incredibly unclear. Her first marriage had been to an Alexander Menken; she had left him and later, thinking he had divorced her, married the prizefighter John C. Heenan. There had been a scandal when Menken announced that he hadn't divorced her but would certainly proceed to do so now; Heenan then had repudiated Adah, and she had applied for a divorce from *him*. And so for at least the first year of her acquaintance with Charles Brown, she would be legally off-limits—married to someone, even if it was hard to tell to whom. This was an incipient romance that in 1861 would have to be marked "To be continued."

It was just as well. There was a bred-in ambivalence in Brown: at one of his psychic poles a desire for a wild, free, unconventional life open to love, pleasure, beauty, passion, leisure; and at the other the belief that a man ought to work hard, get ahead, and not get mixed up in any monkey business—and just then he was feeling conservative. He wrote to a friend in Cleveland that he had never been so steady in his life: "Indeed, I am compelled to be. Promptness and faithfulness in business here are implicitly demanded. It is the greatest mistake in the world to suppose that a man can raise the d——l in New York and still occupy a responsible business position."[9] This might have been his grandfather Thaddeus or his father, Levi, speaking: there were good prospects ahead, so buckle down, work hard, and all would be well.

And indeed, all did go well for a while. In the spring of 1861 he was promoted to chief editor of *Vanity Fair,* Leland having resigned. But the magazine soon ran into rough seas; the political climate was wrong for a liberal comic magazine, paper grew scarce, costs soared, and there were financial troubles. On one occasion Brown suffered the embarrassment of being unable to pay for some verses contributed by his old friend from Ohio, W. D. Howells. Brown began to see that he was not the man to cope with these problems.

"'The poor paper,'" as he put it, had "'got to be a conundrum.'"[10] He decided that he would resign as editor (but continue as a contributor of Artemus Ward letters) and take up the career of a lecturer in earnest. Lecturing still promised to be the best way of capitalizing on his ability as a humorist. Some of the current throng of traveling speakers made as much as $100 or even $200 a night, while Brown was receiving only $25 a week on *Vanity Fair.* There was also the lure of public appearances with all their brightness, excitement, and warmth, as compared with the lonely trade of writing or the usually unrecognized work of the editor.

There was another influence here that came at an important point in Brown's life. Back in Cleveland, when he had considered the idea of lecturing and discussed it with his friends, they had called him a fool. But when he talked it over with the people at Pfaff's, many of whom had had lecturing or theatrical experience, he received strong encouragement. They could see what nobody else had seen—the makings of a great performer on stage.

The initial platforms that Brown set his sights on were those of the athenaeums, literary societies, and lyceums that had been formed everywhere, with the idea, generally, of educating or elevating the masses, a cultural duty that Theodore Parker, Henry Ward Beecher, Wendell Phillips, Horace Greeley, Ralph Waldo Emerson, and others sought to discharge with discourses on science, theology, philosophy, literature, history, politics, travel, temperance, and other improving subjects. This was the sort of thing Brown would never have attempted to do; he doubted whether people could be elevated other than one at a time, by their own efforts.

Brown decided that many people were secretly bored to death with being "improved" and that the lecture platform was ripe for some sort of entertainment. Humor had, of course, been used; there had been readers of humorous works and speakers who lightened their discourses with witticisms and anecdotes. But no one had ever ventured to appear before an audience for an hour with no narrative, information, or instruction—with nothing but the antics of his mind; and this was what Brown seems to have been aiming at from the very beginning, although the comic nature of his performance would greatly evolve as he went on.

Brown had, of course the reputation of Artemus Ward to trade on, and that was a considerable advantage; Artemus was widely known, and this would immeasurably increase the drawing power of advertising and publicity. But Brown had no intention of representing the Old Showman on the platform; his lectures would be something entirely different. Preparing for it, he began putting together in script form the notes he had been jotting down for several months. When completed it was a sort of stream-of-consciousness series of jokes and comments that had very little coherence. For the title, which had not the slightest thing to do with the content of the lecture, he settled upon "The Children in the Wood," which was later sometimes "The Babes in the Wood." This was the name of a well-known children's story that had been the basis of several pantomimes; and although it was completely irrelevant, at least it suggested some of the wide-eyed, childish charm the lecture would attain.

Brown's campaign was carefully prepared. He'd seen enough of show business to know a great deal about it, but he thought that nonetheless he probably needed an agent, and for this service he turned to one of the Pfaffians who had urged him to embark on a lecturing career. This was Frank Wood, an editor then at loose ends, who was described as "fascinating . . . sympathetic . . . amiable,"[11] but whose managerial judgment would prove to be suspect. Wood urged Brown to open at Clinton Hall, on Astor Place in New York, and Brown had to point out that it would be folly to launch an unproved entertainment here and that he had better have a series of tryouts along the lyceum circuit out of town. In preparing for these, and for other engagements that followed, Brown often acted as his own press agent. He knew dozens of writers and editors on magazines and newspapers, and he had no hesitation in writing them tactful, modest, but insistent letters. During all the rest of his career he would always be at work on this task of self-promotion, rarely missing an opportunity to urge some friend somewhere to toot the horn for Artemus Ward, the name he would use as a lecturer in cheerful disregard of the possibility that this might confuse the public. Early in October, writing R. H. Stoddard to tell him about several engagements he had lined up, he suggested, "If you will do the small paragraph for the *World* on Monday. . . ,"[12] and a month later, applying to a prospective sponsor, he was able to report that the *World* was saying nice things about him. In the same letter, dated November 16, 1861, not long before his first lecture, Brown implied that he had not really planned to do anything like this; he was only yielding to a clamor for Artemus Ward to appear on the platform. This was straining the truth just a bit even if it was press-agentry. To be sure, there was a ready-made acceptance for a figure as famous as this, but the public was hardly "clamoring" for Artemus Ward as a lecturer. Yet Brown declared, "I have not sought, in any way, the position of lecturer: it has actually been thrust upon me. I have already some thirty engagements, and they are coming in daily." He added a modest note or two: "It is a wholly new field to me, and I tremble. But not seriously. I open in New London on the 26th, and I conclude that will be a worse day for that place than when the British seized it a number of years ago. But on the second night, at Norwich, I intend to be rather interesting. Newburyport . . . will be my third appearance, and I hope to be easy on my pins (which I am justly proud of) by that time. At least I hope you will not feel called upon to blush for me. My lecture is simply some cheerful paragraphs. As I happen to be acquainted with myself, I have not ventured in where the water is at all deep."[13]

He also added an *e* to his name at about this time; on November 19 he signed one letter "C. F. Brown" and another "Charles F. Browne," so this may have been the day, or near the day, when the change in name took place. However, Artemus Ward would continue moving in on both Brown and Browne, just as Mark Twain took over Samuel Clemens; the author-lecturer would more and more be called Artemus by his friends and would sign many of his letters "Artemus Ward" or "A. Ward."

Along with the classier name of Charles Farrar Browne there developed also a more elegant personal appearance. Besides the intellectual stimulus that New York provided, the city had done much for him outwardly. Here he'd had the opportunity to observe a quality that set the great metropolis apart from most communities he'd been in: a noticeable concern for dress and attractiveness. Brown had an eye for the ladies, and he particularly admired the pretty girls who went tripping along Broadway in multi-colored silks and satins, wearing fine cloaks with rich linings, fluttering their ribbons and silk tassels and holding aloft their dainty, floral-patterned parasols. By gad, this sort of thing made life a little more worth living! He could not fail to observe, too, that many of the men were also exceptional in their grooming: neatly moustached, carefully brushed, clad in fine-textured and well-cut clothing.

One friend, supplementing other descriptions of Brown as he had looked upon his arrival in New York, remembered that he was somewhat old-fashioned in appearance; in fact, if he had been dressed all in red, white and blue he would have looked like Uncle Sam. From this rural, early-American character, Brown—influenced by Bohemianism and a desire to prepare for visual distinction on the lecture platform and, one suspects, yielding to a secret urge just to let himself go—went in a few months to an appearance of exotic splendor. The most spectacular alteration was in what he did to his hair. This, according to most people, was light, flaxen or "hay-colored," although one or two would refer to it as red. Actually, it was conventionally light-brownish-blond, except under artificial light, when it took on a reddish tinge. But there were no natural highlights; his hair was as straight as an Indian's. So Browne (the e now definitely belonged to his name) engaged the services of a *friseur* and had it converted into a mass of curls. In a piece on lectures that the Old Showman had supposedly written, lecturers were described as individuals who "cram theirselves with hi soundin frazis, frizzle up their hare, get trustid for a soot of black close & cum out to lectur at 50 dollers a pop."[14] This is a clue to what Browne was doing—making himself an elaborate representation of the popular lecturer, who sought to be as distinguished and dignified-looking as possible. Besides "frizz[ling] up his hare,"he bought black patent-leather slippers and a funereally dark suit that included a long-tailed coat; a cartoon in *Vanity Fair* also indicates that he wore a white shirt with a furbelow of an elaborately knotted black tie. This costume, combined with Browne's nimbus of curled hair, his bright, luminous eyes, a moustache which, though it drooped at the ends, did so with a devilish, winged flair ("a really killing moustache," one young lady would call it),[15] his big, acquiline nose, a slender frame, and a sort of spread-legged, elbows-akimbo stance that was half grace and half awkwardness, presented a spectacle which could only be regarded as theatrical. In spite of his "better instincts," Browne had gone a long way toward yielding to his secret desire to be a stage performer.

5

The Children in the Wood

On the evening of November 26, 1861, the people gathered in Lawrence Hall, New London, the Connecticut city Browne had chosen for his debut, were utterly astonished when, instead of the rotund, raffish, middle-aged Old Showman whom they'd visualized, a slim, black-clad, solemn creature appeared on the platform. Where is Artemus Ward? they wondered. Has there been an accident? Is this a last-minute replacement?

No, this *is* Artemus. But Artemus Ward is supposed to be funny, and the scholarly-looking young man on the stage is deathly serious. Further, as he begins to speak, it appears that he has prepared himself to give a lecture of the most impressive kind without ever having *been* to a lecture: he seems not to know what he is going to say next; his spoken thoughts dart here and there unexpectedly, some of them absurd, yet delivered with a solemn, fanatical intentness as though they are revelations from God. People begin to laugh. At this the lecturer looks sorrowful and somewhat indignant; he tries to conceal a failing confidence; his mind skitters from one thing to another; and he completely forgets to say anything about his subject, The Children in the Wood. But laughter has seldom ceased, and somehow people have been hugely entertained without knowing, exactly, what they have been listening to!

There is no record of the words Browne actually spoke until after his appearance at Tremont Temple, in Boston, a couple of weeks later. This was recorded by full columns in both the *Transcript* and the *Post*.

Browne was introduced on the platform by his old editorial boss and friend, Benjamin Shillaber, as (according to the *Post*) " 'one of the best fellows of the time, who has done as much as any other man to make people happy.' "[1] According to the *Transcript,* Browne then "stepped to the desk," received "a Boston welcome," and began as follows:

" 'I will state upon the very threshold of the little paper house which I have built, that it is a cold collation rather than a steaming banquet which awaits you within. I can only offer some scraps of salad, a few picnic relishes, and it may be a little whipped cream. But you are very welcome.

" 'The lecture-field has been ploughed, planted and dug; mowed and raked; sowed and reaped; and cultivated, indeed, in so many ways, that I suppose a man of very able mind might not feel too sure of offering you anything strikingly novel or brilliant.

" 'Oblige me, then, by overlooking the shortcomings of a person who has no such thing as a noble mind to his back.' "[2]

There is little reward in reading this or the rest of the lecture, which the *Post* and *Transcript* reporters took down almost word for word, as the similarity of their accounts indicates. There does not seem to be much in what Browne actually said, as recorded, to explain why he caught the fancy of the Boston people and why another paper, the *Daily Advertiser,* was able to report that the audience "was kept in a constant roar of laughter."[3]

The truth seems to be that the contents of the lecture, when separated from their presentation, were as unimpressive as would be the rain droplets that shine in a rainbow after the light has faded. Browne quickly became aware of this difficulty, and he was soon asking reporters not to try to take the lecture down, with the results that verbatim or even near-verbatim accounts of his talks after this date are very hard to find.

There is a hint of what the lecture really was in the account of Boston's *Daily Journal;* it had been, the *Journal* said, an agreeable change from "the old run Lyceum lectures."[4] What Browne seems to have been conducting was a spoof of the lyceum lectures which people had been hearing for years, and of which they were secretly growing so weary. And it seems to have been, in addition, a burlesque of some sermons, and of all solemnly delivered and received utterances which will not stand the light of day when rationally examined. When Browne gave forth, with preacher-like impressiveness and yet with a betrayal of some inner nervous uncertainty, statements that were patently ridiculous, he became the person he had always tried to suppress—the actor—and people's delight in the lecture was largely created by his empathy with the audience and his play upon its reactions. When he stepped out onto the platform and began to speak, something happened in a flash; and what happened was simply the elusive, mysterious magic of a great theatrical presence.

All the newspapers in Boston were enthusiastic. The decisive accolade, however, came in the form of an invitation to attend one of the famous breakfasts at the house of James T. Fields, at 37 (later renumbered 148) Charles Street. This address, at the height of Boston's golden age, represented without any question the most eminent literary and cultural center in the country. Its occupant was the Fields of Ticknor & Fields, publishers of the *Atlantic* and of Longfellow, Lowell, Emerson, Hawthorne, and practically every other then important American writer, as well as of Tennyson, Browning, and other English counterparts. It was presided over by Field's young wife, Annie, whose charm and hospitality, added to similar qualities of her husband, made 37 Charles Street a thoroughly happy and stimulating resort for writers, musicians, artists, actors, and, now and then, an odd celebrity like Charles Farrar Browne. One suspects that Browne was there more at the inclination of the mistress than of the master of the house. Annie Fields had, in the words of Henry James, a "'capacity for incapacitating laughter'";[5] she could laugh herself beyond the power of speech or, almost, of breath. It was she who recorded the event in her diary, and her recollections, added to the several descriptions of the house that came from the pens of its illustrious visitors, make it easy to imagine the scene and the figures in it: the slim young humorist, undoubtedly dressed in his best (it was a Sunday, the eighth of December), knocking at the door of the rather narrow, three-story brick house, and being greeted by the beautiful young hostess and the affable publisher in a small reception room and introduced to two other breakfast guests who arrived shortly afterward, Dr. Oliver Wendell Holmes and his son, the future justice, then home from the war recovering from wounds. These companions were well chosen. The humor of the elder Holmes was sometimes almost as outrageous as Browne's. Any physician who would say that "'the smallest fevers are gratefully received,'" and any Boston Brahmin who would sprinkle into his writings such puns as "When is charity like a top?—When it begins to hum,"[6] would certainly not be a stranger in the world of Artemus Ward.

As they moved to the first-floor dining room, it might have been expected that Dr. Holmes would live up to his reputation as the autocrat of the breakfast table; a frequent guest (he lived just down the street), Holmes usually did dominate these affairs. But this morning, as Annie recalled it, James Fields got started on anecdotes of literary people he had dealt with, with one story leading to another, and the performance was so entertaining that no one else said much. However, Holmes did find an opening in which to compliment Browne on his success, and the young hostess remembered that "Artemus twinkled all over."

Browne seems to have been somewhat abashed. According to Mrs. Fields, he "'said little after the Professor arrived. He was evidently immensely possessed by him.'"[7] Browne's one recorded remark had to do with the audience he had encountered on the tryout tour of his comic lecture. "'I was prepared for a good deal of gloom, but I had no idea they would be *so much* depressed.'"[8] It was just the right sort of thing to say at 37 Charles Street.

As Browne continued through his 1861–62 season, sheer nonsense became more and more dominant in the lecture, and it gradually turned into a performance in which abstract and intellectual humor upstaged everything else. People in a community where Artemus Ward was to appear usually became aware of his coming through paragraphs in the editorial columns which the diligent Artemus, or his manager, planted in advance. Then, a day or so before the lecture, an advertisement would appear in the newspaper, usually one column by five or six inches, and posters would go up at strategic locations. This poster never varied from the beginning to the end of his career. It was reproduced from a reverse plate, with rough, white-on-black letters that said simply

ARTEMUS WARD
WILL
SPEAK A PIECE

A printed slip underneath gave the name of the hall or theater, the time, and other information.

Ward's appearance on the platform was preceded by piano or organ music, or sometimes, as in Manchester, New Hampshire, by the town band. The reporter in Manchester, where Artemus appeared on December 20, 1861, said that a man like this, who had a reputation as a wit from his writing, had a very difficult role to play, for everyone would come expecting him to be unreasonably funny.

This was a perceptive observation, and Browne was well aware of the difficulty. Therefore, he gave a great deal of thought to ways of opening the lecture that would result in a quick conquest. One of his devices was to walk out on the stage and simply stand there without saying a word. As what seemed to be an eternity dragged by, his would-be listeners began to think that he had forgotten his "piece" and were

Artemus Ward as a lecturer in the early 1860s. Courtesy Western Reserve Historical Society, Cleveland, Ohio.

overcome by a sympathetic agony. But time passed, and the impassive figure on the stage just stood there with a fixed, owl-like expression. The agony in the audience increased. People began to get jumpy. They coughed, shuffled, jerked around, and whispered, "What's the matter with him? Why doesn't he say something?" And an anguished lady might cry, "Oh, dear!" Finally the muttering, shifting about, exclamations, and perhaps even stamping and handclapping mounted to a considerable uproar. Artemus then held up his hand. A hush fell over the hall, and he said with sad indignation, "'*Ladies* and gentlemen. When you have *finished* with this unseemly interruption, I shall be glad to continue.'"⁹

This was always followed by a mighty roar of relief and laughter. Obviously, this was not going to be any ordinary lecture but a walk into a wonderful world of foolishness.

Or Artemus might come on with a feather duster, and be mistaken for an usher preparing the stage. And still another gambit was described by a man who was present in a hall at Springfield, Massachusetts, where an audience of skeptical New Englanders had gathered. "Presently the door on the left of the stage was slowly, almost hesitatingly, opened, and the looked-for man appeared. I recall vividly the impression he made upon us all with his tall, gaunt, almost attenuated figure, accentuated to mournfulness by the unrelieved austerity of his black dress . . . and his wistful half-smile, as he glanced deprecatingly at the audience, and then, looking straight before him, strode quite across the platform and took a chair at its farther end. There he sat, his sorrowful visage seeming to breathe the spirit of Cervantes' knight of the weeping laughter. And the audience, as if feeling that it could not come to the relief of this unhappy man too quickly, and assure him of its entire neighborliness and sympathy, broke out spontaneously with handclapping and said plainly enough, 'Welcome, welcome! Be not cast down. We shall laugh at anything you say.' I do not know that I have ever witnessed such a capture of an assembly, so immediate a dissolving of that cold equilibrium which even experienced public speakers dread—and this without a word having been uttered. There could not, it seemed, be a more auspicious moment for his beginning. But the enthusiasm did not, apparently, reach its object. There he sat, motionless; one long, thin leg hanging over the other, his eyes cast down, a picture of irresolution and melancholy. Soon he took out his watch, looked at it, and replaced it; then after a little, he nervously reversed the position of his legs, raised his eyes, and revealed a gaze of anxiety and unrest. Then he distressfully consulted his watch again, after which he resumed his position of resigned waiting. After a few minutes this dumb-show was repeated with distracting variations, until the evident fear and worry of the man infected and hypnotized us all. We could not understand his unrest. We could only sympathize with it."

The reporter went on to describe how the mystery was explained and how, in the explanation, people found themselves plunged into another absurd perplexity. When the town clock was heard striking eight, the figure on the stage got up, gave a sigh of relief, and walked to the lectern. His talk, he explained, had been inadvertently advertised to commence at eight and close at nine. But it was only forty-five minutes long! He therefore simply could *not* decide whether he ought to begin at 8:00 and close at 8:45 or begin at 8:15 and close at 9:00. Browne then led the audience into a typical Wardian rigmarole, solemnly giving the reasons for one course of action and then for the other. Then, abruptly, he paused in this discussion, and in a high-pitched, pathetic voice said, " 'I have come here to lecture in order that I might get money enough to go to Africa. I should feel that I lived in vain if I did not go to Africa and....' " Here he whipped out a handkerchief to smother a sob. " 'I don't want to live in vain. I had rather live in Springfield.' " [10]

He was described as opening in another city as follows: " 'My dear, kind, indulgent friends, I wish to explain to you, before entering upon the Herculean task of speaking my piece, that I have a reputation—a good, yes, most excellent reputation.' " Then, after stopping and fumbling fruitlessly through his pockets for a minute, he said woefully, " 'But I haven't it with me tonight!' " [11]

The audience was always kept off balance. Sometimes, for example, Artemus would seem to be afflicted with a sudden hoarseness or feebleness of the throat and would announce, " 'Ladies and gentlemen, owing to an unfortunate weakness of my voice, I find I must stop and rest it. But—ah—while I am resting my voice I will relate a little anecdote.' " As a variant of his faked voice trouble, Ward might pause in the middle of the lecture, take out his watch, look at it, and announce, " 'We will now have an intermission of fifteen minutes.' " Then, after people had begun to stare at one another in dismay, he would replace the watch, rub his hands, and say, " 'But—ah—hum—during the intermission I shall go on with my lecture.' " [12]

Or he might stop and abruptly inquire if there was anyone in the audience who was dissatisfied with what he had heard so far. If so, that person could have a free ticket for Artemus Ward's next lecture, which, it shortly developed, was going to be held in New Zealand.

The effect of all this, however, was not that of a smart aleck playing tricks on an audience. The impression was one of mental uncertainty and of pitfalls into which Artemus Ward was toppling, dragging a helpless, hypnotized audience in after him. As one critic would write, "He gets hold of two inconsistent and absurdly arbitrary ideas, connects them with a sort of simple fervor in his mind, and presses them on his hearers with an air of plaintive good faith that is quite irresistible."[13]

Thus, with a solemn stare, Ward would say, "I met a man in Oregon who hadn't any teeth. Not a tooth in his head." And then, dropping his voice to a tone of quiet, confidential impressiveness, he would add, "Yet that man could play on the bass drum better than any man I ever met."[14]

The lecturer delivered a piece of nonsense like this with such deathly seriousness that at first people felt they oughtn't to laugh. But they couldn't help it, and when laughter interrupted him, Artemus often reacted with reproachful indignation.

He seemed frequently to be groping for words or thoughts, in the process arriving at what Immanuel Kant, in his definition of laughter, called "'the sudden transformation of a strained expectation into nothing.'"[15] No one had the slightest idea of what was coming next. For example, when Ward began by declaring virtuously, "I prefer temperance hotels...," there was nothing in his demeanor to suggest that he was going to add, "although they sell worse liquor than any other kind of hotels."[16]

Artemus Ward was also an early master of the unspoken joke, consisting of some significant statement followed by an electric pause during which there is a quick flash of nonverbal communication between the performer and his hearers, who can almost see his mind at work. In illustrating, for example, the sensation of being confined in a small compartment such as that of a stagecoach, Artemus would say impulsively, "Those of you who have been in the penitentiary...," and then, by a pause and conscience-stricken expression, indicate that he realized his blunder. He would continue lamely through a few meaningless, time-killing words such as "and stayed there... any length... of time," obviously trying to think of something that would get him out of his predicament, and then say (with sudden hopefulness, as though the rescuing phrase had just come to him), "... as *visitors*," only to indicate, with another expression of distress, that he recognized too late the fact that he had merely substituted one insult for another by implying the imprisonment of the audience's relatives or friends.[17]

After five or ten minutes the audience could begin to read Ward's facial signals (an increase in gloominess, for example, usually meant that he was about to spring something funny), so the pleasure of anticipation heightened their enjoyment. This playful interaction between the audience and a man who was dispensing utter foolishness with the earnestness and solemnity of a minister—the sort of minister or high-minded lyceum lecturer people had been listening to for years—was so tremendously funny to Americans of the 1860s that Ward apparently almost killed some of his audience. There was also an air of delicious sin about it, as though people were, as one man said, "laughing right out in meeting." Here was a black-clad, long-faced preacher type intoning, with impressive pauses between sentences, such things as: "I could draw on wood at a very tender age. When a mere child I once drew a small cartload of raw turnips over a wooden bridge. The people of the village noticed me. I drew their attention." Or: "I remember [a hotel] where they gave me a bag of oats for a pillow. I had night mares of course. In the morning the landlord said, 'How do you feel, old hoss—hay?' I told him I felt my oats."[18]

To people who had experienced little platform humor of any kind, foolishness like this was new and vastly entertaining. It was also an entertainment parents could take their children to. The children couldn't be taken to a "theater" (unless it happened to be called a concert hall); that was immoral. And they couldn't be taken to the ordinary lyceum lecture, which was torture to them. But Artemus Ward's performance simply delighted them, and he often gave matinees for their special convenience. Also, Ward's jokes were always, or nearly always, in good taste. There was, however, at least one exception, recalled by James Ryder, a story told in a lecture concerning a subject on which Ward's usual discrimination had a way of deserting him: death. The essentials of the story were these: Traveling man is trying to take home a few pounds of very high limburger cheese. Freight office refuses to accept it because of the frightful odor. Man puts cheese into an empty coffin he happens to be shipping home as baggage, his wife having died the day before. En route, later on the train, man goes back to the baggage car and finds car attendant with window open, head thrust out, gasping for air. Attendant points to coffin and asks, "Any relation?" Man replies, "Wife." Attendant gasps, "Well, she ain't in no *trance*."[19]

This questionable item disappeared from the script, and many others were eliminated for other reasons. Ward was quick to discover that what looked funny on paper was often not funny on the platform, and that the biggest audience reactions frequently came from phrases that were casually "thrown away." Thus, when he spoke of a photograph of himself as being "rather sweet to look at for a short time,"[20] it was the way he paused and then drawled "for a short time" that triggered the laugh. Effects such as these were greatly facilitated by a remarkable quality of his voice. There were many points in the lecture at which, in delivering an "aside," or in wandering helplessly toward some verbal disaster and losing confidence in what he was saying, or in giving one of his ludicrous soliloquies, "his voice dwindled away" and became, as one reviewer wrote, "sad and somewhat feeble, but clear, so that with little effort he makes himself easily heard by all his auditors."[21] Some sort of extra resonance or amplification, possibly associated with his large nose, produced a clarion-like clearness that carried throughout the largest hall. It was also noted that while his eyes were not actually large, they often seemed to be, indicating that along with his compelling voice went a sort of hypnotic attraction. One reporter wrote of Ward, "One is almost tempted, in listening to him, to regret that he did not adopt the legitimate stage of comedy as a field of display for rare talent . . . and it is easy to imagine the success which his inimitable oddity of voice and expression must inevitably have won in eccentric or character parts."[22]

That Ward did not achieve his effects with a simple deadpan performance, that is, through delivering his jokes with an expressionless face and a corresponding flatness of tone, is indicated by one of his most successful series of lines, which he used throughout most of his lecturing career. This was simply:

> Oh my Maria! Alas! she married another.
> They frequently do. I hope she is happy
> —because I am.[23]

There is nothing funny about these words in and of themselves, nor could there be in a toneless expression. Extrapolating from other descriptions of Ward's performances, it can be imagined that the delivery went something like this:

"Oh my Maria!" This was spoken in the manner of a preacher wailing out some pronouncement of unutterable woe. Then came an extremely long pause, during which Ward stared at the audience in a mood of abstracted gloom and the audience stared back, wondering who Maria was and why the lecturer's life had been blighted because of her. He presently explained this in low, tragic tones. "Alas! she married another." He then seemed to forget his hearers entirely and drift off into a period of meditation, from which he aroused himself with a matter-of-fact, almost casual remark to himself, a sort of verbal shrug. "They frequently do." His voice then mounted on an exalted note of noble self-renunciation. "I hope she is happy!" Then came the snapper as he confided to the audience with a relieved sigh, "Because I am," and people toppled into the aisles.

There was some question as to whether this was all acting or whether some of it was real; that is to say, whether Ward was not actually drawing upon some inner mine of shyness, hesitation, confusion, and most particularly, melancholy, the latter to buttress himself in maintaining the attitude of deepest gloom which in portions of the lecture was so howlingly funny to audiences of the day. As an instance in support of this, it seems very odd that the heroine of the Maria routine should have had that particular name. Maria had been the name of one of Browne's little sisters who had died in the year before he was born. (A reviewer once remarked that behind the humor of Artemus Ward on the platform he sensed something *genuine*—some inner, childlike bewilderment.)

There is a suggestion of such partly-acted, partly-real effects in a reviewer's description of the way Browne's "Children in the Wood" lecture ended. Having mentioned the title only once or twice in a very peripheral way, Ward said, "'I now come to my subject—The Babes in the Wood.'" He then took out his watch, whereupon an expression of great surprise and distress came over his face, and he continued in a perplexed, wandering way, "'But I find that I have exceeded my time, and will therefore merely remark, that so far as I know, they were very good babes.'" Then, on a high-pitched note, very nervous and defensive, "'I really have not time to go into their history; you will find it all in the story books.'" And finally, in a mood changing to dreamy, musing pathos; "'They died in the woods, listening to the woodpecker tapping the hollow beech tree. It was a sad fate for them, and I pity them. So, I hope, do you. Good night!'"[24]

Ward kept his most successful jokes and routines and worked them into each new version of the show as it developed. So, although the show was constantly changing with the inclusion of timely, topical references and other fresh material, a lot of it was the same old stuff, and when Ward returned to a town where he had been before, he usually changed the title. Thus "The Children [or Babes] in the Wood" became "Sixty Minutes in Africa," "An Hour With a Ghost" or "The Ghosts!," and "Robinson Crusoe." It might have been, as far as the content of the lecture was concerned, one of the greatest hoaxes ever practiced on the American public, except for one thing: people weren't attending for the content; they were going to see and hear Artemus Ward, and whatever it was that he had done before, they would love to see him do it again.

Probably one of the things that people enjoyed most about the lecture was the feeling of superiority it gave them, and the wonderful sympathy for the lecturer that somehow accompanied their mirth. Charles Godfrey Leland expressed it well in one of his Hans Breitmann verses about

> . . . de goot oldt lady,
> Ash vent to hear Artemus Ward,
> Und say it vas shames de beoples
> Vas laugh demselfs most tead
> At de boor young veller lecturin',
> Vhen he tidn't know vot he said.[25]

6

Lecturing, Literary, and Other Affairs

Artemus Ward's tour of 1861–62 marked the beginning of a lecturing schedule which for sheer, continuous expenditure of energy would be hard to surpass. Through four such seasons, each lasting roughly from October to June, and through part of another, Ward lectured almost every night except Sunday, even including holidays. As his fame grew and he moved from the lyceum circuit to the big-city halls and theaters, he was able to remain in one place for as long as a week, sometimes longer, but through the first couple of seasons almost entirely and through long periods of his whole career he was rushing through a series of one-night stands, for he overlooked hardly any community where there was an audience large enough to make the lecture a paying propostion. A typical day consisted of getting up very early to catch a train, riding part or, at times, most of the day in cars crowded with soldiers or other war-time traffic, eating irregular meals, checking into a hotel, delivering the lecture, entertaining afterward or being entertained, and getting to bed late at night in time for only a few hours' sleep before the whole routine began over again. And during most of his waking hours he was likely to be a center of entertainment off the stage as well as on it. Although he maintained a sorrowful expression during his performance and was inclined to be quiet and abstracted when not in company, he was what one newspaperman called a "gay and festive cuss"[1] when in a congenial social group, his eyes twinkling and his face alive with appreciation of good humor and good companions. People followed him to a saloon, hotel lobby, or dining room with delighted anticipation, and Ward was always ready to oblige with conversation and conviviality. His enjoyment of the excitement and adulation and his welcoming of new friendships made the lecturing grind more pleasant but no less wearying; it tended merely to anesthetize the fatigue. Nor was his success invariable and automatic during the first lecturing season, when financial reward were sometimes meager.

This is reflected by an agreement Browne made in January 1862 with Charles A. Shaw, a young promoter from Biddeford, Maine, who replaced Frank Wood as Browne's agent. Under its terms, Browne was to get twenty-five dollars per lecture. Shaw was to pay traveling expenses, hotel bills, advertising costs, and hall rents. In his advance work, Shaw usually tried for a contract with a sponsoring group: a young men's association, mechanics' institute, or other lyceum organization which would guarantee a minimum amount, and Browne, coming along behind and delivering the lecture, picked up the money but had no authority to alter the arrangement. The usual admission charge during this season was twenty-five cents, which meant that the hall had to be large and well-filled before Shaw began to make any money. Many halls were limited in size, so neither Browne nor Shaw became rich in this winter and spring of 1862. Yet, at times Artemus Ward could be a big money-maker. For example, after his appearance in Rochester that winter, the *Rochester Democrat* reported that in Corinthian Hall "'no space was left unoccupied'" and nearly five thousand people were turned away.[2]

This sort of crowd was increasingly to be expected as Ward's lecturing career progressed, and he soon became aware that sometime in the future he would be better off financially by controlling the enterprise himself, having his own agent, hiring the halls, and getting an agreed-upon share of the profits rather than a fixed fee.

During that season Browne was making very little use of the pen. In the rush of his traveling about, the lecturer had just about ousted the comic writer. But in spite of his dwindling contributions to *Vanity Fair,* his support from that magazine continued to be firm and friendly. Artemus Ward's first book was due to come out in the spring, and all winter *Vanity Fair* was offering it as a subscription premium. In May it also ran a cover cartoon, "Artemus Ward as a Public Lecturer," showing a slender young man in a frock coat and flowing tie, posed in an earnest and eccentric attitude in front of the lectern with "The Children in the Wood" posted on the wall behind him.

When *Artemus Ward, His Book* was issued on May 17, 1862, it was unexpectedly good, considering the grab-bag nature of the contents. The book included sixteen comic illustrations portraying the Old Showman in various attitudes and adventures, some picked up from *Vanity Fair,* some new, but all similar in spirit and line technique. Excellent typography added to the charm of the pages. In considering the relatively slight amount of manuscript he had to work with, and wishing to make the book bulk up as much as possible, the publisher, George W. Carleton, had told his printers to use plenty of word spacing and plenty of lead between the lines. The result was an open, inviting appearance of almost primer-like readability. All in all, Carleton had somehow made a disorderly collection of articles look like a book, and an interesting book. The response was surprising. According to Carleton, forty thousand copies were eventually sold, with a royalty for Artemus of fifteen cents a copy.

One of the first books published under Carleton's imprint, *Artemus Ward, His Book* soon attracted other humorists to his fold (in one case at least, that of Josh Billings, through Browne's personal good offices). In time, the Carleton office became a sort of hangout for comic writers, and Carleton made his reputation as a publisher of American humor.

As Ward's reputation grew and his dress, grooming, and social facility improved, so did his appeal for young ladies, who would always make up an important part of his lecture audiences. The charm he was capable of exerting on them was indicated on one occasion by an improvisation which was the cause of shrieks of delight. It seems that Artemus was on his way to address a young ladies' seminary, and just as he got there, a runaway horse went down the street, attracting a great deal of attention from the seminary and elsewhere. Ward then began his address as follows: " 'The vehicular elopement which has just taken place, young ladies, has furnished us with a timely topic of discourse. Young ladies' seminaries are ever exposed to runaways. Once, when traveling with my show, I came upon a female institute. There were ladders, and lads, too, as to that, at every window. Manly perpendiculars carrying fainting horizontals to the ground. "Fire!" I shouted. "None of that," replied a solemn voice from the orchard. "There ain't no fire; these are only young fellows running off with their sweethearts." There is moral entertainment for man and beast in this runaway. No horse, if attached to a wagon, that is, if sincerely attached to it, will run away with it, but the more a young man is attached to a young woman the more he will run away with her, leaving no traces, in fact none of the harness behind. Young ladies, since I have stood before your beautiful faces I have lost something, and if you or the boy that sweeps out should find a red object, looking like a coral breast-pin that has been stepped on, you may know it is my poor, busted heart.' " [3]

Ward's heart may indeed have been busted in Boston in the spring of 1862. It was apparently then and there that he loved and lost Adah Isaacs Menken. During the preceding year Adah had risen to a success just as great as his own in a way just as original. She had scored a smashing triumph in *Mazeppa, or the Wild Horse of Tartary*.

The drama was based on the life of Ivan Stepanovich Mazeppa, a Ukrainian of noble descent (died 1709) who, while being educated in the court of a Polish king as a youth, was caught making love to a Polish count's wife. As punishment he was tied naked to the back of a wild horse, which was sent galloping off into the wilderness and which carried him, after much suffering, to the Cossacks, who made him a famous warrior and chieftain, etc. The naked ride incident, romanticized by Byron's poem *Mazeppa* (1819), was the climactic scene of the play, an "equestrian drama" which had been a popular spectacle for several years.

Mazeppa was often played by a woman; it was one of those transvestite roles popular at the time. However, no actress had ever attempted the feat of actually staying on the "runaway" horse. When the trained animal galloped off the stage, shortly to reappear on the first of the inclined runs representing mountain slopes, a dummy was ordinarily substituted for the live actress in the offstage interval. Adah Menken, in June 1861, became the first actress to dispense with the dummy. In all her performances she was really bound to the back of the horse, which then went thundering up into the fake mountains past canvas precipices and stuffed wolves toward the top of the theater—a dangerous ride.

Besides its daring, the feat represented the great sexploitation of the sixties. It was, of course, understood that Adah was stripped only down to flesh-colored tights, and that Mazeppa was supposed to be a man anyway, but the spectacle of the "naked" beauty on the wild horse had an erotic symbolism that was deliciously titillating.

When Artemus arrived in Boston at the conclusion of his 1861–62 season, *Mazeppa* was scheduled for the Howard Athenaeum (in retrospect, the booking was somehow appropriate, for this house was later to become the "Old Howard" of burlesque fame). The play was a great success in Boston, as it had been everywhere. Meanwhile, in April, Adah's divorce from Heenan had been granted. So it was June in Boston, and Adah was free, and a romance quickly blossomed. Ward was never one to record affairs of so personal a nature, but this was not the case with Adah, who was quite accustomed to seeing her love life discussed in public. On July 18 she wrote to a friend in New York, "Charlie and I 'went it' pretty rapid for a few days here." But in the same letter she instructed her friend, a writer for a New York paper, "Contradict all reports of my marriage with Chas. F. Browne ('Artemus Ward'). I see the intelligence in an obscure Boston newspaper. . . . It wouldn't do to be married."[4]

And that was about all. But the letter hinted strongly at an affair, a proposal, and a turn-down that may have been not entirely a rejection of Arterhus but of the idea of marriage, an institution that had caused Adah a series of unhappy experiences and promised more difficulties if combined with not one but two burgeoning theatrical careers. There was also a hint that someone got hurt, and the someone was more likely to have been Artemus than Adah, who had been through the fire before. Nevertheless, the bittersweet days in Boston did not terminate their association; it would continue as a friendship for the rest of their lives.

Marriage probably, as Adah thought, wouldn't have done. The eccentric Artemus Ward in combination with the flamboyant Adah Isaacs Menken, and traveling schedules for both that would have made a life together difficult, suggested formidable obstacles. Yet Ward did favor marriage, at least in principle. In one of the Old Showman's letters he voiced the opinion that "an old bachelor is a poor critter. He may have hearn the skylark ... an' yet he don't know nothin' about music—the real ginuine thing—the music of the laughter of happy, well-fed children. . . . I repeat, he's a poor critter. He don't live here; only stays."[5]

The fondness for children was not put on. Ward was always being attracted to someone's child, and while vacationing in Waterford his best rapport was with the children of the village, perhaps—for one reason—because he was always doing something childlike himself. One morning, during a visit home, he popped out of the front door of his mother's house and, standing on the step, let out a tremendous war whoop which went ringing across the Flat. A neighbor came running to see what was wrong. Nothing was wrong. Artemus had whooped simply because he felt so well and the world around him was so delightful, so perfect (as it may well have been on a summer morning in Waterford) and, having informed the neighbor of this, he whooped several more times and then leaped out upon the lawn, where he turned a handspring and stood on his head. Antics like this by a grown man were incomprehensible to the adults of Waterford, but they enchanted the children.

A man who once kept an inn in Naples, Maine, wrote about an incident involving a child that took place one evening when Ward was staying overnight at his tavern. "For a wonder, the great humorist was about my only guest that night—at least, the only transient guest. Artemus made himself entirely at home. The season was cool, and the flames in the big fireplace leaped and crackled, sending a ruddy glow upon the thin face of the sober-visaged traveller as, leaning back in the old-fashioned, highback rocking chair, he gazed pensively at the glowing heap.

"Presently a bright-eyed little girl, about 8 years of age, who was staying temporarily at the house, entered the room and seated herself near the fire at a respectable distance from the stranger. She had been there only a few minutes when Artemus suddenly turned to her and, with a solemn countenance, slowly inquired: 'Excuse me, my little dear, but please tell me how you spell the word cat?'

"'C-a-t,' was her prompt response. 'Ah! How sad, how very sad,' remarked the great showman, in doleful tones, 'that so intelligent a young lady as you appear to be, should have had your early education so dreadfully neglected! My dear, allow me to set you right. The correct and only true way to spell cat is k-a-t. Now you won't forget it, will you?'"[6]

There followed, according to the innkeeper, a lively discussion, the little girl citing her books, her teacher, and other authorities who upheld the spelling as c-a-t, Artemus bewailing the terrible error into which she had been led and advancing many plausible reasons why the spelling had to be k-a-t. This was an Artemus Ward entertainment in miniature: Artemus persisting in some absurd misconception with the most impressive solemnity and fervor, and his audience, while understanding perfectly the playful nature of the charade, nevertheless having its enjoyment heightened by a delightful sense of superior intelligence.

In other associations with children there was, as one of Ward's friends recalled, a special quality of his mind that made it possible for him to talk with children on their own level; there were long conversations during which he questioned them and discussed the unexpected fancies and notions that the quizzing brought to light. The child's realm of wonder, discovery, and surprise; its delight in the shattering of adult pretensions; its pleasure in the absurd; and the boundless land of childish imagination—all were somehow akin to the inner world of Artemus Ward.

As he would for the next several summers, Ward spent part of the summer of 1862 at his mother's home in Waterford, recuperating from the exertions of lecturing. Caroline had retained possession of the place with some difficulty. In 1855 she had been forced to sell the homestead for $700. By the end of 1859 she had got it back again, with the county records showing a payment of $1 and other considerations to her brother-in-law, C. J. F. Eastman, husband of her sister Mercy, so it seems clear that the Eastmans acquired it and restored it to her. What interfamily arrangements there were for compensating the Eastmans are unknown, but it is known that as soon as Browne was able to do so he began to contribute toward the maintenance of the handsome white house on the Flat and to get reacquainted with his mother and the state of Maine. Caroline was now very proud of him; she once told one of his friends that Charles had been a strange child all the way from babyhood, but he'd been a good boy and good to her. Since Caroline was a practical woman, this undoubtedly reflected his financial help. At any rate, all was now serene at the peaceful, elm-shaded homestead beside Tom Pond, and it was an ideal place for Browne to recover from his exhausting lecture tours: a leafy, quiet place where the loudest sounds were the rattle of buggies passing through the Flat and the splash of wind-driven wavelets against the shores of the pond; a place of long, drowsy afternoons, cool nights, and, for Browne, late mornings. His hours were something of a scandal in the village. One resident remembered that he didn't get up until ten o'clock.

This summertime side of the grown-up Charlie Browne was all that most Waterfordians ever knew. Few of them had ever seen him exercising the fitful but intense energy, the attention to every detail that might further his progress, and the sometimes almost fanatical determination that had together contributed to his success. When he returned to the Flat to recover from the grind of his travels and labors, as far as his neighbors could determine from these interludes, he was simply one of the Sons of Rest. "When Charles was here on his summer visits, he didn't do nothin' except have a good time," one recalled. "He was a lazy critter, and would lay around on the grass or go for a ride or do anything he see fit."[7] The impression grew that he was a likable but shiftless fellow who, for some unaccountable reason, had become famous "outside." A few even feared he might be crazy. Once he and one of his summer visitors, Dan Setchell, a comic actor with an extremely flexible and expressive face, met by prearrangement at the village store, and Browne launched into an excited announcement of some sort to which Setchell responded with expressions of the utmost horror and disbelief. There followed a shouted conversation between the two which gave the impression to bystanders that a frightful disaster had taken place somewhere. But trying in vain to understand, listeners were left with puzzled faces. What they had been listening to was double-talk, an art at which both Setchell and Browne were adept. Setchell also provided Browne with a source of amusement at the homestead. He had a premonition that he was going to die of apoplexy, and so, to get his weight down as a possible preventive measure, he insisted on splitting wood and doing other hard work, activities which Browne loved to watch.

That summer of 1862 Browne worked on his lecture notes and continued to write Artemus Ward letters for *Vanity Fair*. Even though he had been occupied with lecturing, the quality of these letters had not declined. Some of the Old Showman's sharpest observations had to do with the city of Washington, D.C., of which he had a low opinion.

It is easy enough to see why a man goes to the poor house or the penitentiary. It's becawz he can't help it. But why he should woluntarily go and live in Washinton is intirely beyond my comprehension, and I can't say no fairer nor that.

I put up to a leadin hotel. I saw the landlord and sed, "How d'ye do, Square?"

"Fifty cents, sir," was his reply.

"Sir?"

"Half-a-dollar. We charge twenty-five cents for *lookin* at the landlord and fifty cents for speakin to him. If you want supper, a boy will show you to the dinin room for twenty-five cents. Your room bein in the tenth story, it will cost you a dollar to be shown up there."

"How much do you ax a man for breathin in this equinomikal tarvun?" sed I.

"Ten cents a Breth," was his reply.[8]

After another visit to Washington, Artemus concluded:

Washington, D.C., is the Capital of "our once happy country"—if I may be allowed to koin a frase! The D.C. stands for Desprit Cusses, a numerosity which abounds here, the most of whom persess a Romantic pashun for gratooitous drinks. And in this conjunction I will relate an incident. I notist for several days a large Hearse standin in front of the principal tavern on Pennsylvany Avenoo. "Can you tell me, my fair Castillian," sed I this mornin, to a young Spaniard from Tipperary, who was blackin boots in the washroom—"can you tell me what those Hearse is kept standin out there for?"

"Well, you see our Bar bisness is great. You've no idee of the number of people who drink at our Bar durin a day. You see those Hearse is necessary."

I saw.[9]

In addition to his writing, Browne continued with the self-promotion that had become a habit—for the moment in furtherance of *Artemus Ward, His Book*, which had already sold ten thousand copies, something he wanted the public to know. Typically, he wrote to a friend, James Ripley Osgood, of the publishing firm Ticknor & Fields, in Boston. Could Osgood get a paragraph into the *Post* and the *Transcript?* "Only a line you know—a bare statement of the fact. Am I asking too much? Am I boring you? Am I a nuisance, or a pestilence, or a famine or any kind of disorder?"[10] Browne had seen enough of the lecturing and publishing business to know that success didn't just happen, and that no matter how worthy the product was, there had to be a great deal of sowing and planting in advance. Osgood on his part was evidently cultivating Browne with the expectation that he would eventually ripen into an author worthy of appearing on the Ticknor & Fields list. Their friendship would continue on such familiar terms that Browne could later invite Osgood to share his hotel apartment on visits to New York and address to him such remarks as "Write me a letter goddamit all."[11]

All of Browne's affairs and personal relationships were going well that summer. For the first time in his life he had money—enough to help Caroline secure the homestead and enough to help Cyrus, who was ill and needed an operation.

On September 24, 1862, something happened that may also have been fortunate for Charles. Adah Isaacs Menken, her taste for humorists apparently still unsatisfied and her ideas about marriage altered, was wedded to Robert Henry Newell, author of the comic *"Orpheus C. Kerr Papers."* It was a marriage that, while it lasted, would make Newell thoroughly miserable. Like Browne, he was part Puritan underneath, too much so to stomach this delectable but highly-spiced dish, and from Newell Adah would go on to her liaisons in London and Paris with Swinburne and the elder Dumas and then to her final marriage with the wealthy Capt. J. B. Barkley and her early death.

Resting in the shade of the elms at Waterford beside the sparkling waters of Tom Pond, Browne had many personal reasons to be content. But there were, as he well knew, thunderclouds over the southern horizon, and they were growing darker.

7

Forty Nights in California

In Ward's 1862–63 season, the lecture came under the deepening shadow of the war, and this brought problems as illustrated by "Sixty Minutes in Africa," the re-titled performance, as given December 17, 1862, at Bryan Hall, Chicago. Four days previsously the main action had taken place at Fredericksburg. Here, on December 13, under the unfortunate command of General Burnside, the Army of the Potomac attacked fortified heights across open terrain and left the field carpeted with blue-clad figures, shot down or pinned down by the devastating fire. That night the earth itself seemed to be moaning and crying at Fredericksburg; freezing men who were alive stripped the dead of their clothing, and in places frozen corpses were used as breastworks to absorb the sickening strike of Confederate bullets.

Artemus Ward tried to reflect some of the public reaction. His chatter at Bryan Hall followed the pattern of "The Babes in the Wood" in its cheerful disregard of any relationship between title and subject matter. Artemus started out by considering several subjects and rejecting them all until he finally arrived at the statement: "'And so I concluded to speak on Africa. True, I know but little of Africa, but according to the standard recently established in this country, that fact only makes me all the more competent to speak upon the subject I have selected. According to this standard I am liable at any moment to be dragged from the bosom of my boarding house and made a Brigadier General.'"[1]

The *Chicago Times* said that the hall was densely packed, with hundreds unable to get in; that Artemus "enchained the attention of the entire auditory"; and that everyone was delighted with the lecture. It neglected to say that people who had just lost relatives or friends through the incompetence of Union leadership at Fredericksburg might have applauded but would not have fully enjoyed Ward's jokes on the subject.

In Louisville, on January 2, 1863, he used another joke about Northern leaders, a ploy and entrapment that began, "'We have among our officers one good general, Stonewall Jackson. . . .'" At this there was a cry of protest from the audience, which Ward allowed to die down before he concluded his sentence, "'but he is among our officers a little too often to be pleasant.'"[2]

All very well, but it was an hour's oblivion that people were beginning to look for, and this is what Artemus would eventually give them, although he had not at this time found the complete formula for humor of forgetfulness. His "Sixty Minutes in Africa" still contained too many topical references of a sore nature, too much reality, and not enough of the fantasy at which Ward excelled. There was not yet enough of "absurdities and infirmities abstracted from persons"[3] which Hobbes had said was the essence of pure and perfect laughter.

And yet it was the best thing going, and Artemus Ward had become celebrated in show business, as anyone could tell who read the *New York Clipper,* where his rise to eminence had been traced. Besides reporting weekly on the ring, the turf, "ball play," cricket, quoits, pedestrianism, billiards, chess, other such diversions, and—most important—the drama, circuses, minstrel show, variety acts, and all the other activities that made up an astonishingly variegated entertainment industry, the *Clipper* also contained a modicum of literary content, usually something of a highly popular nature, and in 1862 it had reprinted some of Ward's writing. But in that year it had taken very little notice of him as a performer, comparatively speaking; Ward had been classed mainly as a humorous writer and lyceum lecturer.

Then had come Lincoln's delighted and widely publicized interest in *Artemus Ward, His Book,* with the publicity probably helped along by Artemus himself. Somebody also remembered and pointed to the fact that in one of the pieces in *His Book,* "Interview With President Lincoln," Ward's advice on the cabinet had been asked by the president, and Artemus had replied, "Fill it up with Showman, sir! . . . They know what the public wants, North & South."[4]

On February 3, 1863, the *New York Herald* further promoted the cause in an editorial headed "Artemus Ward and the President," which read, in part: "Upon somewhat the same principle that Alexander the Great read the Iliad before beginning a battle, the President now reads a chapter of Artemus Ward's book to his cabinet before beginning business. The result is that the members are so convulsed with laughter and chuckle themselves into such an extremely good humor that they willingly endorse whatever the President proposes. We scarely know which most to admire, the simplicity, the sublimity or the success of the idea."

With all this Artemus became a show-business celebrity, which must have delighted his secret soul. The *New York Clipper* began reporting his movements and activities as diligently as it did those of Laura Keene, Edwin and John Wilkes Booth, Edwin Forrest, the Wild Men of Borneo, Campbell's Minstrels, General Tom Thumb, the Fakir of Ava, Dora Dawson the Double-Voiced Singer, Bihin the Belgian Giant, Carter's Zouave Troupe, and all the rest. If it was significant news that so-and-so had suffered a fatal fall from the top of the center pole while helping put up a tent at Greenpoint, Long Island, it was also news that Artemus Ward was confined to his hotel room at Newark, Ohio, with a bad throat. If it was to be noted that the Bedouin Brothers had knocked them dead in Baltimore, it was also essential to report that Artey Ward had a good house in Binghamton. In the *Clipper* pages Artemus Ward was here, Artemus Ward was there, Artemus Ward, "like the soul of John Brown," was marching along through various states with overwhelming successes. "Everybody understands of course," said the *Clipper*, "that it is a burlesque upon popular lectures and popular lecturers, and viewed in that light it is perfectly inimitable. Mr. Browne is entitled to the credit of originating a purely original and successful form of entertainment. No other man in America would have succeeded in it however."[5]

The *New York Clipper* continued to follow Artemus Ward's schedule closely. On one occasion it made a mistake about the size of one of his houses and ran a correction the very next week, probably after getting a hot telegram from Artemus, for he could scramble as hard as any good professional to keep his name in favor. The correction read: "We are glad to learn that Artemus Ward's lecture in Pittsburgh *did* draw a crowded house, and our correspondent there was in error in saying otherwise. The place was not only crowded but 'more too,' for many persons were turned away, being unable to gain admittance. We thought it strange that Pittsburgh should prove an exception to the general rule, for wherever the great showman has figured, the houses have always boiled over.... On the 2nd inst. [February] Artey lectured in

Brant's Hall, Harrisburg, Pa., and the house was crowded to its utmost capacity. One of the local papers states that so great was the interest to hear him 'speak his piece,' that the Legislature adjourned at an early hour for that purpose, and repaired almost en masse to the lecture room. We are not surprised at this, after hearing that A. Lincoln reads A. Ward's book to his Cabinet, to get them in good working order."[6]

Even Ward's professional opinion now had great weight in the *Clipper*. One minstrel group got a good notice because "Artemus Ward has said they were the best troupe he ever saw."[7]

That so mild a form of entertainment as a lecture should achieve such success, even on the basis of an implied presidential endorsement, was a phenomenon—and another indication that it was not a lecture at all but a theatrical performance, a sort of intellectual vaudeville show. Ward's competition was formidable. Major cities in the 1860s were likely to be offering more places of entertainment than they would be a century later, and certainly more *kinds* of entertainment. As a humorist Ward had not only human but chemical competition. A Dr. Colton was going around giving his Laughing Gas Entertainment; people inhaled the gas and "were exalted"; the inhalees "sang, danced, laughed, made speeches, became affectionate, patriotic and so forth."[8] The *Clipper* in all serious-ness reported on these performances not in terms of attendance or gross but somewhat as follows: "Dr. Colton expended sixty gallons of gas daily last week in Brewster Hall, New Haven."[9] Ward was, of course, aware of this and sometimes featured himself as a "gas man;" he could furnish gas, and the audience the laughing.[10]

Extremely rough competition faced Artemus when he came east and into Philadelphia on Valentine's Day, 1863, for a lecture at the Musical Fund Hall, on Locust Street. This was, at the time, one of the main centers for Philadelphia's cultural and civic life, antedating the Academy of Music. With superb accoustical qualities, it had rung to the voices of Jenny Lind and Adelina Patti and the oratory of the first Republican National Convention, nominating Fremont there in 1856. It was one of the largest halls in the city.

In venturing to fill the seats, Artemus Ward was going in against these and other attractions on February 14: at Mrs. John Drew's Arch Street Theater, Miss Jane Coombs and her company in the tragedy "Fazio" followed by a nautical play, "The Lost Ship"; at the Walnut Street Theater, a Spanish dance program preceding the popular drama "The French Spy"; at another theater, Shakespeare's "The Merry Wives of Windsor." And at others, Carncross & Dixey's minstrel show; the Bohemian Glass Blowers and their Glass Steam Engine; Dr. Kane's

Immense Panorama, "Arctic Voyage"; Signor Blitz, magician and ven-triloquist, and his Learned Canary Birds; a "classical soiree", a gymnas-tics exhibition; and at least seven musical variety shows, featuring among them such performers as Signor Bliss, the Antipodean Walker promising to walk the ceiling head downward fifty feet from the ground, the Celebrated Educated Trick Dog Jenny Lind, and various unrivalled banjo players, singers, dancers and comics. There was also a circus playing at the local amphitheater.

To see how Ward would make out against big-time competition, the *Clipper* sent a reporter to the Musical Fund Hall. He wrote that "the place was absolutely packed to its fullest capacity. The seats were all filled, and every inch of standing room occupied. It was a monster mass meeting. . . ."[11]

E. P. Hingston, an English show-manager whom Browne had met about sixteen months previously, happened into Philadelphia that night, and he decided to have a look at the performance. The lecture was already underway when he arrived. Hingston estimated attendance at two thousand "and there was that description of standing-room left which has been defined as no place for standing." The hall manager, as a professional courtesy, escorted Hingston to a place in the wings where he could observe the lecturer from the side as well as get a partial view of the audience. On the stage he saw Artemus Ward performing, "a tall, thin, gentlemanly-looking young man, with light-coloured flowing hair. He wore a black coat ... his waistcoat was a white one, and in his hand he carried a roll of white paper, which he twitched nervously in the course of his lecture." There was a large map of Africa suspended at the back of the stage, but it seemed to have no relation to the content of the lecture. Hingston afterwards ascertained that "Sixty Minutes in Africa" was practically the same lecture as "The Babes in the Wood;" he described it as "a grand display of mental fireworks . . . rocket-flight following rocket-flight, without giving his audience time to think." Hingston noticed that "all that the lecturer said was spoken by him as though it fell from his lips without premeditation; but from the position in the hall which I chanced to occupy, I could notice that his eyes were keenly fixed upon his audience, and that he carefully watched the manner in which every sentence was received."[12]

After the show Artemus invited Hingston to his room at the Continental Hotel for a few rounds of bourbon. They'd hardly settled themselves beside the bottle when half-a-dozen young men with traces of burnt cork on their faces rushed in. Ward was a hero of the minstrels.

There was even an "Artemus Ward, Jr.," described as a blackface burlesque lecturer, who was traveling around on the variety-show circuit capitalizing on Ward's fame. The fellows who had come into the hotel room were from Philadelphia's great Carncross & Dixey minstrel organization; their show had just let out and they had hurried over to see Artemus. After inviting the admiring minstrels to sit down and have a drink, Ward informed them that he'd had a new joke in the show that evening, and went on to say that if George Christy (of Christy's Minstrels, in New York) had known about this he would have traveled all the way to Philadelphia to borrow it—but no matter, someone would probably telegraph it to him next day. At that, one of his minstrel friends informed him that Carncross & Dixey had been taking no chances; they'd had a man in Ward's audience that very night making notes of everything new he said.

A few months later there were developments that brought Ward and Hingston together professionally. By the summer of 1863, the lecture was getting played out in the East; in its current form it couldn't be kept attractive forever simply by changing the title and adding a few new jokes. So Artemus began thinking about a tour of the West. The same idea was occurring to other people, as indicated by a telegram he received from Thomas Maguire, owner of the Opera House in San Francisco and other theaters. The telegram read: "What will you take for forty nights in California?"

The answer Ward sent back over the transcontinental telegraph line was: "Artemus Ward, New York City, to Thomas Maguire, Opera House, San Francisco, California, Brandy and water."[13]

This reply was widely circulated in California, where it created amusement and further interest in Ward's show. It may also have suggested to Maguire that Ward was not inclined to hire himself out to an entrepreneur. If so, he had correctly sensed the hidden meaning of the telegram. Ward was thinking about engaging a new agent or manager to accompany him on a tour of the West. He sent word to E. P. Hingston, and the two met at the Revere House, on Broadway.

Hingston had been serving for several years as agent for Prof. J. H. Anderson, a magician, actor and producer of elaborate stage illusions in America and Australia, and he had met Ward for the first time more than a year and a half previously. He had been on a train approaching Cincinnati in mid-November, 1861, when a fellow passenger ventured the opinion that they must be on the railroad Artemus Ward had written about. The sketch he was referring to was this one.

In the Ortum of 18–my frend, the editor of the Baldinsville *Bugle,* was obleged to leave perfeshernal dooties & go
& dig his taters, & he axed me to edit for him doorin his
absence. Accordinly I ground up his Shears and commenced. It
didn't take me a grate while to slash out copy enuff from the
xchanges for one issoo, and I thawt I'd ride up to the next town
on a little Jaunt, to rest my Branes which had bin severely rackt
by my mental efforts. (This is sorter Ironical.) So I went over to
the Rale Road offiss and axed the Sooprintendent for a pars.
    "*You* a editer?" he axed, evijently on the pint of snickerin.
    "Yes Sir," sez I, "don't I look poor enuff?"
    "Just about," sed he, "but our Road can't pars you."
    "Can't, hay?"
    "No Sir—it can't."
    "Becawz," sez I, lookin him full in the face with a Eagle
eye, "*it goes so darned slow it can't pars anybody!*" Methinks I
had him thar. It's the slowest Rale Road in the West. With a
mortified air, he told me to git out of his offiss. I pittid him and
went.[14]

The story had achieved wide currency among Midwestern travelers
who, in spite of the frequent wrecks that killed many of them, never
thought the trains were going fast enough. The passenger who mentioned it also said that he knew Artemus Ward and was going to meet
him that evening at the Burnett House, in Cincinnati, and he would
introduce Hingston if he wished. At the hotel Hingston had been led to a
tall, slim gentleman who looked, he thought, like "a youthful member of
one of the learned professions," and he had been astonished to learn that
this slim, scholarly-looking young fellow was Artemus Ward. He had
expected to see an elderly man with a shrewd, wrinkled face, a brassy
voice, and the rough-and-tumble look of a traveling showman. Instead,
here was a man "not more than twenty-five years old, slender in build,
frank, open and pleasant in demeanour, with ruddy cheeks, bright eyes,
and a voice soft, gentle and musical."[15]

Hingston, although a traveling showman himself, did not entirely
look like one either. A high forehead surmounted by a mass of wavy, dark
hair, large, dark eyes, a moustache, and a full beard which parted at the
chin into two curly, pointed wings—all this bespoke the man of letters
which Hingston was at times, as an occasional editor and author. But
there was also an unliterary smartness of dress and grooming about him,
as befitted a theatrical advance man.

In Cincinnati, the two had become immediate friends. Artemus Ward was an Anglophile, and Hingston had strong pro-American leanings. For example, he was a Longfellow enthusiast. A friend of his, G. L. M. Strauss, remembered that Hingston once cornered him in a small office at the top of the Lyceum Theatre, in London, and read him, Strauss thought, the entire *Song of Hiawatha*, in spite of all the doctor's anguished efforts to escape; at the end of it Strauss didn't care if he ever again heard of Minnehaha, Pau-Puk-Keewis, Old Nokomis, or even Longfellow. But at the finish, when Hingston asked him, in an emotional voice, what he thought of *that* for a poem, Strauss recalled his reaction: "Well, he was such a sterling good fellow, I hypocritically expressed my delight to him."[16]

One reason why Hingston liked America was that its whole atmosphere was more congenial to his profession. The conservative British, in his opinion, tended to look down their noses at anything in the nature of a "show", although they liked to attend one well enough, and they also disliked pushiness—but if a man was an agent, he *had* to push, and in America aggressiveness of this sort was considered a virtue, not a fault.

A few minutes after they had been introduced at the Burnett House, Artemus had said, "'This is the hotel where your Prince of Wales stopped at when he came through here last summer. Suppose we go down and hoist to him'".[17] At the bar they had toasted the health of his Royal Highness, and that evening they had made a survey of Cincinnati entertainments. Two days later Ward had accompanied Hingston on a steamboat trip down the Ohio to Louisville, where Ward had followed the agent on his rounds: to the theater, where Anderson's show "A Night in the Wonder World" was opening; to City Hall, where Hingston deadheaded the mayor, aldermen, and city clerk with free passes; to the newspaper offices to arrange for advertising and publicity; and on other promotional errands.

It had struck Hingston at the time that Ward was being unusually attentive to all these details, and on the night before they parted there had been a hint of why. "'Suppose one day you manage me,'" Ward had said. And when Hingston wanted to know what there would be to manage, Ward had replied, "'A moral lecturer.'"[18] This had puzzled Hingston. In that November of 1861, as far as he knew, Ward was simply a magazine editor and a writer. But, unknown to Hingston, Ward's lecturing career started only a few days later. And now here he was, in the summer of 1863, a great show-business success. Since Hingston's association with Prof. Anderson had now ended, he was open to an invitation to become Ward's manager.

Ward began their interview at the Revere House by wanting to know what Hingston thought of going to California. Hingston thought well of it if Ward didn't stay too long, for although San Francisco was flourishing, the gold-rush bloom was fading and the interior mining regions were not as prosperous and carelessly prodigal as they had been a few years previously. Hingston advised "a brief visit, a rapid march through the State, lecturing at one town tonight and at another tomorrow evening, and a speedy return to New York with the dollars resulting from the enterprise." Ward then offered him the job of agent and manager, and after some discussion Hingston accepted. The subject of route came up, and then it began to dawn on Hingston that Ward was not thinking just of California; it appeared that he wanted to make the return journey across the mountains and plains, dropping in on the Mormons at Salt Lake City, instead of returning as they would go, by sea and the Isthmus.

Hingston was appalled at this prospect. They'd be going to California in autumn, and by the time they finished there and started back toward the Rockies, it would be winter. A midwinter journey by stagecoach and sledge through frozen and uninhabited wastelands was nothing to be undertaken lightly. So there was an argument between Ward and Hingston about the return route, and it was finally left for later decision; they'd come back on the Overland Stage if they found the route to be "open, practicable, and comparatively free from danger."[19] Hingston evidently felt that the agreement was sufficiently hedged so that Ward, when he came up against the realities of the terrain and the season, would see reason.

There were preparations for the journey. Hingston, who was going in advance, got a hundred copies of *Artemus Ward, His Book* to use as handouts to editors, politicians, preachers, and other prominent people in California. He obtained lithographed portraits of Artemus and had another batch of "Artemus Ward Will Speak a Piece" posters printed. Ward made an arrangement with Carleton for a book he intended to result from his travels in the West, and took one final shot at the Eastern public with the old "Babes in the Wood" lecture, refurbished with a few new jokes and advertised as "an entirely new comic oration" under the title "An Hour With a Ghost." This was inspired by a new stage effect that was all the rage in New York in the summer of 1863: an illusion depending on sheets of plate glass, black cloth, a darkened stage, and special lights and reflections whereby the audience was made to see horrible apparitions. Several of these ghost shows were playing, and Artemus believed they were ripe for a take-off. The come-on worked. On

September 30 there was a good house at Niblo's Saloon, a hall adjoining Niblo's Garden Theater on Broadway, and good reviews which Hingston gathered up for reprinting and distribution out west. Three days later, with Artemus lecturing a few more times in Newark and New England and going to Maine for a final visit with Caroline, the Englishman boarded the steamer *North Star* and was off to California, along the route on which Artemus would follow him later: southward by sea to the Isthmus city that was then called Aspinwall and would later be Colon; across the Isthmus about fifty miles on a busy little railroad to Panama; and thence by steamer in a long curve up past the coasts of Central America, Mexico and California.

Reaching San Francisco some ten days after Hingston's arrival there, Artemus checked in at the sumptuous Occidental Hotel, where Hingston was already well settled, and received an account of his manager's activities. Many things had happened. Uncertain at first, but with a plan for finding out whether it would be more profitable to stage the lecture at their own risk or put it into the hands of a local entrepreneur, Hingston had seen to it that a paragraph appeared in the newspapers announcing that Artemus Ward was coming and that his advance agent was at the Occidental. He had then called at the Opera House to see Thomas Maguire, "The Theatrical Napoleon of the Pacific Coast" and the man to whom Artemus had sent the brandy-and-water telegram. Maguire had made an offer for the show, and Hingston had told him he'd think it over.

The manager reported that he had also been around to see the newspaper and magazine editors, and they were all heralding the visit of Artemus. Bret Harte had promised the support of the literary weekly, *Golden Era*. Good use had been made, also, of a peculiar San Francisco institution, the barroom bulletin boards, which were often ahead of the newspapers in posting telegrams from the East.

(And, by the way, Ward's old girl friend, Adah Menken, was in town. She and Newell were living in grand style at the Russ House.)

The result of all this, Hingston said, had been a series of offers from theater managers, association secretaries, and speculators. Finally there had been a call by Mr. Maguire. He and Hingston had driven out to the Cliff House and had gotten down to business while watching the seals over a bottle of champagne. Maguire had offered to let Artemus Ward have the Opera House one night for nothing; he had other theaters on the West Coast, and perhaps he had hoped to book the lecture for its entire tour. But Hingston by now had the feel of the situation. He decided that he could get a larger crowd into Platt's Hall, on Montgomery Street, and that he and Artemus could better take all the risks (and profits) themselves.

And there were a few other details to add to the account of Hingston's work. The minstrels were all touting the lecture; each end man in the city had been supplied with one of Artemus Ward's books with permission to use the jokes in exchange for mentions of the lecture. As for bill-posting, at every principal street corner there was a printed strip bound around the curb-boarding of the sidewalk: ARTEMUS WARD WILL TROT OUT HIS BABES IN THE WOOD—PLATT'S HALL, NOV. 13.

For the Western tour, Artemus was charging one dollar; back East it had been twenty-five or fifty cents for general admission, with fifty or seventy-five cents for reserved seats. The increase made not the slightest difference to the citizens of the Golden Coast. On the evening of the thirteenth the people poured into Platt's Hall in such numbers that the pressure of the crowd carried away and overturned the money-taker's stall. The police were called. Men holding hats were stationed at the entrances to collect admissions, but one of the hats burst under the weight of the silver dollars thrown into it and "cartwheels" went rolling away over the floor and under the tidal wave of people. Hingston never did learn how many people paid, but he got his hands on more than $1,600, and estimated that it would have been $3,000 if the hall had been large enough to accommodate everyone who wanted to get in. Financially, the lecture had equaled the success in San Francisco of Adah Menken's opening night there in "Mazeppa," and it would have exceeded even that success if all admissions had been paid and everyone had got in who wanted to. Artemus Ward was a better draw than "The Naked Lady"!

"The Babes" was re-scheduled for November 17 at the Metropolitan Theater, leaving Artemus four days in which to disport himself around San Francisco. He visited one of the great banking houses, where he was asked if he would like to walk on a floor of gold. " 'I should like to dance on it,' " was the reply.[20] Ward was then taken to a room where the floor was covered with a layer of gold ingots awaiting shipment, and while his companions whistled and clapped hands, he danced a breakdown on the golden floor. He met some of the literati who had grouped themselves around Bret Harte, Joaquin Miller, and the *Golden Era*—San Francisco's modest attempt at a Bohemia of its own—and found time to visit a Chinese theater.

From San Francisco, lecturer and manager then set out on a tour of Stockton, Sacramento, and other California towns that was to take them well into December. The proceeds of the lecture in the Metropolitan

Theater, in Sacramento, on the evening of November 20 was $600, but of this the widow of an actor of that city, whose house had just burned, got $100. There was a subscription going around for the unfortunate lady, and Ward told Hingston to contribute the $100 but not to let his name be put on the list. Instead, the donation was to be listed as "Subscribed by a religious Indian."[21] It was typical of an anonymous generosity whereby a great deal of money found its way out of Ward's pocket.

After Sacramento, there were lectures at Folsom, Marysville, and Oroville. At Marysville, Ward and Hingston held an important conference sitting on a pile of timber beside the railway track. The question of which route they would use on the way back to New York—overland or by sea—had finally come up, and Hingston was surprised to learn that Ward still considered it a question. California, even including some of its more remote mining towns, represented a fairly well-worn theatrical circuit and many show people had traveled this path before them, including such actors as the Booths. But when it came to the route to and from California, the oceans and Isthmus provided the only practical way, and even mad old Junius Brutus Booth hadn't been crazy enough to start back across the continent in the dead of winter. Hingston pointed a warning finger at the ice-covered Sierras looming up on the eastern horizon, their white tops providing chilling support for what he now had to say: that they were likely to perish if they attempted to reach Salt Lake City this time of year. It was no place to take a show anyway. It was like Tibet, and beyond it, in a stretch of more than a thousand miles along the stage route, there was probably only one town big enough to give a lecture in—the mining community of Denver, in the Colorado territory, which had, what? perhaps three or four thousand people?

And Hingston had other arguments to advance against the overland route. For one, there had been continuing and worsening reports of Indian disturbances. Hingston was correct in his estimate of these as sources of trouble. The Civil War was occupying most of the government's soldiers, and the overland route could be protected only by a few detachments of state militia stationed here and there. Tired of being pushed around, the Indians had acquired many horses and firearms during 1862 and 1863. Many of them had also acquired from traders who sold them liquor in circumvention of the law quantities of "pilgrim rum," a horrible mixture of alcohol, water, molasses, and red pepper which, as one observer noted, "made a compound that would bring out all the bad qualities of the consumer."[22] The year 1864 would be one of bloody massacres and running battles all across the plains, with the operation of the Overland Stage brought to a halt at times.

All of this information seemed to have not the slightest persuasive effect upon Artemus Ward, so Hingston sought to turn him from the cross-country idea with an alternative suggestion. If he wanted to make such a hazardous trip, why risk the extra hazards of winter? Why not return to Panama, visit the West Indies, come back to California in the spring, and then make the overland journey in warm weather?

"'We'll toss for it,'" said Artemus. He took a gold piece out of his pocket. "'If it comes down eagle, we'll go to the Mormons.'"[23] The coin spun briefly in the late-November sunlight, fell, and came to rest with the eagle side up. And that was that. The return trip would be overland.

With that important question settled, the lecture tour of mining towns and other inland communities continued—through North San Juan, Nevada City, Grass Valley, Auburn, Placerville, Drytown, Jackson, and Murphy's.

Around December 10, Ward returned to San Francisco for a few days before starting out on his transcontinental journey eastward, which was planned to include a few days lecturing in the mining region of Nevada before striking out into the western wilderness. In San Francisco, Adah Menken gave a farewell party for him; there was also a brief time for other merrymaking with the literary colony of which Adah was the temporary queen, and Ward's personality, along with the character of his work and the evidences of his success, seems to have made a profound impression on these writers who were striving for recognition in this cultural outpost.

After Artemus had departed, Bret Harte wrote for the *Golden Era* of December 27 a long article about him that was part defense and part appreciation.

The defense seems to have been called for to counteract a reaction among certain people that was not uncommon as Ward dispensed his new form of humor across the land. These people had paid good money to attend a lecture—they laughed, they enjoyed themselves—but after it was all over, what had they been laughing *at?* What was the *substance* of the lecture? In his *Golden Era* article, Bret Harte pointed out that Ward had come to California known as the author of an admirable series of sketches exhibiting a special type of humor—a humor that had never pretended to serve any purpose "beyond the present laugh" and that had "no wrongs to redress in particular, no especial abuse to attack with ridicule, no moral to point"—and that all this had been a quality of Artemus Ward's reputation that everyone had understood. "And yet," Harte wrote, "some people are surprised and indignant that his late lectures exhibited this lawless construction—that he gave us fun without application." It was a revealing comment on the reactions of some Americans to their first taste of abstract humor on the platform—fun for the sake of fun alone—as it replaced the informative lecture, the didactic lecture, or the lecture in which humor had only a subservient role. Harte's appraisal was this: "His strength does not lie simply in grotesque spelling—that is a mechanical trick suggested by his education as a printer—and those who have gone to hear him in this expectation have been properly punished—but it is the humor of audacious exaggeration—of perfect lawlessness; a humor that belongs to the country of boundless prairies, limitless rivers and stupendous cataracts. In this respect Mr. Ward is the American Humorist, *par excellence,* and 'his book' is the essence of that fun which overlies the surface of our national life, which is met in the stage, rail car, canal and flat boat, which bursts out over camp fires and around bar-room stoves—a humor that has more or less local coloring, that takes kindly to, and half elevates slang, that is of to-day and full of present application."[24]

These words have been most often taken as meaning something about Artemus Ward, but they may have meant even more about Bret Harte. Such is the interpretation of Franklin Walker in his *San Francisco's Literary Frontier.* Mr. Walker makes the point that to Bret Harte, Artemus Ward was a revelation of a quality that was truly native to America; and that taking direction from this, Harte himself turned from the life of books to the life he found around him, seeing for the first time in the rough and vigorous mining camps possibilities for the material that was soon to form the basis for his own writing fame.

On December 17 Artemus Ward headed toward Nevada, pausing in Sacramento, where he was presented with a request signed by most of the legislature urging him to give another lecture in that city. But Artemus had to refuse. The indefatigable Hingston, who disliked a night without a booking almost as much as nature abhors a vacuum, was already on his way to Nevada ahead of him, and he would be making dates that would have to be kept.

8

Virginia City

At Placerville, the western terminus of the Overland Stage, Artemus Ward and E. P. Hingston began their eastward trip on one of the most remarkable transportation systems the country would ever see—a route nearly two thousand miles long over which stagecoaches, sleighs, and sledges were moving day and night, summer and winter, through the wild, largely uninhabited country between Placerville and Atchison, Kansas, where the railway from the East ended. The first part of the route, over the Sierras to Carson City, Nevada, was a good road, by all accounts—good at least in summertime. But when Ward and Hingston passed over it (with Hingston traveling in advance), snow was falling from time to time, and as their Concord coaches ascended into the glacial grandeur of the mountains the wheels slewed wildly, often coming dangerously close to the edge of a precipice. Hingston saw at the bottom of one ravine the remains of a coach he thought must have fallen five hundred feet. He began to understand why the coach had leather blinds instead of glass windows; it was arranged, he decided, to prevent wounds from knife-like fragments when the coach toppled over.

There were breathtaking views from the summits of the road. Hingston never forgot a sunrise that changed snowy peaks and domes into "ruby monuments . . . silver spires . . . gigantic opals, iridescent with every tint of crimson, green, violet, and gold." The wildness and solitude seen from the heights awed the Englishman, as did the monster pines which shadowed the trail in the valleys. From the final summit, looking out across Nevada, the view was more somber. "Far as the eye can see is one broad expanse of brown, arid, treeless, cheerless, solemn desolation. . . ."[1]

At a point about a dozen miles beyond Carson City (where Artemus paused to deliver a lecture), a road branched off from the main route of the Overland Stage and ran northward to Virginia City, up through barren hills and mountains that were throbbing with the great silver boom of the early 1860s—past mouths of tunnels and piles of excavated earth and through a continuous thunder of the steam-powered stamping mills crushing the ore. Clinging to the side of Mount Davidson astride the great Comstock Lode, more than six thousand feet above sea level and only a few hundred feet below the gray dome of the mountain top, Virginia City was in a boom period, boasting banks, hotels, theaters, gambling halls, breweries, jails, restaurants, stores, newspapers, large brick buildings with ornamental iron balconies, and saloons with mahogany bars and oil paintings. Streets were lighted by gas jets on iron poles; the city blazed with illumination at night. Sides of cliffs were painted with spectacular advertisements. Maguire's Opera House, on "D" Street, had an enormous stage, gas footlights, gilt chairs, velvet railings, boxes brocaded in scarlet, and a sparkling crystal chandelier.

The roads were jammed with ore wagons, freight teams, buggies, Chinese coolies, Piute Indians, Mexicans, Frenchmen—people from every country on earth: miners in blue jeans, bankers in top hats, gamblers with gaudy vests. The earth shook from the blasting that was going on in the mines deep underground and from the pounding of the ore crushers. The thunder of hoists, shrieks of steam whistles, curses of teamsters, rumble of wheels, and clanging of freighter bells added to a cacaphony that could be heard miles away, far out in the desert. The tinkle of pianos echoed from honky-tonk saloons, and often shots cracked out. Inside Maguire's Opera House, on its opening night, two men fired at each other from opposite sides of the house.

A corresponding frenzy seethed in the brains of Virginia City inhabitants. Everyone had a get-rich-quick scheme, and many of the schemes were succeeding. Money was as plentiful as sand; the problem was not how to get it but how to spend it. One man who was there wrote, "Everybody had money to burn, and it might as well have been burned for all the good the bulk of it did—squandered as fast as made."[2] It was a good town for show business or any business, and Hingston, arriving in advance of Artemus Ward, went on his customary rounds of newspaper offices (there were three in Virginia City) to whip up publicity. At the *Daily Territorial Enterprise,* housed in a fine new fireproof brick building, he handed editor Joseph T. Goodman a little card which read: "E. P. Hingston. Ars est celere Artem-us." Goodman didn't get it. Hingston had to explain that this was his own version of the old adage "Ars est celare artem" ("True art is to conceal art"), changed to mean "True art is to hurry up Artemus,"[3] and the editor agreed that the *Enterprise* would do its part in the hurrying. Joe Goodman's Latin may have been rusty, but he was the king of everything else that had to do with the written and printed word in Virginia City. Handsome, talented, and a daredevil, Goodman had come here from San Francisco with one journeyman printer, and a borrowed forty dollars about three years previously. Since then he had assembled a staff of reporters, twenty or thirty compositors, a crew of advertising solicitors, and a battery of steam-powered presses; now the paper was making big money. Part of the reason for its success was that it dispensed exactly the kind of journalism Virginia City wanted. Along with the news of shootings, brawls, and other commonplace affairs, and the highly technical news of mining that depended on a reporter's knowledge of geology and mineralogy, there were stories that sprang largely from the writer's imagination—tall tales, burlesques, humor, and other flights of fancy.

One of Goodman's discoveries was young Samuel L. Clemens—really not so young, as he was then twenty-eight—who had caught his attention while contributing letters from an outlying mining region. Clemens had received an invitation to join the staff in the late summer of 1862, and to take the job he had walked more than a hundred miles to Virginia City, since he was just about down and out at the time. He had come into the *Enterprise* office dusty and dirty, wearing a slouch hat, blue woolen shirt, pants stuffed into miner's boots, and a heavy suit of whiskers.

Up to that time Clemens had been wandering along a path that seemed to promise no great success. He had worked in various places as a printer, been a river pilot for a spell, served briefly in the Confederate army, and come out West as private secretary to his brother, Orion, whom Lincoln had appointed territorial secretary for Nevada. But since there had been nothing for the secretary's secretary to do, and no salary, Clemens unsuccessfully labored for a while as a miner. He had been glad to get Goodman's invitation, because he had hardly enough to eat. Now, a little more than a year later, signing his articles "Mark Twain," he was a valuable man on the *Enterprise* staff, but his work was still largely unformed, he had no literary reputation except around Virginia City, and he gave evidence of no great literary ambition. Somewhere under his rough exterior lay one of the greatest writing talents in America, but

Mark Twain had not awakened to its possibilities. Goodman had another man on his staff who, he thought, was Twain's equal: William Wright, who wrote under the name of Dan de Quille. Goodman would persist in this opinion even after Mark Twain had become famous; the only difference, he believed, was that Wright lacked Twain's commercial instincts.

To Artemus Ward, Virginia City, with its reckless mood and the kindred souls he found there, represented one of the high spots of his life. In excellent health and spirits at the time, he was performing off the platform as well as on it. Jared Graham, a printer for the Virginia City *Union,* later wrote about an impromptu entertainment that Ward gave in the *Union* print shop soon after he got off the stagecoach in Virginia City. As he recalled the incident, Ward marched into the composing room still wearing his travel attire, an old slouch hat and an ankle-length linen duster, and carrying a big carpetbag. Pausing in a dramatic pose, he gazed around at the printers until his eyes came to rest upon Graham. "Then the bag dropped to the floor as though released by an automatic spring. With a movement like Hamlet's ghost he advanced to my side, seized my arm, stripped it to the shoulder, and tragically pointing to a vaccination scar exclaimed, 'Behold the mark! It is, it is my long lost brother!' "[4]

Because of the years Artemus Ward had spent in the printing trade, printers all over the country had a special feeling for him, as he had for them. To celebrate the "reunion" with his long-lost brother (he and Graham had worked together on the *Cleveland Daily Plain Dealer*), Ward invited the *Union* printers to join him at a nearby bar for a drink.

He then got a large sheet of newsprint and with a blue crayon wrote upon it

ARTEMUS WARD
WILL
SPEAK HIS PIECE
HERE
TONIGHT

He tacked the sheet on the door of Maguire's Opera House, and that, with the publicity work Hingston had already done, was all that was necessary to assure a full house. On the *Enterprise,* it had fallen to Mark Twain to write the advance notice of the lecture. He gave evidence of thorough familiarity with Artemus Ward's writing by doing the piece in imitation of the Old Showman's eccentric phrasing and spelling, and on the evening of the performance he was in the "printer's pew," a row of seats close to the stage at Maguire's, usually reserved for printers and newspaper reporters.

The lecture was a revelation to Mark Twain. Apparently he absorbed it with two parts of his mind; one part examining and marveling at the technique, the other belatedly enjoying the humor. Jared Graham, who happened to be sitting right beside him, said that Mark Twain watched with his mouth literally wide open, and that there would sometimes be a general explosion of laughter in the audience following one of Ward's jokes and then, after the uproar had subsided, suddenly a burro-like "Haw, haw, haw" from Twain. Once, when one of these delayed "Haw, haws" had interrupted the lecture and attracted all eyes to the "printer's pew," Artemus Ward glared in that direction in mock anger and asked, "'Has it been watered today?'"[5]

Ward lectured in Maguire's Opera House, in Virginia City, on the evening of December 22, 1863. The house couldn't accommodate everyone who wanted to get in, so there was another show on the evening of Christmas Day. In the second lecture Artemus illustrated in a striking way his talent for adapting his lecture to current events. In this case he had to deal with news which was so bad that it might have killed his entire performance. A shock wave of dismay and disappointment had been moving toward Virginia City for many days. It had started on a hill in Sussex, England, at about ten o'clock on the morning of December 10, when the great prizefighter John C. Heenan, the pride of America and particularly of the western mining regions, beaten almost senseless by Britain's Tom King, had been unable to come out for the twenty-sixth round of a much-heralded match.

Two steamships had immediately started for the United States with the grievous intelligence, and the outcome would be unknown there until one of them arrived.

In Nevada the news was awaited with great anxiety. Many of the miners knew Heenan personally; he had come from Benicia, California, and was popularly known as the Benicia Boy. Heavy bets had been made in Virginia City.

The ship *Jura*, after battling high winds, reached Portland, Maine, early on the morning of December 23, and the sorrowful news was immediately flashed to wherever it would go by the not-always-reliable telegraph system, the speed of which was something less than that of light. The calamitous tidings reached Virginia City just prior to Artemus Ward's second performance at Maguire's Opera House. Privately, Artemus could not have been less interested. In fact, he disliked prizefights. However, on the stage of Maguire's that evening, Ward had to forget his own prepossessions and show concern for the mood of the audience. According to Joe Goodman, the gloom which pervaded the Opera House could not have been greater had an army on which the liberty of the country depended been conclusively defeated. An atmosphere of despondency hung over the audience like a pall.

When the curtain went up Artemus advanced falteringly to the footlights with a handkerchief over his eyes, shaken by paroxysms of grief. In an instant he made everyone's distress seem ridiculous, and Goodman, remembering the lecture nearly thirty years later, described how Artemus followed up on this opener and a reference to the outcome of the fight: "But instantly a bright and hopeful look sprang into Artemus's eyes. He said he was aware it was a low thing to stake so much feeling on a contest of this kind; that he knew he ought to be ashamed of himself; but he confessed to the universal weakness of desiring, even in a dog fight, that his dog should win, but, though his dog hadn't won in this case, he did not despair. He believed the nation would survive the defeat, and that there were many happy days in store for us Americans yet."

The ludicrous performance brought enough of his listeners to their senses to inspire laughter and applause. In Goodman's words, he had "neatly relieved an embarrassed situation."[6]

From Virginia City, Ward made short side trips to lecture at mining towns in the vicinity, but much of the time was taken up by a binge that was not altogether alcoholic. On Artemus Ward, Virginia City seemed to have the effect of a strong hallucinogen. The throbbing of the blasting underground, the rarefied air, the oddity of the situation—a mountain-top city from which an endless panorama of hills and desert stretched away sharp and clear in the December sunlight—the noise, the devil-may-care spirit of the place, the throngs of bizarre characters in the street, all combined to stir him intensely. In Joe Goodman's words, "He was as if strung on wires, vibrating to every impulse of its tumultous life. Every alarm, every excitement, every killing—and these were things of almost incessant occurrence in Virginia City in those days—shook him with a force at once exhilarating and exhausting." He was at that time, Goodman said, 'bright and handsome as a young Apollo, but exhausting himself by foolish excess and feverish activity. . . ."[7]

Ward's unofficial headquarters in Virginia City was the office of the *Enterprise,* to which he had immediately gravitated with his sure instinct for talented and convivial company. From here, guided by Mark Twain and Dan de Quille, he ranged all over the town and under it as well; miners laboring hundreds of feet beneath the surface looked up to see Artemus Ward entering the illumination of their lamps; drinkers and gamblers made a place for him at the bars; and he mingled with Indians, Mexicans, and Chinamen in the street. Now and then he popped into the *Enterprise* office, and if the work was not done at a decent hour of the evening, he took off his coat and wrote an editorial or otherwise helped finish up the chores. Afterward he and Goodman, de Quille, Twain, and others went out to dinners and all-night drinking bouts.

There is no coherent day-to-day or night-by-night account of this time in Virginia City. And there is no exact agreement among the stories the participants wrote in later years, although all were professional reporters (this undoubtedly indicating the effects of an alcoholic fog as well as the haze that time and failing memories cast over the events). When Mark Twain was an old man dictating notes for his authorized biography, to be written by Albert Bigelow Paine, he gave Paine to understand that Artemus Ward was in Virginia City three weeks, indicating that in his memory at least, a great deal had happened. But Artemus was in Twain's company only one week. He arrived in Virginia City about December 22 and left there on the morning of December 29. From the accounts of his companions, there emerges a rough consensus concerning what happened within that week, but accounts of exactly how and just when it happened would be something else again.

Mark Twain remembered one scene at Barnum's restaurant at 2:30 A.M., with Artemus Ward proposing a standing toast only to discover that no one could stand. Dan de Quille recalled a dinner at the International Hotel, where the group engineered an elaborate prank at Twain's expense. The plot was that after they had had a few drinks Artemus, who was an expert at something akin to double-talk, was to say something that sounded highly literary and intellectual but that would actually be senseless, and everyone would pretend to understand it perfectly while, it was hoped, Mark Twain would be baffled. At the proper time Artemus, who had seated himself beside Twain, began his rigmarole in a voice that was loud enough to halt the general conversation and cause everyone to listen. De Quille's recorded impression, which of course could not have been entirely accurate, was that Ward said something like, "'Ah—speaking of genius, Mr. Clemens, now, genius appears to me to be a sort of luminous quality of the mind, allied to a warm and inflammable constitution, which is inherent in the man, and supersedes in him whatever constitutional tendencies he may possess, to permit himself to be influenced by such things as do not coincide with his preconceived notions and established convictions to the contrary.'"

All the men around the table nodded in solemn agreement, except Twain. Artemus then gravely asked him if the definition was not a good one. "'I don't know that I exactly understand you,'" Twain replied. Ward looked at him with just a slight elevation of the eyebrows, as though politely concealing his surprise and impatience. "'Why that is very singular. However, I will try and express my idea more clearly.'" He restated his concept a couple of times in increasingly incomprehensible terms, with Mark Twain getting more and more befuddled and the rest of the company faking disgust at his obtuseness, until finally Twain yelled, "'For God's sake! If you go at that again, you'll drive me mad.'"[8] What had been done to him was then revealed, and Mark Twain was sore for the rest of the evening. The incident later appeared in his collected works as "First Interview With Artemus Ward," but with Twain's own reconstruction of a garbled conversation in an altogether different situation: he and Ward and Hingston having breakfast in Virginia City, drinking whiskey cocktails; Artemus talking about a silver mine and posing questions Twain couldn't understand; and Twain attributing his growing confusion to the effects of the whiskey cocktails and finally, when he sees Hingston laughing, admitting that he had been swindled by "a string of plausibly worded sentences that didn't mean anything under the sun."[9]

On Christmas Eve (according to an account by Joe Goodman), after a lecture in a nearby mining town, Artemus appeared in the *Enterprise* office about midnight, helped put the paper to bed, and then took Mark Twain, Dan de Quille, Hingston, Denis McCarthy, and Joe Goodman to dinner at Virginia City's French restaurant. The drinking and wisecracking began, and this time, Goodman noticed, Mark Twain was more than holding his own. Held to a draw by Twain, Artemus turned to work on Goodman, and Goodman said to let him alone and go on with the mammoth contest of wits; he'd continue with the ordering and have a little joke for them later on. Many courses and wines later, the waiter brought Ward a bill for $237. "That is *my* joke," said Goodman. Ward picked it up, saying he was surprised at the moderate amount; he had thought it would be at least twice as much.

Dawn was just breaking when they left the restaurant. "'I can't walk on the earth,'" said Artemus, "'I feel like walking on the skies.'"

He settled for something in between, clambering up on a shed and mounting from there to the top of a building. Mark Twain scrambled up after him, and the two went clattering away over the roofs along a row of the closely packed structures, leaping from one rooftop to the next, with their companions running along the street below. Goodman was worried because patrolmen in Virginia City usually shot first and asked questions afterward. Just in time he ran into a policeman who had his revolver cocked and was about to fire at the two figures silhouetted against the sky. When restrained, the officer of the law protested, "'Don't you see those burglars up there?'" And when told the burglars were Artemus Ward and Mark Twain, he said, "'Well, I'll be damned.'"[10]

That was Joe Goodman's recollection of the affair. According to Dan de Quille, it happened somewhat differently: they had been in Virginia City's Chinatown, where they were drinking rice brandy, when a tong war broke out and bullets began to fly, killing one man and wounding others. Escaping from the melee, they started back up the hill to the main part of town, and it was then that the march over the roofs began, until a night watchman armed with a shotgun, not a revolver, brought them to earth. After that they danced with the girls in a dance hall to the music of a hurdy-gurdy and then went on to a tour of bars and saloons under the guardianship of one Kettle-belly Brown, a burly miner who went along after deciding that they were too drunk to take care of themselves. And—still according to de Quille—the night's spree wound up in front of Hooper's Saloon, where Kettle-belly Brown, alarmed at his estimate of the mixture of Oriental and Western liquors inside the bellies of his charges, gave, or tried to give, them an emetic of mustard and water. Then Mark Twain, Artemus Ward, and Dan de Quille went to the boardinghouse where Twain and de Quille lodged, and all piled into one large bed to sleep off their colossal binge, just as the sun was rising on Christmas Day, 1863.

After he had attained an end-of-the-century perspective, Mark Twain could look back on his Nevada period as a sort of watershed. Behind it lay the morning-time of the republic when, as in one of his remembered dawns on the Mississippi, there was serenity, poetry, romance, and time to listen to the awakening birds and watch the colors of the foliage freshen in the changing light—while downward from Nevada and ahead into the rest of the century flowed what almost seemed to be an extension of the money-madness in Virginia City: the hurry, clangor, smoke, and greed of an increasingly industrialized America.

But of the Virginia City days themselves he would say, "They were so full to the brim with the wine of life; there have been no others like them."[11] He might also have said, if he had cared to admit it, that Artemus Ward's visit marked an important upward turn in his creative career.

9

Mark Ward and Artemus Twain

To Mark Twain, Artemus was in many respects a physical demonstration of his own unrealized possibilities, all the more striking because of the remarkable similarities between the two men. Both had been born into good families (Twain's Virginians, Ward's New England Puritans) who had moved to remote, near-frontier areas—the Clemens family to Missouri, the Browns to inland Maine. The fathers of both had died in the same year, 1847, leaving their wives and children in straitened circumstances. As a consequence, both had been put out to work as printer's apprentices, Twain at the age of twelve, Ward at the age of thirteen. Soon afterward, both had worked for elder brothers who were temporarily in the printing-publishing business, but neither had found shelter under these fraternal wings: Twain's brother Orion was incompetent and Ward's brother, Cyrus, a boozer, and so they had failed.

After the collapse of their brothers' enterprises had turned them out into the world again, both Twain and Ward had become itinerant printer boys, wandering and working their way here and there for several years. It is not unreasonable to trace to this early insecurity some of the roots of Mark Twain's inner disquiet and some of Artemus Ward's frequent despondency. For both men, humor may have been more than a commercialized talent; it may also have been a necessary item in their survival kits. On another and not unrelated point of comparison, both Twain and Ward seem to have had a real need for the applause, the welcome, the encompassing warmth, and the love of an appreciative audience. Each had inside him a submerged actor, and in Ward, at least, there was an inner conflict between this supressed performer and his "respectable" half.

One of the Virginia City nights when Ward got particularly intoxicated—drunker, as he said, than Alexander the Great in his "drinkinist days"—his inhibitions dissolved and he yielded to his secret urge: the desire to be a real performer in a real stage production. In the manner of one about to perform an unspeakably shameful but irresistible act, he sneaked away from his companions, joined the minstrels playing at one of the Virginia City theaters, blackened his face with burnt cork, and appeared as an end man. The audience, discovering who he was, called for a lecture, and Artemus responded with what he in his own anguished account of the affair termed "a gibbering, idiotic speech. Godamit!"[1] He scourged himself for several days about this episode and identified Mark Twain as someone who, along with himself, ought to be blamed, later writing to Twain, "Why did you not go with me and save me that night?" He told Dan de Quille that he had thought of being a comic actor, but now he was too old (a ridiculous statement—Ward was then only twenty-nine).

For Mark Twain, Ward provided almost a mirror image of his own capabilities and possible future success. Here was a man only a year older than Twain, a man who was not a product of the academic world but who had risen out of the printshop and newspaper office to become editor of the sophisticated *Vanity Fair* in New York, publish a best-selling book, consort with literary lights, and lecture to delighted audiences all across the nation. What was particularly impressive about all this was that Ward had made his reputation as a *humorist*. With him humor was not incidental—it was the whole show, and a highly intellectual show at that. He had raised humor to a new level of respectability that must have been instantly apparent and enormously appealing to Mark Twain. Further, Ward was proving that humor could make money; anyone who could pick up a dinner check for $237 was certainly well-to-do. And what was particularly aggravating about all this was that Artemus Ward, who was known from one end of America to the other, was not as good a writer as Mark Twain, even then, must have known himself to be.

So much for what was undeclared. The overt, intentional influence of Ward came from his seeing in this unknown writer a talent that few others had fully appreciated, and from his urging the young reporter to try to market his literary products on the East Coast. As a result of his own days as an editor of *Vanity Fair,* Artemus was well connected in Manhattan, and he promised that if Twain would send some articles or stories to New York, he would pave the way by writing to editorial friends on the *New York Mercury*. This was a good suggestion for getting Twain started. The *Mercury* was not too high-toned. In fact, there was a faint air of sin about it, for its city and suburban editions, containing sporting and theatrical news, local and national reports, serial romances, market information, and the like, were issued at an early hour on Sunday, when respectable people were supposed to be reading their Bibles, not worldly, weekday fare such as that of the *Mercury*. Mark Twain's stuff might easily find a place in this miscellany, and if it did he would be assured not only of New York but of national readership, for the *Mercury* had early editions, starting to come out on Friday afternoon, that went all over the country.

Ward left Virginia City with Hingston on the morning of December 29, 1863, to continue their journey eastward, and Mark Twain next heard from him in a letter written at Austin, Nevada, on New Year's Day 1864. The letter assured Twain that he would follow through on his promise to intervene for him in New York. "I shall write, soon, a powerfully convincing note to my friends of 'The Mercury.' ... Good-bye, old boy . . . and God Bless you! The matter of which I spoke to you so earnestly shall be just as earnestly attended to."[2]

A demijohn of whiskey Ward had taken along on the stagecoach may not have been a good idea. Nipping on the whiskey, and being subjected to the constant jarring and jouncing of the vehicle, may have placed a strain on his urinary system. He said in his New Year's Day letter to Mark Twain that his kidneys were affected, but it was difficult to tell whether or not he was serious. The letter rambled in places. For example, one sentence read: "I shall always remember Virginia as a bright spot in my existence, as all others must or rather cannot be, as it were." Mark Twain extracted a portion of the letter ending with these words and published it in the *Enterprise*. In his accompanying remarks he was not quite so considerate of Ward's reputation among the temperance-minded as Artemus Ward would be zealous to promote his in the literary world. He said that he couldn't understand the sentence, implied that Artemus must still have something left in " 'that old basket-covered jug,'" and wished him a safe continuing journey " 'drunk or sober.' "[3]

The two men never saw each other again, but they were destined to have, in spirit, a long association, the complexity of which was determined in large part by the complicated nature of Mark Twain. He was capable of warm friendships and yet of turning on his friends over imagined slights or misdealings. Within him humility warred with the pride of an eagle. It was pride as much as anything that was to affect Mark Twain's attitude toward the departed Artemus Ward.

W. D. Howells, who knew both men well, wrote in an introduction to a 1912 edition of Ward's works, ". . . I think that whoever renews or makes acquaintance here with the fun of the earlier humorist will be struck with the fact that in some of his beginnings Mark Twain formed himself from, if not on, Artemus Ward. The imitation could not last long; the great master was so immensely the master; but while it lasts it is as undeniable as it is curious, and it by no means impeaches his superiority. I think him incomparably the greater talent, and yet not always."[4]

Howell's opinion that Ward represented at least an initial influence upon Mark Twain is borne out to an extent by a comparison of their writings. There is some resemblance of spirit between the two authors, something of the same instinct for realism and a deriding of sentimental illusions. There is much of the same sportive, droll style. For example, consider the following passage: "Industry is a very fine thing. It is one of the finest things of which we have any knowledge. Yet do not frown . . . when I state that I don't like it. It doesn't agree with me. I prefer indolence. I am happiest when I am idle. I could live for months without performing any kind of labor, and at the expiration of that I should feel fresh and vigorous enough to go right on in the same way for numerous more months."[5]

This sounds so much like Mark Twain that it is hard to believe he did not write it. In truth, it was composed by Artemus Ward three years before Mark Twain launched his real writing career with the publication of *The Innocents Abroad.*

Since Ward's writing career was over before Twain's really began, one might suspect that the latter borrowed certain substantive bits and pieces from the older writer's work, but a warning is in order. Tracing the antecedents of a joke is a tricky business. (According to Twain, even the supposedly unique jumping-frog story was once attributed by a professor to a Greek who had lived two thousand years before Twain heard it.) Perhaps all that can safely be said is that the two often borrowed from the same sources; the same sort of material appealed to them both.

For example, in one of his books Mark Twain used a story that Don C. Seitz, author of *Artemus Ward, A Biography and Bibliography,* attributed to an incident involving Artemus Ward himself. It seems that one day Artemus was riding on one of the nation's slower trains when he summoned the conductor and, with the passengers as his audience, made a plea for a new safety measure. It was evident from the speed of the train, he pointed out, that it could not possibly catch a cow if one chanced to be traveling on the track in front of it, but there was nothing to prevent a cow from running into them if it happened to be following behind. "'I beseech you, therefore,'" Artemus cried, "'to remove the cow-catcher from the locomotive and place it on the rear car and so save us from disaster.'"[6] Mark Twain used this story, illustrating it with line drawings, in *The Gilded Age.*

So great was the remarkable retentiveness of Mark Twain's mind that he apparently never forgot anything he saw, heard, or otherwise experienced; sooner or later it would be turned into literary output. He may even have got the title *The Gilded Age* from "The Babes in the Wood." This is very much a speculation, for just what the lecture consisted of that night at Maguire's Opera House was not recorded (by then, reporters had been well warned against trying to take it down), but a year earlier, in December 1862, it had included the following passage having to do with moneyed people: "'It is often the case that gilded idiocy passes for gentleness, gilded impertinence passes for wit, gilded vulgarity passes for honest bluntness—in a word, if you want your base coin to pass for the true and ringing metal, simply gild.'"[7]

Further instances are found in comparing the works of the two authors. In Ward's work there is the boring minister whom he advised to enlist in the Union medical corps as 160 pounds of morphine and preach while surgical operations were being performed. In Twain's there is the summation of a piece of dull writing as "chloroform in print."[8]

In at least one of Ward's lectures there was a joke about a baggage-car man who said of a shipment of limburger cheese (thinking that a deceased lady was inside the coffin containing it), "She ain't in no *trance!*" In Twain's work there is "The Invalid's Story," a tale about exactly the same situation in a baggage car spun out to twenty-five hundred words or more.[9]

What was little more than a passing incident with Ward (as in the case of the double-talk prank in Virginia which became Twain's "First Interview With Artemus Ward") Mark Twain could elaborate into a whole article. One of Ward's two-liners Mark Twain could make the climax of a story several pages long. Typically, the summer of 1860, Ward published the following joke:

Scene at Restaurant
Waiter: *Please sir, how will you have your steak cooked?*
Serious Gentleman: *Well done, good and faithful servant.*

And that was all there was to it. But with Mark Twain, the "Well done, good and faithful servant" was the punch line for a long sketch called "Riley—Newspaper Correspondent,"[10] in which Riley proposed this as an epitaph for a faithful old Negro woman, long devoted to her mistress, who had met her end by falling asleep over a red-hot stove. (Twain's taste often left something to be desired.)

Given just a slight running start, Mark Twain could carry one single incident or character into the development of an entire book, and the fact that he made off with a few morsels from Artemus Ward takes as little away from his work as certain borrowings from Chaucer and Plutarch take away from Shakespeare. As far as can be discerned, the influence of Ward's writing on Twain was negligible. The influence of Ward himself may have been something else again. In summary, it seems that during his meteoric passage through Virginia City Ward did three important things for Mark Twain. He helped make him more aware of the literary and commercial value of humor, particularly of humor derived from American frontier life. He presented him with a living example of success within his own capabilities. And he encouraged him to send some of his writings to New York.

With, presumably, Artemus Ward's introductory note running on ahead, Twain followed up on the New York suggestion almost immediately, sending articles which were published in the *New York Mercury* on February 7 and 21, 1864. However, these two pieces, excellent as they were, did little to establish his reputation.

But then came "The Celebrated Jumping Frog of Calaveras County."

It would be pleasant to relate that the frog leaped to recognition entirely through the interest of Artemus Ward in his friend and protege, and indeed friendship did play a large part in his good offices. But so did self-interest, to some degree. When Artemus arrived back in the East in the spring of 1864 and started to write *Artemus Ward, His Travels,* the book about his western trip he had promised his publisher, he found that his notes were inadequate, and he began writing to people he had met on his journey, asking them to send him descriptions of things he had failed to note carefully, or to verify details or make other contributions, for which he offered payment. He asked Mark Twain to send him something to put in the book, and when Twain got around to it, he sent Ward the story under the title "Jim Smiley and His Jumping Frog." But the manuscript arrived too late, and Ward's publisher, Carleton, very casually gave it to Henry Clapp, editor of the failing *New York Saturday Press,* where it finally appeared in the issue of November 18, 1865. The story made something of a sensation and was reprinted all over the country. The name of Mark Twain became known as the author of the sketch, but he was still four years away from the work that began his lasting literary reputation, and it was, as he complained, only the frog that became famous in 1865, not he.

Concerning the jumping-frog tale, Mark Twain once wrote, "I used to tell the story of the Jumping Frog in San Francisco, and presently Artemus Ward came along and wanted it to help fill out a little book which he was about to publish." (There is a mix-up of chronology here that may be attributable to loose wording or a failure of memory. It was not Artemus Ward that came along but a letter from him. Mark Twain wrote the jumping-frog story around the end of January 1865; he and Artemus had met and parted more than a year previously.) Twain continued, "So I wrote it out and sent it to his publisher, Carleton, but Carleton thought the book had enough matter in it, so he gave the story to Henry Clapp as a present, and Clapp put it in his *Saturday Press,* and it killed that paper with a suddenness that was beyond praise. At least the paper died with that issue, and none but envious people have ever tried to rob me of honor and credit of killing it."[11]

Mark Twain's report of the death of the *Saturday Press* was, as he once said of a report of his own demise, greatly exaggerated; this was not the last issue, and the paper staggered on for a while afterward. As illustrated by this and other matters, Twain was a master in making often questionable details somehow add up to an unquestionable truth. It was another contradiction of his character that his biographer, Albert Bigelow Paine, remarked upon. In spirit, Paine said, Mark Twain was the very essence of truth, but he often made no real pretense as to accuracy of time, place, or circumstances as long as he could tell a good story. "When I was younger," he once said, "I could remember anything, whether it happened or not, but I am getting old, and soon I shall remember only the latter."[12] As was often the case, he was clowning about one of his human frailties. Yet, for all that, he could usually manage what might be called impressionistic veracity, and in this sense Mark Twain was entirely truthful in conveying the idea that the jumping-frog story involved both an accident and the friendly assistance of Artemus Ward.

In his excellent books *Mark Twain in Virginia City* and *Mark Twain on the Lecture Circuit,* Paul Fatout attributed much of Mark Twain's development as a lecturer to Artemus Ward, pointing out that Twain borrowed not only lecturing techniques but some of Ward's accessory devices. In his scholarly study of Ward, Prof. James C. Austin concluded that it was perhaps the pose of Artemus Ward the lecturer that influenced Twain the most. "In the mask of sober innocence Clemens discovered an approach to his audience both in speech and writing."[13] Twain was already known as a fascinating talker when Ward first came to Virginia City, but his status was strictly that of an amateur. Afterward, he was on his way to becoming a professional. From his front seat in the "printer's pew" at Maguire's Opera House he had watched Ward's performance with a craftman's intentness, looking for the techniques that lay behind the seeming artlessness—the mock gravity, the look of innocent surprise when the audience laughed, the anticlimaxes, pauses, nonsequiturs, wanderings of thought, and all the other tricks Artemus Ward had perfected in many appearances and through long observations of audience reactions.

Later on, in one of Twain's sketches, "How to Tell a Story," he gave Artemus credit as the exemplar of at least one bit of comic art—a delayed-fuse way of putting across the nub of a story not through emphasis but "by dropping it in a carefully casual and indifferent way, with the pretence that he does not know it is a nub."[14] As time went by Twain would develop and enlarge upon his stage personality, but in the beginning he undoubtedly borrowed much from Ward and was often compared with him when he began lecturing on the West Coast in the fall of 1866. Also, apparently, he was still using Ward techniques seven or eight years later, when he was a celebrity. A man who heard Twain lecture in London wrote, "The hall was crowded with fashionable people in evening dress, of whom few if any had ever seen Mark. He came on the platform in full dress with the air of a manager announcing a disappointment and stammered out apologies. 'Mr. Clemens had landed at Liverpool, and had fully hoped to reach London in time, but, etc.' The murmurs were deep and threatened to be loud, when Mark added that he was happy to say that Mark Twain was present and would now give his lecture."

This manner of sneaking up on an audience was pure Artemus Ward. So was the relation of Mark Twain's lecture that night to its title, "The Sandwich Islands;" the one had little or nothing to do with the other. But the lecture also demonstrated that Twain was beginning to develop his own manner as when, in a narrative about a duel, he said in an exalted tone: " 'But I never fight duels now. If a man insults me, do I challenge that man? Oh, no! I take that man [uplifting his eyes piously] by the hand, and with soft persuasive words lead him to a dimly lighted apartment and—kill him!'"[15] This was not in Ward's style, yet the audience reportedly enjoyed it hugely.

In 1910 W. D. Howells summed up Mark Twain's lecturing career by saying, "He was the most consummate public performer I ever saw, and it was an incomparable pleasure to hear him lecture; on the platform he was the great and finished actor which he probably would not have been on the stage."[16] It is undoubtedly correct to believe that Mark Twain eventually far surpassed his mentor on the platform and had little to fear from any comparison with him.

However, for many years, his debt to Artemus, both as a literary man and a lecturer, did not rest easily on his shoulders. After their boozy companionship in Virginia City the two men had parted on the best of terms. The letter Artemus wrote him from Austin had begun (with Ward's usual airy disregard for conventions) "My Dearest Love," and had ended on an equally affectionate note. And Mark Twain, writing of their brief association years later, appeared to remember the genial, kindly Artemus as "one of the best fellows in the world and one of the most companionable."[17]

But the fact remains that Artemus Ward haunted him most unpleasantly for at least a couple of decades. He would always be compared with Ward, sometimes unfavorably, and this was galling to a man of Mark Twain's fierce pride. Also, all of his associations with the memory of Artemus seemed to rub him the wrong way, and Twain's curious character seemed to turn these into a resentment that had no logical relationship with Artemus himself.

To begin with, the linking of his name with "The Jumping Frog" displeased Twain. He asserted that it was a "villainous backwoods sketch" that stamped him as a rube writer; that he ought to have become known for something better; that he wouldn't have written the sketch in the first place if it hadn't been for Artemus Ward; and that he was glad it arrived in New York too late to be included in Ward's book, which was a "wrechedly poor one."[18]

Then such recognition as "The Jumping Frog" brought him failed to make him any money; and when he visited Artemus Ward's publisher in February 1867, with the idea of making it the titlepiece of a book of sketches, Carleton turned him down in an interview that left a long aftermath of exasperation. There were two sides to the story. Mark Twain said that Carleton had snootily declined to publish his book on the ridiculous grounds that he had enough books already. Carleton said he turned it down because the author looked like a bum. Nine years afterward Mark Twain wrote that Carleton had insulted him, and that "when the day arrives that sees me doing him a civility I shall feel that I am ready for Paradise, since my list of possible and impossible forgivenesses will then be complete." When the book Twain had offered

Carleton was published in 1867 by C. H. Webb under the title of *The Celebrated Jumping Frog of Calaveras County and Other Sketches,* its sales were small and it was full of "damnable errors of grammar."[19] He must have thought for many years that Artemus Ward had done him no favors in bringing this seemingly unfortunate work into the light of day.

On a lecture tour in 1871, when Mark Twain's talk was not going well, he threw out his script and hastily wrote a new one entitled "Artemus Ward, Humorist." It was partly an account of Ward's life as it might have been delivered by an old friend who by reason of his friendship was entitled to indulge in a certain amount of affectionate and amusing disparagement. Unfortunately, however, his jests came through with a slightly malicious tone, as though Twain could not help himself. He would begin to say something favorable about Artemus: humor was born in him; he took the country by storm; he was a man of good impulses; and so forth. But then there would be a subtle downgrading: Ward had been thrown so suddenly into success that he did not develop into the polished wit he might have become; he did not live in vain, but he was not deep, not great-brained; his humor was not refined, and not up to that of Holmes, Lowell, Harte, or Warner.

Twain also offered descriptions of Ward's personal appearance which were intended to be funny but which were unflattering. And he contributed mightily to an impression that Artemus was indolent, saying, for example, that Ward never had any schooling because he was too poor to afford it and too lazy to care for it; that he hated work and even hated to see others work; and that his success was a freak—he had gone to the top of the ladder without touching a single rung.

In the lecture, the account of Artemus Ward's life served as a framework upon which to mount bits of humor and comic stories, some by Mark Twain but many by Artemus—including a joke that was widely known as part of the Wardian legend, his "brandy and water" reply to Thomas Maguire. Twain had overlooked the fact that Ward had lectured practically everywhere and that this, plus the widespread reprinting of his written sketches, had given his material great circulation. But the borrowing did not escape the notice of the newspapers. One reporter refered to the lecture as "Mark Ward on Artemus Twain",[20] and others severely criticized him for trying to lean on Artemus and collecting lecture fees for Ward's old jokes. When he lectured in Ward's home state of Maine the *Portland Daily Press* chastised him for a number of grave errors in regard to Artemus Ward's early history, condemned the lecture generally, and suggested that "Mr. Clemens's forte is not the platform. He does better with the pen."[21] The talk was finally discontinued, with

Mark saying he hated it and with Artemus Ward getting a good deal of the blame; the material Ward had written was no good, Twain asserted—it was only the part he had written himself that audiences laughed at.

Public comparisons of Ward and himself represented a cross that Twain had to bear for years, and even his old friend Joe Goodman did not spare him. In an article published in 1892, Goodman observed that people of that day might well be astonished at the reputation Artemus Ward had achieved thirty years previously, "but, nevertheless, it was genuine and well deserved. Aside from being a poineer in his line of literature, there was about him a personal charm that none of his successors need ever pretend to."[22]

Also typical was a review by the *Spectator,* in 1873, which concluded that though a perfect calm and assumed earnestness of manner was common to the two humorists, "there was something much more comically child-like, much more of a serious inward embarrassment and bewilderment at the core of the humor of Artemus Ward than in that of Mark Twain," and that on the whole Mark Twain could not be regarded as "so remarkable and rare a humorist as Artemus Ward."[23] In 1876 the *New Quarterly Magazine* of London made about the same sort of comment: Mark Twain was a bit too smoothly professional, but the humor of Artemus Ward had always seemed completely spontaneous.

When he visited England—having been preceded there by Ward—Twain had to overcome a strong personal bias on the part of many London newspapermen to whom Artemus had already endeared himself, both on and off the stage, only a few years previously. One of the fraternity, after attending a Mark Twain lecture, wrote, "His coming had been heralded by much flourishing of trumpets; but, speaking for myself, I was greatly disappointed. Perhaps it was that I was prejudiced. Anyway, I compared him with Artemus Ward, greatly to the disadvantage of Twain, who seemed to me to copy Ward's methods without success."[24]

Another comment made by the *New Quarterly Magazine* touched more closely the real difference between the two men. Mark Twain, the magazine said, was more diffuse in his composition; he would take a whole page to bring a jest home, whereas Artemus Ward would do it in a line, a phrase, or a misspelling of one word. It was soon to be proved that Twain was not just more diffuse; he was enormously larger. In his performances as an author and a lecturer he would soon surpass the impression left with the Londoners in the early 1870s.

After he had risen to the heights of his greatness and had been acclaimed throughout the world, Mark Twain probably made his peace with the ghost of Artemus Ward. There is a suggestion of this in the aftermath of an episode that took place at a gathering for Mark Twain in London in 1872, as related by Albert Bigelow Paine. In 1870, John Camden Hotten had brought out a pirated version of *The Innocents Abroad* with an introduction, highly complimentary to Twain, by E. P. Hingston. Twain, by now quite famous, was angry with Hingston, but Paine does not indicate why except to say that "Twain's views had undergone a radical change,"[25] a remarkably unclear explanation. Paine does not make it appear that Hingston was blamed for being associated with the piracy, and he really does not seem to understand the reasons for Twain's ill will.

There is a hint, however, in Hingston's introduction to the book, which concludes: "I believe that Mark Twain has never visited England. Some time since he wrote to me asking my opinion relative to his giving an entertainment in London. He has appeared in New York and elsewhere as a lecturer, and from his originality would, I have no doubt, be able to repeat his lectures with success here were he to visit this country. But I never met him in the character of a public entertainer, and can only speak from experience of his remarkable talent as a humorous writer, and of his cordial frankness and jovial good-fellowship as a friend and companion."[26]

There is reason to believe that Hingston was being very tactful in this statement—and that concerning the proposed lecturing tour in England, Twain had asked him for something more than his opinion. In the *New York Clipper* of November 17, 1866, there had been an item reporting on Artemus Ward's debut in England which said, "Hingston is engineering for him."[27] In the same issue there was another story about Mark Twain's beginning to lecture "in the mountain towns of California." And there exists a letter from Mark Twain to the English manager in which Twain says his book is about ready for publication (evidently *The Celebrated Jumping Frog of Calaveras County and Other Sketches*), refers to what appears to have been a previous proposition that Hingston "engineer" for *him,* and asks Hingston how he feels about it now. From the circumstances and the use of this word "engineer," an unusual one to employ with respect to theatrical management, it seems very likely that Twain, who arrived in New York from the West Coast in January 1867, saw the *Clipper* items and began a correspondence with Hingston, referring to or enclosing them along with a proposal that Hingston act as his manager; and that since nothing came of it, he placed the Englishman on his list of unforgivables.

At any rate, what happened at the meeting of the two men in

London was that Hingston came toward Mark Twain, his hand out-stretched and his face aglow, ready to greet his old friend from Virginia City, and Twain cut him dead—refused even to look at him. As an example of Mark Twain's occasional behavior this was not too exceptional, but what *was* remarkable was Paine's observation that "in after-years his conscience hurt him terribly for this. He remembered it only with remorse and shame. Once, in his old age, he spoke of it with deep sorrow."[28] This is rather mysterious. Distress of this sort did not afflict Mark Twain very often. One can only wonder if, in a confused and troubled memory of that evening in London, he did not see stepping forward in an accustomed place beside his old manager someone who had not actually been there, Artemus Ward, the young humorist whom he could think of in his old age as his true friend, but whose incorporeal presence had been at one time his most annoying competitor.

On that same visit to London in 1872 Mark Twain was entertained by the Savage Club, a group that had welcomed Artemus Ward, made him a member, and become greatly attached to him in 1866. It is quite possible that this was the gathering at which Mark Twain met Hingston. If so, the puzzling aspect of the incident deepens. When Twain arose to speak to the Savages, he knew perfectly well of their emotional involvement with Ward, and if he were going to say anything about Artemus, it would have to be something pleasant. On the other hand, he could have said nothing. What he did express was thanks for the hospitality and help the club had extended to his "old friend," and he proposed a toast to Artemus Ward.[29]

It is the more fond and friendly attitude expressed in the toast that Mark Twain seems to have developed toward the memory of Artemus Ward, after that memory had faded in the public mind and once Twain himself had become "the most conspicuous person on the planet."[30]

10

The Wild Humorist
of the Plains

Heading eastward into the wilderness from Virginia City, Ward and Hingston were continuing a winter journey on the Overland Stage that would have been arduous even in summertime. About 1,800 miles of rough trail lay between them and the railroad terminus at Atchison, Kansas. Along the route there were stations every twelve miles or so. At "line stations" horses were changed. "Home stations," which were reached at noon and night, served meals and offered rude lodgings, but these were so bad that most travelers started out carrying as much food as they could with them and planning to travel night and day, sleeping on the coach. Because of the danger from hostile Indians in that winter of 1863–64, both drivers and passengers were armed. In Virginia City, Ward and Hingston purchased revolvers. Artemus, who had a nervous dislike of firearms, bought a case for his weapon, put the revolver inside, and locked the case. Each bought extra clothing to protect himself from the bitter cold: a pair of thick blankets, with straps for binding them around the body; a fur hat; fur gloves and fur boots. Ward obtained a big buffalo robe to wrap around them both at night. They purchased a large boiled ham, six roast chickens, a bag of biscuits, a bag of coffee, a coffee pot, and a lantern. Someone gave them a demijohn of whiskey.

To Hingston, all of this had a decided sense of unreality. What seemed so odd, he thought, was that they were not explorers or missionaries starting out to convert the heathen Indians; they were going into this howling wilderness with a show!

They left Virginia City early on the morning of December 29, 1863, riding in a vehicle known as a mountain mud-wagon. This was a lightly built but strong wagon much lower than a standard coach and therefore less likely to tip over. Entered from the rear, it had seats along each side, a canvas roof, and leather curtains in place of windows. The floor was covered thickly with straw, which served not only to insulate against the cold but to cushion the fall of travelers when they were jounced off their seats while asleep. In this uncomfortable vehicle they rode night and day some 175 miles, arriving on the morning of December 31 in Austin, Nevada, a mining town in the Toiyabe Mountains. There had never been a lecture or any other kind of a show in Austin. Two miners and a friendly Indian were sent to distribute Ward's handbills to outlying camps. On the evening of New Year's Day, an unfinished store, still smelling of wet plaster, was made into a lecture hall with borrowed chairs and lights. Artemus Ward himself entered carrying an oil lamp. The lecture was enthusiastically received, with a dance following that lasted the rest of the night. It was a scene that struck close to the base rock of American humor, this gathering of miners and Indians, the raw building in a remote settlement, with the sound of laughter and fiddles reaching out along the rays of yellow lamplight into the darkness of the lonesome Nevada mountains. Ward also made a side trip to lecture at Big Creek, a mining camp twelve miles from Austin. The only reason, Hingston thought, was that "it was the wildest place he could go for lecturing purposes."[1]

Before leaving Austin, where there was a second lecture on January 4 to take care of people who hadn't been able to get into the store for the first one, Artemus prepared to carry out an odd idea. This was suggested to him by the utter desolation of most of the stations along the Overland Stage route, which sometimes were merely mud huts or even dugouts, with a covered excavation to serve as a stable and another as a dwelling for the isolated wretch who kept the station. Where the company obtained its station-keepers, and why they were content to live in such misery and danger hundreds of miles from civilization, was something of a mystery, but it was suspected that many of them were either fugitives from justice or insane. Hingston remarked to one of these pariahs—who was typically gaunt, dirty, long-haired, and shaggily whiskered—that he must be sadly in want of company in such lonely and dreary surroundings. "'Not while I can talk with Martin Luther and Daniel Webster,'"[2] was the reply. He was a benighted spiritualist from Melrose, Massachusetts. It struck Artemus Ward that it would be an epic joke to post a show bill on each of these lonely specks in the vastness of western

America. He dictated the wording: "'A lecture will be delivered here, in a sweet voice, by Artemus Ward, the Wild Humorist of the Plains,'"[3] and he had the bills printed in Austin. These were later posted, as planned, at stations along the way, and it always delighted Artemus to believe that some of these notices probably remained tacked to isolated hovels for years, bleaching in the sun and wind, stared at by uncomprehending Indians and astonished travelers, with a background of windswept wasteland emphasizing the absurdity of the message.

But the sixteen-hundred-mile ride that still lay ahead of Ward and Hingston was no joke. They left Austin in a Concord coach on January 5, rolling northeast into a wintery landscape with the cold growing more and more intense. About eighty miles from Austin they came to the formidable Diamond Mountains, deeply covered with snow. But this was no barrier to the intrepid and ingenious operators of the Overland Stage. The passengers were transferred to open sleighs, four to a sleigh. This vehicle, as Hingston described it, was nothing more than a wide, shallow, open box mounted on runners, with a little plank platform, on which a man could stand, projecting on each side. The sleigh was drawn by a team of mules harnessed wide, their neck yokes keeping them at least six feet apart. Two men, one on each of the outrigger platforms, assisted the driver; by quickly shifting their weight they could keep the sleigh from tipping over. The mailbags and other pieces of baggage were placed in the bottom of the sleigh. The four passengers, warned to hang on, lay on top of these, faces uppermost, covered with blankets and buffalo robes. Hingston and Ward made this part of the trip at night, so a guide with lanterns and a long pole went ahead; the pole was used to probe the snow for possible pitfalls, the lanterns to mark danger points. And so over the Diamond Mountains they went, all but eyes and noses covered against the freezing cold, the sky and the stars tilting suddenly in great swoops above them. Hingston remembered that although they were lying horizontally with respect to the sleigh, they were every now and then "almost vertical with the zenith."[4]

Then it was back into a coach and onward over bumpy, frozen ground toward Utah territory. The threat of attack by Indians continued. They found the guard doubled at all stations where horses were changed. The passengers kept their firearms at hand. One day there was an alarm and a general snatching for weapons, a procedure which, with Artemus, consisted of reaching into various pockets in search of the key to his revolver case. The locked-up case, his fellows were annoyed to learn, was outside on the luggage rack. Someone pressed a pistol into Ward's hand,

and he accidentally discharged it, becoming a much greater danger than the Indians until he was disarmed.

Fortunately, the Overland Stage depended more on speed than on firepower. At one stop the station-keepers, normally an inhospitable lot, asked them to stay on the basis that "the more hands we have the better stand we shall make against the sons of bitches."[5] But the driver elected to keep moving. Most of the time the main enemies were boredom and fatigue. There was little to look at except acres of barren land and sagebrush stretching away to distant mountains. The eye grew tired of this dreariness, and the nostrils wearied of the camphor-like odor of sage as it mingled with the smells of harness oil, horse droppings, dust, and the raw, wild-animal odor of robes made of buffalo hides. As described by Hingston, they traveled "day and night, cramped up in our narrow coach, jerked forward, tossed backward, jolted from side to side, tumbled over, thrown out, bruised, battered, and sore all over, irritable through want of sleep, nervous with continuity of excitement, and weary of the cheerless monotony of the scenery . . . too jaded to talk and too drowsy to be convivial."[6]

By the time they arrived at Schell Creek station, although they still had around 225 miles to go to reach Salt Lake City, Ward decided that he could not continue without a night's sleep in a bed. Schell Creek, just inside the Utah border, was a large, fortified repair and maintenance station operated for the Overland Stage by the Mormons. After supper at Schell, Ward and Hingston retired to crude beds in a loft over the telegraph room. The loft was cold, for there were portholes all around it for firing through at the Indians. They stuffed the holes with rags. Before wrapping himself in his blankets, Hingston placed his revolver near at hand and asked Ward where his weapon was. "'In the case,'" was the reply. "'Is the case unlocked?'" "'No,'" said Artemus. "'Where is the key?'" "'I don't know'" Ward replied drowsily. "'When the Indians come, blow open my case with your revolver.'"[7]

In the morning they boarded the next coach. At Spring Valley station, twelve miles farther on, they found the keepers going about their work under arms. Two days later they heard that the men who had harnessed their horses here had been killed and scalped and the station burned to the ground.

They ploughed through sand along the southern edge of the Great Salt Lake Desert—a vast and lonely old seabed from which the covering water had long ago evaporated—and then turned northeastward again, across a series of hills and intervening flatlands seen in their dreariest and most desolate mood under the silent grip of winter. One station was completely invisible. The coach stopped, for no reason that anyone could see, in the middle of a barren plain. Suddenly a man and two horses rose out of the earth. It was Dug Way station, with stables and sleeping quarters, as the name implied, dug into the ground. By now Ward and Hingston had used up the supplies of food they'd been carrying and had to depend on meals obtainable at stations such as this, which were abominable, consisting usually only of black coffee, bread baked at the station, and strongly flavored bacon. It was a rancid joke among travelers that you could tell you were coming to a station long before you saw it; the smell of the bacon carried at least two miles. But Dug Way had fooled them; they'd been smelling bacon and still couldn't see any station.

As they crossed the frozen Jordan, a river flowing northward into the Great Salt Lake, the ice under them broke, there was a sudden flood of water into the coach, and they got a cold baptism while the team thrashed its way through the river and up the opposite bank. There was a halt for drying out at the next station and then, after a journey of nearly four hundred miles from Austin, they found themselves approaching Salt Lake City around January 10. As they neared the capital of Mormondom, Artemus grew apprehensive; in one of his sketches he had once allowed the Old Showman to rank Salt Lake with Sodom and Gomorrah while calling its residents "a set of retchis." The sketch had been widely read, appearing in *Artemus Ward, His Book,* and Ward began to fear (a little late in the day, Hingston thought) that they might not be hospitably received by the Mormons. But all appearances seemed to be contradicting the Showman's derogatory statements. Although the ground was covered with snow, there were indications of neatness and industry everywhere as the coach rolled on—smoothly now, over good roads and bridges—into Salt Lake City itself. The streets were wide and clean. There were no slums, no hovels. Each tidy house, with its garden, occupied more than an acre of land. There didn't seem to be any poor people—none, anyway, that looked like retchis. Considering that the city was only fifteen or sixteen years old, the public buildings were impressive: a theater, the building housing the territorial legislature, stores and hotels, a tabernacle. Stonemasons were at work on a new temple which, by the extent of its foundations, promised to be a towering structure. Salt Lake City looked as little like Sodom or Gomorrah as anyone could possibly imagine. Its one claim notoriety was, of course, the institution of polygamy, and this made it as interesting to mid-century America as a city of nudists. Hence, visits of prying journalists were nothing new, and those who served as the Mormons' public-relations men were well prepared to deal with such visitors.

But it took the nervous Ward and Hingston some time to be reassured on this point. They checked into the Salt Lake House and there talked with a cavalry captain, an officer from nearby Camp Douglas. Troops were stationed at this post primarily, it was said, for protection of the territory and the Overland Stage against the Indians, but the officer made it appear that there was also an uneasy relationship between the Mormons and their military neighbors. The captain pointed out that the Mormons would probably treat them courteously, but only because they wanted to be written about favorably, and "'if Uncle Sam didn't keep us up there in Camp Douglas to protect you, you might find their hospitality to be a *grave* matter.'"[8] Following their conversation with this alarmist, Artemus took to his room while Hingston went out to talk with people and get some idea of how they felt about the humorist. He returned gloomily. "'Thank God, *I* never wrote against the Mormons.'"[9] Presently they were visited by an individual who was so well cloaked and bundled up against the cold that he seemed like a masked messenger of evil to the super-sensitive Hingston, who also noted that "his step was of a gliding character." But when a large comforter was unwound and cap and cloak were removed, this proved to be one of Brigham Young's elders. The elder, chatty and urbane, said he was an old newspaperman himself—used to work on the *New York Herald*. He wanted to make them happy during their stay in Salt Lake City. After a while he got down to business. "'The President [he meant Brigham Young] has your book in his library. He has all the books that have been written about him. You ought not to have made ridicule of our Church.'"[10]

Artemus replied that he'd known very little about the Mormons at the time of that writing; now that he had the opportunity to learn more, he'd try to do them more justice in the future, and he hoped that Brigham Young would allow him to lecture in the Mormon theater. The elder left, saying that he'd try to arrange for a meeting with the head of the church. The meeting, which took place soon afterward, went well. The offending Sodom and Gomorrah piece was not mentioned, and Young was "affable, gracious and conversational,"[11] according to Hingston, who was delighted when they received permission to use the theater.

Then Artemus came down with what Hingston, who had a smattering of medical knowledge, thought was typhoid fever. He was soon out of his head and raving. Hingston rode to Camp Douglas and brought back an army doctor. The physician was pessimistic, advising, "'When that delirium quits him you had better say a few words to him about how he wishes to dispose of his affairs.'"[12] Distracted, Hingston began looking about for a coffin and went to the office of the Overland Stage to find out how, if it came to that, he could transport the remains eastward. The agent said it couldn't be done. "'The last time we sent on the body of one of our people, the wolves smelt it and attacked the mules. Our orders are never to send on another.'"[13] Walking out of the stage-office and into the snow, thinking of the thousand miles of wilderness that still lay between him and civilization to the east, Hingston felt that he was stumbling around in a nightmare.

But next morning the doctor reported that Artemus had taken a turn for the better, and that with care he might pull through. A curious corps of nurses attended the invalid, including an old Englishwoman Hingston located, the Mormon landlady of the hotel, and Jerome Davis, a roughhewn, burly Californian who had met Artemus and taken a fancy to him. Gradually Artemus grew stronger, with the aid of appetizers and nourishment sent from many well-wishers. Brigham Young contributed dried fruit and homemade wine. The general in command of Camp Douglas sent champagne. Mormon ladies brought eggs, jellies, jams, and sweetmeats. Jerome Davis ransacked the stores and found a dozen cans of oysters which had somehow reached Salt Lake City from Baltimore. After his first meal of oysters Artemus Ward said, "'Get out the bills for the lecture.'"[14] His illness lasted about three weeks, but on January 21 he was well enough to write Mark Twain a letter in which he said, "The Saints have been wonderfully kind to me. I could not have been better or more tenderly nursed at home. God bless them!"[15]

The lecture was delivered on the evening of February 8, with Artemus Ward standing in an elegant drawing-room scene which the stage manager had set up and Brigham Young beaming from his rocking chair in the pit, seeming to enjoy "The Babes in the Wood" thoroughly. "I can only say," Artemus recalled, "that I was never listened to more attentively and kindly in my life than I was by this audience of Mormons."[16]

By now, so keen was the public perception of Ward as a humorist that people were able to catch even the thinnest of puns. A story in the *Daily Vedette* (the Camp Douglas newspaper) of February 11 said,

> Artemus Ward left for the East in yesterday's coach, fully
> recovered from his recent illness. . . . Artemus carries with him
> an enormous board, which he says is a woodcut for his show

bills. Just as the coach was drifting off, a friend in the crowd halloed out, "You have left the board behind." Artemus quickly responded, "All right, I expected to, the stage can't carry an entire people," gracefully intimating that *the bored* were the good folk of this city.

With this final jest Artemus—well bundled up in furs and cheerfully puffing on a cigar—took his departure from Salt Lake City. Twelve miles out, encountering deep snow, the travelers changed from coach to sleigh. That night in the Wasatch Mountains a sudden lurch threw Ward and the driver from their seats, the horses ran away, and the two thrown-out men waded through snow two miles before they came up with the horses, the vehicle, and the other passengers, all piled up in a snowbank.

A week later, they were crossing the Continental Divide by way of Bridger's Pass in dire peril of their lives. At midnight on February 17 their sleigh broke down in the pass, forcing a four-mile walk by the passengers. The darkness, the far-below-zero temperature combined with a piercing wind, and the struggle through the deep snow made this a nightmare experience. It was here on the roof of the continent, in the middle of the winter and the night, that Hingston seems to have been convinced—if he had not been convinced previously—that Ward was possessed of a self-destructive madness. Why hadn't he turned back from Salt Lake City? He had already accomplished his announced objective—that of visiting the Mormons. From Salt Lake City it would have been about 775 miles back to San Francisco, from which port they could have returned to New York by sea in less than a month. From Salt Lake City eastward to the terminus of the railway was much farther—about 1,250 miles, over storm-swept mountains and across plains peopled by hostile Indians. Yet Ward had gotten up out of a sickbed and continued. Now here they were, struggling through snow and darkness, in danger of freezing to death in a wilderness as remote from civilization as the dark side of the moon. In *Artemus Ward, His Travels,* Ward later wrote that "it occurred to me, as I wrung my frost-bitten hands on that dreadful night, that for me to deliberately go over that path in mid-winter was a sufficient reason for my election to any lunatic asylum, by an overwhelming vote."[17] There is also a hint in that account that Hingston told him that he was insane, and they were not, on that particular night, in a situation that would have called for a joke.

Sometime that night, according to Ward in *His Travels,* a German boy who was among the struggling passengers sank down in the snow, resisted all attempts to keep him moving, and froze to death. Next morning, according to Ward's story, they got the boy's body onto a sleigh and buried it farther on. But no one knew who the boy was; he had no baggage, identification, or money, although his fare had been paid to Denver. It was a strange story, not referred to by Hingston in his own written account of the trip and not reported in the Denver press in subsequent days—so strange a story that it may be wondered if it really happened and if they boy may have been a dream within a nightmare, perhaps a vision of the boy Ward himself, a lingering fantasy of his teen-age wanderings; somewhere, he wrote in *His Travels*, a poor mother was crying for a son who would never come home.

Once they were across the Medicine Bow Mountains and turning southeastward, through Little and Big Laramie stations, the weather improved; so did the food, and Ward's quick powers of recuperation were at work. The country was alive with antelopes and other game. At one station they enjoyed a breakfast of antelope steak, hashed deer, ham, boiled bear, honey, eggs, coffee, tea, and cream. It was the best meal they'd had on the trip. "A better couldn't be found at Delmonico's or Parker's," Artemus asserted.[18] Soon they were heading almost due south into Colorado, with the dramatic peaks of the Rockies, now safely passed, off to their right and a dull, far-reaching brown plain on the left.

By the time they reached Denver, on February 22, Ward was looking rather ratty. Some of his hair had dropped out during his illness in Salt Lake City, he was still thin from the effects of that illness, and his unbathed days in fur clothing while on the trail for twelve days had depressed him. After cleaning up and shaving at the Planters' House in Denver, he visited a hardware store and bought a pair of curling irons. Hingston helped him frizz up his hair into the distinctive mass of curls, and, thus restored, Ward took to the platform again. He lectured at the Langrishe and Dougherty Theater in Denver, and afterward the citizens gathered outside his hotel to salute him with a serenade. There were other lectures in nearby Central City and at the mining town of Black Hawk. The Central City *Daily Miners' Register* was ecstatic: "The arrival of Louis Napoleon or the Dey of Algiers could hardly create a greater sensation in our mountain circles than the entrance among us of this king of humorous writers, and prince of good fellows."[19]

From Denver, the trail of the Overland Stage led generally along the South Platte River in a great arc, swinging up through the northeast corner of Colorado and then across southern Nebraska, finally departing from the Platte near Fort Kearney to descend across a corner of Kansas to Atchison, on the Missouri, the western terminus of the railroad. The prairies in March presented by far the least inspiring section of the overland route. Of the Platte—a wide, muddy, exceptionally shallow river lined in places with scrubby willow and cottonwood growths—Artemus Ward said, "'It would be a good river if stood on edge.'"[20] The ground, sandy on the tablelands, grassy in the swales, generally low and flat, was swept by winds that often drove gravel through the air like birdshot. To the naturally dreary and desolate aspect of the terrain, the ruthless western rush of the pioneers had added its own touches of devastation. In places the road was three hundred feet wide, beaten and rutted by wagon wheels and the hooves of animals, many of which had left their skeletons beside the trail. In wide swaths on both sides the ground was gnawed bare by grazing or burned black over thousands of acres. This time of year the dry grass was like tinder. One cavalry officer Ward met on the plains remembered how a companion lit a cigar, threw the match away, and "in a flash a blaze started—the flame went with the speed of a railway train; went with a hoarse rumble and was one half mile wide by the time it reached the river."[21] In certain areas the plains were white with the bones of slaughtered buffalo, and carrion birds circled overhead; it was the trace of expansionists who were in many respects an army of looters, out to plunder half a continent.

Artemus Ward's crossing of the country was proving itself to be in almost every way an odd experience, and not the least odd of its aspects was the fact that it was proceeding from west to east. On this course, entirely in keeping with his humorist's mind that tended to look at things upside-down or wrongside-to, Ward was seeing America backward as compared to the pioneers he was meeting, people to whom the land of the future, the future itself, was the West. For them the tops of the far-off mountains that shone like promises of distant glory were touched with the light of dawn. For Artemus it was the setting sun that gilded the peaks ahead, and he was gazing into the past along the trail of devastation the wagon trains had left.

At least by the time he had arrived in Salt Lake City, Artemus Ward had conceived of the idea of illustrating his next lecture with a painted panorama of his Western trip, and there would be paintings to suggest the prairie fires and the brooding and ominous sense of desolation. But what interested him most, as usual, was not terrain but people. Somewhere just beyond Julesburg, Colorado, which they reached on March 1, he and Hingston paused to visit a camp of Sioux who happened to be friendly at the moment. One of the customs of the Sioux and the Pawnees made a lingering impression on Ward (it would be pictured twice on his panorama). This was represented by a not-uncommon sight in that country: four poles set in the ground and supporting, high in the air, a platform of stretched thongs on which an Indian body lay, tightly bound in a buffalo hide. It couldn't properly be called a grave since there can be no interment in air, nor could it be referred to even as a burial platform for the same reason—in fact, there was nothing in English to describe it. In his lecture Ward would finally call it a "mid-air tomb",[22] but that was not quite right either. The mid-air tombs would appear, along with the bleached buffalo bones and buzzards, in his panorama with little comment, but they were symbolic enough of an ancient tribal society that was vanishing as Artemus Ward passed, like the handfuls of dust that mourning medicine men threw with their incantations toward the sun.

The Sioux, however, were not prepared in that spring of 1864 to vanish without a fight. As Ward and Hingston passed through Nebraska, raiding parties were watching from the hills overlooking the Platte valley, and the Indian war of 1864 was about to flare up. The coach bearing the two men and their companions went through the troubled area at high speed, making close to a hundred miles a day. There was one brief stop at Cottonwood Springs—a little cluster of buildings consisting of a log store, fortified corral, stage station, blacksmith shop, cavalry barracks, and saloon—accompanied by an episode that remained long in the memory of a 7th Iowa Cavalry lieutenant stationed there. He and his company commander had heard that the famous Artemus Ward was on the stage, so when the coach came pounding in out of a dusty sunset, the two officers were waiting at the station. Artemus promptly invited them to have a drink at the little saloon. The only beverage available in the saloon was Hostetter's Bitters, which was advertised as a cure for rebellious livers but which was also popular for its high alcoholic content. Ward and the cavalrymen had a drink, and then Ward bought out almost the entire stock of Hostetter's. When the driver yelled for him to come back and get aboard, Artemus ran to the coach with eighteen bottles, leaving only one in the saloon. The passengers greeted him with a cheer, the driver cracked his whip, and the coach disappeared eastward into the gathering dusk, leaving Cottonwood Springs virtually a dry community. Considering that he stopped only a few minutes and made off with everything there was to drink in the place, Artemus left a remarkable testimony to the knack of instant friendship he possessed. "We bade him," the lieutenant remarked, "an affectionate adieu."[23]

On the evening of Sunday March 6, they rolled into Atchison, Kansas, their coach and sleigh journey of close to two thousand miles completed. After a day's rest in Atchison, there were side trips to deliver lectures at Lawrence and Leavenworth. Then Hingston and Ward took a steamer up the Missouri and boarded a train at St. Joseph. A newsboy came through the cars selling copies of Tennyson's latest work, *Enoch Arden,* and Hingston, settling thankfully back in his seat, felt for the first time that he was back in civilization. As for Ward, he summed it up with: "An overland journey in winter is a better thing to have done than to do."[24]

As Longfellow once observed, scenery has little or nothing to do with literature. Nevertheless, the West had colored Artemus Ward indelibly. He would return to it frequently in his thoughts. And as a public figure—further tinted, perhaps, by Bret Harte's characterization—he would often be imagined against a background of deep-clefted mountains, sand, sagebrush, and lawless, limitless prairies: "The Wild Humorist of the Plains."[25]

Back in Manhattan, Ward found that much had changed. Pfaff's had disappeared and had been replaced by the House of Lords, on Houston Street, as the gathering place of Bohemians. The House of Lords was described by George Augustus Sala, who was in America as a war correspondent from England, as a "queer, comfortable hostelry very un-American in its aspect . . . a tavern, and therefore beyond the pale of gentility; but I shall ever preserve a kindly remembrance of the place, for there I first met Artemus Ward. . . ."[26] The meeting was right after Artemus had returned from the West, and Sala thought he looked "very sunburnt, but quite fresh." Sala was impressed. "As a rule," he wrote, "one feels inclined to look upon a man who has 'done' the overland stage route between California and the States, with the same amount of curiosity mingled with awe which one might regard a Christian who has made the pilgrimage to Mecca, and come back alive."[27]

That Ward had come back alive was indeed remarkable, but his escape had been not so much from western perils as from those within him. By this time E. P. Hingston had a knowledge of Artemus built up from a close association of several months, and he was to record an almost clinical impression of him. Among its details: Stature—tall, slender. Weight—disproportionate to height. Long, graceful hands, of which Ward took meticulous care. Very white teeth. Thin, fine, soft hair. Large forehead. Eyes that had an "undue brightness." An excitable and sometimes irritable disposition. Alternating spells of jubilation and despondency. A capricious appetite. And with his poetic leanings Hingston had to add that in some of Ward's darkest spells of depression he cast about him a sense that "the abhorred fury with the shears" was waiting to snip a slender, shining thread.[28]

11

Adoo! Adoo!

For the 1865–66 and subsequent seasons, Artemus Ward conceived of the idea of using a panorama to illustrate his lecture. Panoramas—the moving pictures of the day—had been part of the American theatrical scene for many years. One of the first and best had been "Mississippi," the result of a tremendous labor and venture of faith on the part of John Banvard, who had spent months traveling the Mississippi River, making sketches of scenes along its banks, and months more in his studio converting his sketches to giant paintings on ten- to twelve-foot-high rolls of canvas. Completed, the canvas was thousands of feet long, and when unrolled across a stage with an accompanying travelogue, it was, for the audience, the next best thing to a trip down the river itself. Banvard exhibited his panorama with great success everywhere, including twenty months in London's Egyptian Hall in 1848 and a command performance before Queen Victoria. Since Banvard there had been many panoramas picturing far-off places for theater-chair travelers. The eventual loss or destruction of these paintings would be a historical disaster: while they may not have been "art," they did show what a great deal of the country looked like before photography became general and before many features of its life and landscape vanished, otherwise uncaptured forever. But disaster was something that panoramas were prone to. To begin with, they were hideously expensive to prepare, each scene half as big as the side of a barn but requiring a genuine artist instead of a barn-painter. Then a mechanism had to be constructed for displaying the paintings to an audience, a device capable of drawing the canvas across the stage from one upright roller to another. Also a man or men had to be hired to operate the thing. And finally the whole business was costly to transport, and to set up and take down in going from one place to another. For Artemus Ward a panorama represented a large financial gamble, but he saw in it an opportunity to add visual humor to the lecture. Panoramas had been around for a long time and were about due for a burlesque. While in Salt Lake City he had engaged photographers to provide him with views of Mormondom, and he had their pictures with him in New York, ready to reproduce in colors on canvas. Dodworth Hall, at 806 Broadway, was engaged for a fall opening, and three scene-painters were set to work on the panorama in a painting room next to Wallack's Theater.

It was going to be a busy summer for Artemus Ward. He had to write the lecture and the lecture program (always an important part of his show), prepare advertising and promotional material, and write the book on his travels which he had promised Carleton. On June 5 Ward was writing to one of his many correspondents, "'I am popularly supposed to be rusticating here, but it is a ghastly mockery. I am working very hard.'"[1] It was also a time of sober reflection and sadness. Ward's brother, Cyrus, had died on April 22 at the age of thirty-seven and was lying in a new grave in Elm Vale Cemetery, South Waterford. There had been a real affection between the two brothers and a considerable likeness in character. Several of the Pfaffians and other companions had been swept away by early deaths, some of them killed in the Civil War. Ward wrote a eulogy for one which began, "I seem to be standing in a grave-yard, so many of my friends have fallen around me during the past few years."[2] To an extent, his mood reflected that of the entire nation, now in the fourth year of devastating war. From now on Ward's lecture would not make much use of current events; these had ceased offering any root-ground for real humor, and henceforth topical references, excepting those concerning the Mormons (who were isolated from the lives of most people by sheer distance), would be rare, and not remindful of unpleasant events. Ward sensed with his usual sure instinct that his audiences from 1864 onward would simply want him to entertain them, to make them forget for an hour, if he could, that the world around them existed. Thus, his new lecture would eventually take a long step into the airy realm of abstract humor, although at first he visualized the panorama and much of his talk as semi-serious or informational.

Back in New York by the first of September with opening night scheduled for October 17, Ward and Hingston hired a group of Irishmen, dressed them up as Indians, and sent them war-whooping and dancing down Broadway, carrying large white umbrellas on which were stencilled ARTEMUS WARD—HIS INDIANS—DODWORTH HALL.

For his newspaper announcements Artemus devised a take-off on the sort of panorama promotion that had been going on for years. In 1858 one of the more popular panoramas had been advertised as 1800 feet in length, but after that the figures bandied about by competitors had been progressively larger and more vague, with such phrases as "covering 10,000 feet of canvas," "15,000 square feet" and so on.[3] Artemus Ward's panorama was advertised as follows:

ARTEMUS WARD AMONG THE MORMONS
YOUR ATTENTION IS CALLED
TO
A MILE OF PICTURES
FIVE SQUARE YARDS OF JOKES
SIXTEEN CUBIC FEET OF FINE MORAL SENTIMENT
FOUR RODS OF SAD AND BEAUTIFUL PATHOS
ETC. ETC.

In the same flamboyant and whimsical vein the copy also spoke of Stupendous Scenery and Steam-Moved Mechanism, but this was a product of Ward's hyperactive imagination; his panorama was moved by a man turning a crank. In a printed flyer the panorama scenes were described as each being twenty feet long and sixteen feet high, "six feet higher than any panorama ever hitherto unrolled." Since there were eighteen paintings, presumably with some separation, the entire canvas must have made a tremendous bundle, unrolling to more than four hundred feet in length. Readers were also informed that the panorama had cost Ward nearly $10,000 in addition to "months of laborious and perilous travel."[4]

Since the show would be opening in New York, a great many distinguished deadheads would have to be provided for, and Artemus, who neglected nothing that offered an ounce of promotional value, created a complimentary ticket that became a classic. It read simply:

ARTEMUS WARD AMONG THE MORMONS
Admit the Bearer and One Wife[5]

When people entered Dodworth Hall on the evening of October 17, they found the entertainment beginning with the most curious printed program anyone had ever looked at. There was a cast of characters including "Secretary of the Exterior—Mr. E. P. Hingston" and "Secretary of the Treasury—Herr Max Field." The latter was Horace Maxfield, an old schoolmate and friend from Waterford, whom Artemus had brought down from Maine to handle the sale of tickets and other business arrangements. Maxfield was a man of great financial integrity in Ward's eyes; he would later name him as trustee of his estate, even though Maxfield's occupation—he owned and drove the stage in Waterford—had given him no special qualifications. Other members of the "cast" included a Crankist, Assistant Crankist, Reserved Chairist, Moppist, and Broomist. There was also a Doortendist, listed as Mons. Jacques Ridera. This was James F. (Jack) Ryder, Ward's old friend of Cleveland days.[6]

With all this, Artemus suddenly found himself with a full-sized show on his hands. Going around the country as a lecturer had been simple. But now he had what amounted to a complete stage production, with rather massive scenery, music, stagehands and all the rest—a show that had to be carefully scheduled, financed, transported, and arranged for in many details. So, with Hingston planning to return to England, Ward had called in two of the men he trusted most, Horace Maxfield and Jack Ryder, to help him get the show started and on the road. About the only part that would not have to be transported was the piano; Ward's practice would be to borrow a piano or organ from a local music store, giving the store a credit line in the program. But he did engage a regular pianist, a lady who, for a time at least, also functioned as a curlist. Getting Artemus Ward's hair properly curled with the iron he carried along for that purpose was an important step in the preparation of every performance.

The program included notes on each of the panorama scenes depicting Ward's western journey, such as "Town in the Silver region—Good quarters to be found there." And "The Indians on the Overland Route—are an intemperate people. They drink with impunity, or anybody who invites them." Artemus would keep working on the program and would later add such audacious notes as:

"Appearance of Artemus Ward, who will be greeted with applause. The Ushers are particularly requested to attend to this."

"Children in Arms not admitted, if the Arms are loaded."

"Ladies and gentlemen will please report any negligence or disobedience on the part of the Lecturer."

"If the audience do not leave the Hall when this entertainment is over, they will be put out by the police."[7]

Artemus opened the lecture in the usual Wardian manner, owl-eyed and solemn, spinning off atrocious gags, conjuring up ludicrous images, dropping incongruous asides, warming the audience up with an assortment of jokes, some of which he had used before.

If the audience wondered what these preliminary pyrotechnics had to do with the Mormons, they were quickly reassured. "One of the principal features of my entertainment," Artemus explained, "is that it contains so many things that don't have anything to do with it."[8]

When Ward did reach that part of the lecture having to do with his travels in the West—the panorama coming into play at that point—his manner, which had been one of grave and earnest thought through his nonsense routines, did not change. But from here on there was a certain amount of information, along with his verbal pranks.

With respect to the Mormons, who had treated him so kindly during his illness and at his lecture in Salt Lake City, Ward was in a delicate situation. He had left the city of his benefactors well regarded and was apparently still in their good graces. On April 20 the *Deseret News* had declared that Artemus Ward had been a perfect gentleman while in Utah, and it was hoped that there would be no occasion for the Mormons to change their good opinion of him.

Ward's problem was complicated by the fact that being neutral or factual about the Mormons would not be acceptable in the East; something unfavorable had to be said—otherwise he would not be standing up for church and womanhood. Ward partially got around the problem by saying, of polygamy, "I fancy it isn't at all necessary for me to grow virtuously indignant over something we all know is hideously wrong."[9] He was careful to point out that the Mormon people were not the sinful ignoramuses that many writers had said they were; they appeared to be industrious, neat, and humane, and there were no poor among them. Neither was there anything coarse about Brigham Young. He was a man of great mental powers and administrative ability who had, Ward admitted, treated him most kindly. Most of the references in the lecture to the multiplicity of Mormon wives and to Young were lighthearted. A typical remark was, "I saw his mother-in-law while I was there. I can't exactly tell you how many there is of her—but it's a good deal."[10] Generally the lecture was accepted in the spirit Ward intended.

"Artemus Ward Among the Mormons" ran in New York from October 17 through December 23, 1864, and was a critical but not a financial success; Dodworth Hall was far too small to yield adequate receipts. The performance also made Ward aware of another and more basic difficulty. Much of the fun of an Artemus Ward lecture had always come from its playfulness, its incongruities and unexpected turns, and he had hoped to apply some of this humor to the panorama. But the

Artemus Ward after his trip to the West Coast, c. 1864. The heavy watch chain appears to be of gold given him by Nevada miners. Courtesy Library of Congress.

painters had done their job altogether too well. Their carefully rendered scenes tended to be taken seriously, and the whole thing had become too much like a conventional panorama show.

Then there was the bulk and awkwardness of the canvas and its display mechanism, as well as the cost of shipment. Going to Boston, where he opened at the Melodeon on December 26, he made a promotional asset of the packing cases. One large box was marked in big letters "Artemus Ward's Valise," another was labeled "Artemus Ward's Carpet Bag," and so on. The arrival of this equipment in Boston was reported as "the cause of considerable merriment."[11] But during or just prior to the move, Ward made a courageous decision—to junk the panorama on which he said he had expended close to $10,000. What was needed, he believed, was a less "artistic" version—in some places a caricature of a panorama—of a size that he could travel with more easily and inexpensively. This work was done rapidly by scene-painters in Boston, and the new panorama caught up with him in Providence around the middle of January. It was just what the show needed. The scenes were still accurate enough to illustrate what Artemus was talking about, but now and then there were ridiculous errors of proportion, perspective, or rendition, and there were several patently phony devices of transparency and illumination.

Artemus and his audience had great fun with these offbeat portions of the panorama. One of Ward's approaches was to deny all responsibility. He would point out that he hadn't drawn the panorama. The only picture he had ever drawn was one he once drew in a lottery. It showed Gen. Winfield Scott entering the city of Mexico. The only trouble with it was that people couldn't tell which was General Scott and which was the city of Mexico—the sort of weakness his panorama shared.

Or he might begin by praising one of the paintings extravagantly. He wished the audience were nearer to it, so they could see it better. He wished he could take it to their residences to let them see it by daylight. Celebrated artists of the city came every morning before dawn to look at it with lanterns, saying they had never seen anything like it before—and they hoped they never would again. The panorama included absurd special effects. For example, the windows of the Mormon Temple, shown as it would look when completed, were cut out and filled in with colored paper so that when lighted from behind they gave the effect of a tremendous inner illumination. Another scene was supposed to represent the moon shining down on the Great Salt Lake, with a pathway of moonlight stretching across the surface of the water. Part of the fabric here was made to be diaphanous, and when a bull's-eye lantern was held up behind the panorama it showed not only as the moon but as the reflected path of light across the lake. But the lantern always whirled or moved around in such a way that when the illumination appeared, Artemus became visibly dissatisfied. With embarrassment and distress he would leave the rostrum and disappear behind the panorama, whereupon there was an immediate worsening of the situation. The moon danced around, the reflected light shifted here and there, and the Great Salt Lake was thrown into chaos. After a few moments Artemus would return dejectedly and ask the audience if anyone didn't know of a respectable boy of good parentage and education; he would pay such a boy a good salary to serve as a "moonist."[12]

The moon bit became one of the most laughed-at parts of the show. There was a similar business with another scene that had been suggested to Ward by one of the prairie fires he had seen while crossing the plains. A painting (also illuminated from the rear) depicted one of these fires, but the flames kept springing up and dying out in ways that were obviously shocking and displeasing to the lecturer.

During the performance the pianist was usually playing selections that were absurdly inappropriate to the scenes being displayed. In one sequence the pianist had a key role. This had to do with a scene portraying what appeared to be the culmination of a horrible disaster of some sort on the plains. When this segment of the panorama appeared, the apparent effect on Artemus was to excite him terribly. He would begin to give an animated description of the events leading up to the scene, but at the same time the pianist began to hammer out such a thunder of loud, dramatic accompaniment that Ward's voice was completely drowned out. The audience could see the lecturer's lips moving and his arms waving wildly as he pointed here and there at the painting as the events being described (whatever they were) mounted to their awful crescendo, but no one ever gained the slightest notion as to what had happened. The piano stopped just as Artemus reached his breathless conclusion, "—and she fainted on Reginald's breast!"[13]

Ward was also well aware of, and used the comic possibilities of, inanimate objects. The closest he ever came to declaring a theory of humor took place one day when, as related by a friend, Artemus came upon a group of black men grinding their hoes on an old, dilapidated grindstone. The stone had been mounted a bit out of balance, and hard use had worn it from its originally perfect circular shape into an eccentric ellipse, so that as the grindstone turned it wobbled and swayed up and down alarmingly. Seeing it, Ward burst into laughter and said, "'There is wit personified—or thingified.'"[14]

In "thingified" humor he had the same instinct for the intrinsically ridiculous that he had in the use of words. For example, he discovered or at least recognized the principle that using an object for something it is obviously not intended for, or to serve a purpose for which it is ineffectual, can be humorous. In early performances of the Mormon lecture he indicated scenes on the panorama with an umbrella or a fishing pole instead of a regulation pointer. Later he used a droopy riding whip. Another device he adopted was a pair of white gloves; he calculated that a man lecturing with white gloves on would be comical, and it was. He had, one man remembered, "a way of making quotation marks in the air with his left and right forefingers, on occasion, that was irresistibly funny."[15]

Foolishness such as this, and in particular Ward's self-involve-ment—his willingness to make himself as well as his discourse seem ridiculous—had an ameliorative effect upon his comments on the Mormons. Somehow the impression arrived at was that Ward was not laughing at the Mormons but with them, as in reality he had been with them, in sickness and in health.

Artemus kept improving the show, introducing new touches as he went along. The printed program continued to be enjoyed. One of the selections of piano music serving as an overture was listed as "Dear Mother, I've Come Home to Die by request." A note was added saying, "The Mormon's religion is singular, and his wives are plural," and another declaring, "The pretty girls of Utah mostly marry Young."

And Ward inserted a whole new section headed "Answers to Correspondents," which included such exchanges as "I have an unfortu-nate tendency, even on trivial occasions, to shed tears. How can I prevent it?" "Lock up the shed." And another: "How long was Artemus Ward in California?" "Five feet ten-and-a-half."[16]

To the blend of clowning and information that was "Artemus Ward Among the Mormons" audiences responded enthusiastically, as the lecturer knew they would. Artemus had been confident of success even before leaving New York—confident enough so that he'd used some of the revenue for kindnesses to a friend and to himself. On December 15 he had made his performance a benefit for Edward Mullen, an artist and an old friend from *Vanity Fair* days who was having a long illness. On December 20, about a week before he left New York with the show, he'd taken a step toward settling down by buying a house at 44 Pine Street, in

Yonkers, for $5,000. That he ever established a household for any duration there seems doubtful, but he often talked about it, and in his nomadic wanderings the house in Yonkers became a sort of symbol. Someday he could give up the grimy railway rides, the worn hotel rooms, the unpredictable meals, and all the other discomforts of the lecturing grind and sleep in his own bed, eat in his own dining room, and work in his own book-lined study. And he'd give up the role of the literary and lecturing clown. There'd be no more bad spelling and platform posturing; for all his fascination with the stage, he was beginning to long for literary and personal "respectability," and, as would be the case with Mark Twain, to want the best of two worlds.

But before any of these possibilities could be realized, the harlequinade of Artemus Ward the comedian had to pay off financially, and Ward did not do all that he might have done to capitalize on his great popularity. Considering the demand, tickets to his show were relatively low in price. Typically, fifty cents was all that the people of Pittsburgh paid when they thronged to his lecture in the middle of February 1865, and the *New York Clipper* reported: "'Ye God's what a house!' says our correspondent. 'Why hundreds were turned away unable to gain admittance; every seat was sold during the day; in the afternoon it set in to rain and continued all day and evening. Yet that did not seem to dampen the feelings of the people, as the door was literally blocked one hour before they opened.'"[17]

By now Hingston had gone back to England and Ward was associated with a new manager, Thomas Warhurst, who was traveling ahead of him, setting up a schedule that would have taxed the endurance of the most durable lecturer imaginable. Ward was in good health, but for him, good health was something to burn—fuel for flights of living. Nearly every day he was traveling or lecturing—an unremitting, night-after-night grind that had begun in October and would continue through June before there would be any rest. During this period he would appear in sixteen states, usually in a series of one-night stands that meant hurrying to catch trains, gulping meals, getting to bed late at night, and arising early the next morning. This would have been more than enough exertion, but on top of it there was his delight in companionship and conviviality, so that on some nights there would be social activities until dawn.

By now Artemus Ward's lecture had become a fashionable event; it had social status, and it was safely daring as a hallucinatory flight into a wonderful world of nonsense in which the audience surrendered its sanity at the door and was carried off on swoops of airy, subtle foolishness through an evening of gaiety and charm. During his engagement at the Masonic Temple, in Louisville, March 13–18, the *Louisville Daily Journal* commented, "Artemus Ward has been the most successful lecturer in the United States. He has earned and received a very large fortune, and has used large portions of it as a good and generous man always will. Let us all greet Artemus Ward tonight and every night of the week. We may not look upon his like again." And in another issue, "Masonic Hall has been transformed into a palace for the reception of fashion, intellect and beauty. Artemus Ward is the great magnet around which this brilliant array centres."[18]

In reading so many reviews of this nature, Artemus Ward could not have failed to grasp the idea that he had attained a unique place in America's affections—that he was now a sort of national resource. Deep down in the submerged but still unconquered Puritan half of his soul, he did not quite approve of this, for in a mood of curious detachment he once told a man in Cleveland that he felt "a sadness and a sort of . . . humiliation" that foolishness of this sort should be greeted and honored by audiences so much larger than those which went to hear men of more literary, cultural or other merit.[19] But as a showman, he made the most of his popularity. He was now promoting his lectures as "farewell appearances" being made prior to a departure for England, and heading his advertisements "Adoo! Adoo!" At the end of a six-night run which had kept the Masonic Temple packed to capacity, with many people turned away, the Kentuckians called for him to come before the curtain and make a farewell speech. It was gracefully done, in the simple, unassuming manner people liked. " 'Thus I close my season in Louisville. Before I shall again have the pleasure of appearing before you I shall have tried my fortunes in England. I certainly hope to come back to you again, and I shall come gayly, because I shall know I am returning to my friends.' "[20] There was something about the thought of Artemus Ward going away that touched a sentimental note in everyone. At about midnight that night, as Ward was preparing to retire in the Louisville Hotel, there was a sudden burst of music and cheering down below. A crowd and a band had come to serenade him, and he had to go out on the balcony and make another farewell speech.

From Louisville the lecturer continued west to St. Louis, and north to Iowa, and then headed east at a pace that was increasingly demonic, considering that he had to move not only himself but his panorama. His schedules through May and June called for him to lecture fifty-three evenings in forty-three places, every day but Sunday, along a route from

Fort Wayne, Indiana, to Portland, Maine. By the time Ward got back to Waterford early in July, he was ready for a rest.

And besides fatigue, something else was creeping up on Artemus Ward—the realization, somewhat hinted at in his odd Cleveland confession of "sadness and . . . personal humiliation," that he had taken a cheap shot at fame. Seven years later, in 1872, when lyceums were beginning to run into financial trouble, Dr. Josiah Gilbert Holland, one of the old-line speakers of the instructive and "uplifting" sort, would take his editorship of *Scribner's* as a pulpit from which to denounce the "jesters," "triflers," and "mountebanks" who in his opinion had ruined the lyceum system. One of Holland's comments was, "Artemus Ward 'lectured' and he was right royally paid for acting the literary buffoon. He has had many imitators; and the damage that he and they have inflicted upon the instituion of the lyceum is incalculable."[21] Dr. Holland's thesis was that the nonsense vendors drove away from the lyceums the thoughtful and sensible people and attracted only those who wanted entertainment; in the next phase of decline those who wanted entertainment decided that they were better served by the comedy of the theater or the minstrel shows; and in the final phase, everyone had departed, after the brief but deceptive success that the clown-lecturers had stimulated.

It would fall to Mark Twain, by then the leading humorous lecturer, to reply to this accusation Holland had leveled at all comic lecturers, and Twain would fulminate briefly and not too effectively, calling Dr. Holland a "perambulating sack of chloroform"[22] and saying it was dull stuff like his, not comic entertainment, that was tying the crepe on lyceum doors. But Twain could not, at that time at least, seem to make an adequate defense of humor as a worthwhile contribution to thought and culture. Nor was his personal attack on Dr. Holland justified. Although some would later call Holland a bigot and a moralist, he was the sort of moralist of whom a great many Americans approved—a tall, keen-eyed, virile New Englander whose ancestry was of the 1630 Puritan vintage and whose lecturing and writing had commanded the interest and respect of an audience so large that even Mark Twain might have envied it.

The sort of criticism that Dr. Holland put forward in 1872 must have been a matter of concern to Artemus Ward even in 1865, for he could perceive well enough the sort of landslide he had started. When, as a solemn, hesitant young man he had stepped out on the lecture platform in 1861, diffidently saying that his ideas of what a lecture ought to be were very confused because he had never attended one, and then with seeming innocence had led his audience into a series of screaming fits with his owlish burlesque of lyceum lectures, he had become the father of buffoonery, whether he liked it or not. And for one who, underneath, had a serious literary capacity and ambition, it was not an entirely comfortable reputation. In America, this sort of humor was not yet "respectable."

On April 14, 1865, there occurred a tragedy, the assassination of Abraham Lincoln, which must have deeply affected Artemus Ward, who had treated Lincoln affectionately as "Old Abe" in early sketches. If Ward ever made any public reference to this event, the author has been unable to discover it. It is highly unlikely that he would have mentioned it in his lecture; to do so would have dealt the evening's entertainment a death blow, and, besides, Ward had long since ceased to make topical remarks in the lecture. However, in *Artemus Ward, His Travels,* a book written in the spring of 1865 about Ward's Western journey, padded out with a section of "Perlite Literatoor," there is a letter from the Old Showman entitled "Artemus Ward in Richmond." The president had toured the conquered capital of the Confederacy not long before his death. In the Showman's account of his own fictional visit to that city, purportedly a week or so later, one may find echoes of the compassion Lincoln is reported to have felt toward the people of the defeated and devastated South. One passage describes an encounter in a Richmond eating-house between Artemus and a slender young Southerner with long black hair who is ragged, thin, and hungry, but who defies the Old Showman, calling him a "'low-lived Yankee,'" declaring his undying hate, and saying, "'So—Sir—you come here to taunt us in our hour of trouble, do you?'" "'No,'" says Artemus. "'I cum here for hash!'" Artemus then buys a meal for the young man, and here is what follows:

> He et very ravenus. Poor feller! He had lived on odds and ends for several days, eatin' crackers that had bin turned over by revelers in the breadtray at the bar.
>
> He got full at last, and his hart softened a little to'ards me. "After all," he sed, "you have sum peple at the North who air not wholly loathsum beasts?"
>
> "Well, yes," I sed, "we hav' now and then a man among us who isn't a cold-bluded scoundril. Young man," I mildly but gravely sed, "this crooil war is over, and you're lickt! It's rather necessary for sumbody to lick in a good square, lively fite, and in this 'ere case it happens to be the United States of America. You fit splendid, but we was too many for you. Then make the best of it, & let us all give in and put the Republic on a firmer basis nor ever.

"I don't gloat over your misfortins, my young fren'. Fur from it. I'm a old man now, & my hart is softer nor it once was. You see my spectacles is misten'd with suthin' very like tears. I'm thinkin' of the sea of good rich blud that has been split on both sides in this dredful war! I'm thinkin' of our widders and orfuns North, and of your'n in the South. I kin cry for both. B'leeve me, my young fren', I kin place my old hands tenderly on the fair yung hed of the Virginny maid whose lover was laid low in the battle dust by a fed'ral bullet, and say, as fervently and piously as a vener'ble sinner like me kin say anythin', God be good to you, my poor dear, my poor dear."

I riz up to go, & takin' my young Southern fren' kindly by the hand, I sed, "Yung man, adoo! You Southern fellers is probly my brothers, tho' you've occasionally had a cussed queer way of showin' it! It's over now. Let us all jine in and make a country on this continent that shall giv' all Europe the cramp in the stummuck ev'ry time they look at us! Adoo, addoo!"

And as I am through, I'll likewise say adoo to you, jentle reader, merely remarkin' that the Star-Spangled Banner is wavin' round loose agin, and that there don't seem to be anything the matter with the Goddess of Liberty beyond a slight cold.

ARTEMUS WARD.[23]

12

And Again, Adoo

In the summer of 1865, Artemus finished work on the proofs of *Artemus Ward, His Travels.* Carleton published the book in September of that year. Before the month was over John Camden Hotten had brought it out in England under the title of *Artemus Ward (His Travels) Among the Mormons.* One of Hotten's specialties was in spotting an American work he believed would be popular, then issuing it by the tens of thousands in cheap editions sold by railway-station bookstalls for as little as a shilling. Hotten had watched a British interest in American humor building up for several years; seemingly growing was an opinion that while most American literature was only imitative of England's, American humor was different and distinctive. In 1859 Hotten began publishing English editions of Lowell's *The Biglow Papers,* and these were extremely successful. He had then seized upon *Artemus Ward, His Book,* issued it early in 1865, and struck a rich vein of profit. The Old Showman was greeted with excitement and enthusiasm; rival publishers rushed to bring out competing editions of Artemus Ward; and Hotten wrote to a friend in America asking him to send anything more he could find, any scrap, written by Artemus Ward.

On the whole, there were advantages for Ward in the publication of his works by Hotten. Produced in large numbers, the Hotten books would do much to establish a reputation that Ward could later capitalize on in England as a lecturer. And yet Artemus was not making his literary appearance in England under the best of auspices. Hotten was described by a contemporary as a man with a passion for books, an almost clairvoyant ability to judge what would sell and what wouldn't sell, and a prodigious store of energy. He worked nine or ten hours a day in his Piccadilly office and his mind never stopped to rest, according to this associate. "A man of his time, he felt that he must keep pace with the railroad speed of his age, or leave others to outstrip him in the race."[1]

Actually, Hotten not only kept up with the railroad tempo, he managed to forge a hundred years or so ahead into the jet era in issuing, for a selected list of clients, well-printed works of pornography. It was mainly this that blackened his reputation in the world of Victoria. In America there was added cause for disfavor. Hotten was perhaps the most prominent retaliator for the piracy that American publishers had been practicing upon British authors for years in a situation for which America was mostly to blame. There was in England legal machinery whereby it would have been possible to extend copyright protection to American authors—but only if the United Staes would reciprocate, and so far the U. S. Congress had declined to do so. The tide of advantage was flowing westward, and from the larger stores of England's literature the American masses could be provided with "intellectual food" at a much lower cost if reciprocity was avoided. When English publishers began extensive pirating of American works and the anguished cries of American authors began to be heard, it was toward Hotten that many of the howls were directed.

In reply, Hotten asserted that the howlers were charging a crime that did not exist, for rights are the creation of public law, and in the absence of such law there could be no rights and therefore no infringement. It has also been generally forgotten that Hotten was a strong advocate of an Anglo-American copyright agreement. Suppose, he wrote in a book on the subject, that England was divided into seven districts, and an author could obtain protection only in his own district; then few people would go the the labor and pains of writing a book which could be published without compensation everywhere but in the author's own too-small and therefore unprofitable bailiwick. Apply the same principle to the English-speaking world (also divided into districts), Hotten pointed out, and there was still a large discouragement to literary production, and anything that was bad for writers was bad for publishers and, in the end, bad for the reading public.

Undoubtedly, Hotten's publication of *Artemus Ward, His Book* in the winter of 1865 was an out-and-out piracy, with no royalties to Ward. The travel book, since it involved Ward's cooperation—possibly arranged by Hingston, who was then in England and who wrote an

introduction to the book for Hotten—may have been paid for. A couple
of the stories in these two books were of special interest to the British.
Both concerned Albert Edward, Prince of Wales, later to become King
Edward VII. The first told of Ward's visit to the Prince when he was
touring Canada and the United States in 1860. Artemus saw the Prince
sitting on the piazza of a Canadian hotel and tried to approach him, only
to be violently repulsed by a colonel of the Queen's troops.

"Good God!" yelled the Kurnal, "the idee of a exhibiter of wax
figgers goin into the presents of Royalty! The British Lion may
well roar with raje at the thawt!"

However, the Prince spots Artemus and comes to his rescue.

"Never mind," sez Albert Edard, "I'm glad to see you,
Mister Ward, at all events," & he tuk my hand so plesunt like &
larfed so sweet that I fell in love with him to onct. He handid
me a segar & we sot down on the Pizarro & commenst smokin
rite cheerful. "Wall," sez I "Albert Edard, how's the old folks?"
"Her Majesty & the Prince are well," he sed.
"Duz the old man take his Lager beer reglar?" I inquired.
The Prince larfed & intermatid that the old man didn't let
many kegs of the bevridge spile in the sellar in the coarse of a
year. We sot & tawked there sum time abowt matters & things,
& bimeby I axed him how he liked being Prince as fur as h'ed
got.
"To speak plain, Mister Ward," he sed, "I don't much like
it. I'm sick of all this bowin & scrapin & crawlin & hurrain over
a boy like me. I would rather go through the country quietly &
enjoy myself in my own way, with the other boys, & not be
made a Show of to be garped at by everybody. When the *peple*
cheer me I feel pleesed, fur I know they meen it, but if these
one-horse offishuls cood know how I see threw all their moves
& understan exackly what they air after, & knowd how I larft at
'em in private, thayd stop kissin my hands & fawnin over me as
thay now do. But you know Mr. Ward I can't help bein a Prince,
& I must do all I kin to fit myself fur the persishun I must
sumtime ockepy."
"That's troo," sez I; "sickness and the docters will carry
the Queen orf one of these dase, sure's yer born."
The time hevin arove fur me to take my departer I rose up
& sed: "Albert Edard, I must go, but previs to doin so I will

obsarve that you soot me. Yure a good feller Albert Edard, &
tho I'm agin Princes as a gineral thing, I must say I like the cut
of your Gib. When you git to be King try and be as good a man
as yure muther has bin![2]

Another letter, entitled "Artemus Ward to the Prince of Wales,"
followed the Prince's marriage to Princess Alexandra, and gave him
some advice on how to get along with her. For example, she might
object, Artemus said, to getting up and lighting the fire in the morning.
His own experience had been that when he first proposed that idea to
Betsy Ward, on a rather cold morning, she had kicked him out of bed and
he had lighted the fires himself since then.

> I never attempted to reorganize my wife but once. I shall
> never attempt agin. I'd bin to a public dinner, and had allowed
> myself to be betrayed into drinkin several people's healths; and
> wishin to make 'em as robust as possible, I continuerd drinkin'
> their healths until my own became affected. Consekens was, I
> presented myself at Betsy's bedside late at night with con-
> sid'ble licker concealed about my person. I had sumhow got
> perseshun of a hosswhip on my way home, and rememberin'
> sum cranky observations of Mrs. Ward's in the mornin, I snapt
> the whip putty lively, and, in a very loud voice, I said, "Betsy,
> you need reorganizin'! I have cum, Betsy" I continued—
> crackin' the whip over the bed—"I have cum to reorganize you!
> Ha-ave you per-ayed to-night?"
> ... I dream'd that night that sumbody had laid a hosswhip
> over me sev'ril conseckootiv times; and when I woke up I
> found she had. I hain't drank much of anythin' since, and if I
> ever have another reorganizin' job on hand I shall let it out. ...
> There's varis ways of managin' a wife, friend Wales, but
> the best and only safe way is to let her do jist about as she wants
> to. I 'dopted that there plan sum time ago, and it works like a
> charm. Remember me kindly to Mrs. Wales, and good luck to
> you both![3]

The 1865–66 season for Artemus Ward's lecture show opened in
Irving Hall, New York, on August 28 and ran for twelve nights with a
"Standing Room Only" placard at the entrance. On one of these nights
Adah Menken, who had long since parted from Newell, appeared at the
hall escorted by John Augustin Daly. She seems to have had no involve-
ment with Daly other than as a friend, so this might have been the time

for rekindling an old romance with Ward. But some sort of intestinal infection had Artemus in a condition in which he could be neither very attractive or attracted, although he was gamely going on with the show. In his spell of illness Adah went to see him once more, at his rooms, again accompanied by Daly. How much of this visit was ascribable to lingering affection and how much to Adah's desire to learn how Ward was coming along on a farce he was writing for her was a question. At any rate, one outcome was that Ward turned the farce script over to Daly to complete and thereby put it into more than capable hands. John Augustin Daly would go on to become a famous playwright and producer, his theatrical genius magnificently evident from the fact that he was the first to bind the heroine on a railway track in the path of an approaching train or on a sawmill log in imminent peril of being sliced in two by a buzz saw.

After New York, the lecturer took a swing down through Washington, Philadelphia, and Baltimore, and the *New York Clipper* observed with astonishment that he was going over the same ground he had traversed the year before, with much the same show, and his business was better than it had been the first time around. No wonder he had postponed going to England!

In October, Artemus was in Canada, and from time to time there were signs, following upon the illness in New York, that all was not well with him. Under the stress of life on the road, he was living somewhat in the manner of a pulse-jet rocket, experiencing periods of depression and exhaustion from which his remarkable powers of recuperation would rescue him and propel him onward through spells of euphoria and energy. In Toronto, Ward hired a valet to assist him with his clothing, baggage, and other personal chores, most important of which was using the curling iron that was the principal item in his make-up kit. The valet was a boy named George H. Stephens who had been working as a bellboy at the Queens Hotel, in Toronto, and he was about sixteen. Someone asked young Stephens if he could remember Ward's first words to him, and he said they were, "'George, bring me a gin cocktail.'"[4]

The campaign in Canada was a very satisfactory success. In Montreal, people who couldn't get into Mechanic's Hall stood outside in the street just to catch a glimpse of the famous Artemus Ward. In Toronto, the Music Hall was packed, with a hundred or so standing. Ward proceeded through Hamilton and along the northern shore of Lake Erie, made a two-night stand in Detroit, and then went on through Ohio and western Pennsylvania. Then he started down the Ohio River, hitting the high spots along the old circuit before heading into the deep south. The fact that many people had heard the Mormon lecture before made not the slightest difference. Dr. Robert Morris remembered going to one of these repeat performances. An old friend of Ward's, he had been given a special pass of admission. Morris recalled that although it was a cold, stormy, winter night, the hall was crowded and the audience was completely under the spell of Artemus Ward. Most of those present, he was sure, had seen the panorama and heard the lecture before, but they were enjoying it no less the second time around. In fact, the performance seems to have become a sort of ritual that no one wanted changed, "I think I have heard that 'Panoramic Commentary' five times," Morris said, "and I could not detect any variation in word, syllable, letter or gesture during the repetition."

Apparently there was, however, one new prop on the night Morris described. Although the lecture was being delivered word for word exactly as everyone expected and wanted it to be, and although all must have realized that Ward knew it by heart, having performed it more than two hundred times, he was now pretending to read it out of a huge book. As Morris remembered it, "I never saw anything so ridiculous as that scene. Artemus stood on a little platform or dais three feet square. His enormous nose loomed up in grandest proportions. Before him, on a trestle, was a folio volume professedly containing his address, at which he gazed with an earnestness so absorbed that you would verily suppose he had never read it before. But the fact is, there was not a word of print or writing in the book. The leaves were blank. Once, in turning over a leaf, he made an absurd break in a sentence, stammered, looked confused, turned back, apologized with a half bow for the blunder, and resumed the subject."

In entering the hall, Morris had paused for a moment to watch from behind the audience. Ward spotted him and made a quick gesture, pointing over his left shoulder. Morris knew what this meant. Artemus was nearing the "moon bit," which called for him to go behind the panorama, and he wanted Morris to join him backstage.

Presently the night scene of Great Salt Lake came on, and after a brief description of the scene and the standard joke ("They say a Mormon farmer drove forty head of cattle in there once, and they came out first-rate pickled beef"), the moon, which was rising over the water, began to veer and yaw eccentrically, and Artemus, with great annoyance and embarrassment, solicited the indulgence of the audience while he went behind the scenes to regulate the errant satellite. He then disappeared with the routine result—a worsened performance of the moon and heightened screams of laughter from the audience.

Making his way around the wings, Morris found Ward seated at a little table ready to entertain him with a bottle of whiskey, while working the moon with one hand by means of a string attached to it. They had a drink, and Artemus began a long, detailed account of something that had happened to him the night before. This lasted, Morris remembered, at least ten minutes, and meanwhile Ward kept the laughter going by knocking with a hammer on the machinery of the panorama now and then and jerking the disobedient moon with his string. Then, "being thus rested and refreshed he returned to the dais and finished the lecture to the boundless satisfaction of his hearers."[5]

On December 18 Ward returned, unembarrassed, to Louisville, where there had been a touching "farewell" as recently as March—and he packed the Kentuckians in again for two nights. The campaign continued through Nashville to Memphis and down the Mississippi in what the *Clipper* reported as a "blaze of glory."[6] At Memphis he was joined by Melville D. Landon, a former Union officer Ward knew, and Landon invited Ward to take a much-needed rest at his plantation in northern Louisiana, where he was raising cotton. The two men embarked on a river steamboat out of Memphis. As a national celebrity, Ward was constantly being pestered by complete strangers, and people knew he was on the steamboat because they had seen the eccentrically marked containers for his panorama being carried aboard, labeled "A. Ward's Valise," "A. Ward's Sunday Clothes," etc. However, Artemus managed to shield himself for a while by creating an immense confusion. He went around pointing out Landon as the famous lecturer, meanwhile explaining to Landon, when he wondered why he was the object of so much attention, that people were mistaking him for Nathan Bedford Forrest, the great Confederate general.

Going on to New Orleans, after lectures at Vicksburg and Natchez, Ward gave a benefit—or at least a semi-benefit—for the family of Jefferson Davis. The ex-president of the Confederacy and his family had been captured by Union troops in May 1865, and had been the focus for a time of all the vengeful anger of the North. Confined to Fortress Monroe, weak and emaciated from illness, Davis had nevertheless been placed in manacles and otherwise abused. Mrs. Davis and their four children had been separately detained for a time in Savannah. Much of Mrs. Davis's money had been taken from her, as well as her provisions and most of her children's clothing. Now, in January 1866, Mrs. Davis and the children were back among friends in the South, but Jefferson was still in prision at Fortress Monroe, and the family was without funds or a breadwinner. On the evening of January 13, Ward gave what was announced as a benefit lecture for the Davis family and presented $250, half of the proceeds, to the Ladies Southern Aid Association for that purpose. But if Ward's heart was correctly tuned, for once he made an error in the manner of his charity. He should have slipped someone a few banknotes for the Davises in the way he had handled a similar situation in Sacramento when his donation was labeled as "subscribed by a religious Indian." With some justification, the *Daily True Delta* criticized Ward for having given only half and not the entire proceeds of the lecture; it had, after all, been advertised as a benefit, and there was some implication that Ward had "used" the plight of the Davises as a come-on. This of course was not true. By now Ward did not need any extra inducement to fill his lecture halls anywhere. Shortly afterward a Boston newspaper chastized Ward for being down South "toadying to the rebels." This hurt Artemus, and he wrote an aggrieved letter to the newspaper, saying, "I acted purely in a spirit of charity and without the remotest idea that the affair could possibly assume political appearances. I certainly did not suppose it would induce any newspaper in the North to doubt my loyalty."[7]

Ward's managing to get into the bad graces of both the Northern and (to some small extent) the Southern press was enough to make him feel, as he had once had Artemus Ward say of Jefferson Davis himself, that "It would have bin ten dollars in his pocket if he'd never bin born."[8]

In New Orleans there was another rather edgy episode related by a man who said he had been the managing editor of a New Orleans newspaper when Artemus Ward came to town. The staff, he said, hadn't been able to attend the lecture, and so, in order that the newspaper people could meet Ward before he departed, the proprietor of the paper prevailed upon Artemus to visit the city room on his last night in New Orleans, right after the Jefferson Davis benefit. Everyone was having a fine time when a one-armed ex-Confederate colonel who, it had been noticed, had only bowed stiffly to Ward instead of shaking hands with him, said, "'Mr. Browne, I should like to ask you a question,'" and there was something about the way he said this that caused the atmosphere to become very formal.

Ward's air of gaiety was instantly replaced by one of seriousness as he replied, "'I will answer you, Colonel, if I can; if I cannot, I shall regret my inability.'"

"'I have not attended your lectures, Mr. Browne'" the Colonel said, "'because to be frank with you, whenever I look at my empty sleeve I do not feel as friendly as might be toward the people from your part of the country. You can readily understand that.'"

Ward nodded and the ex-officer continued: "'And to be still franker with you, I did not like a Northern man to be coming down here so soon after the war, and carrying off what little loose change we have. That is why, when you were introduced to me just now, I did not offer you my hand. But I remembered, the next moment, that you had this evening given proceeds of your lecture to the Confederate soldiers' widows and orphans. I wish to thank you for that and to ask you to take my hand.'"

Ward's face lit up, he grasped the colonel's hand, and there the matter might have ended. But the proprietor of the paper, not willing to let well enough alone, had to ask, "'What is the question, Colonel, that you wished to ask friend Browne?'"

"'Well, simply this. Pray, Mr. Browne, did you fight against us during the war?'"

The air began to get slightly chilly again. Artemus Ward straightened up and folded his arms, and his face was composed and sober but his eyes twinkled as he answered, "'Since I came South, Colonel, I have frequently been asked that question. Permit me to answer it in my own fashion. I did my duty faithfully, Colonel, by sending a a substitute to the war. I have never met him since. Doubtless, he will yet return to his family's bosom, to draw a pension in my place. I was therefore excused from further active service.'"[9] Ward closed his statement with a pleasantry to the effect that he had often publicly proclaimed that if Lee stayed away from him and his mother and their old homestead in Maine, he would promise to stay away from Lee, and the general must have heard of this, because he had never come near the place. At this there was laughter, and Ward made his departure leaving all in good humor.

This is the only discovered explanation of why Ward did not serve in the Union armed forces. With his aversion to firearms and his physical frailty, he may have realized that he would have been of little military use. There would have been, at any rate, no legal obligation for him to serve until the national draft act was passed in the spring of 1863. After that he had three choices: serve, pay a sum of money as "commutation," or send a substitute. Aside from going himself, sending a substitute was the more constructive course; the government was getting all the commutation money it wanted as a result of this faulty draft act but not enough good soldiers. And if the substitute practice would later seem to be morally questionable, it could be justified by the fact that the hired man would soon have to go anyway, and he might as well go with several hundred extra dollars in the family treasury. The draft act also provided exemption for anyone who was the sole support of a widowed mother, and after the death of Cyrus in early 1864, Artemus would have qualified for this exemption. But whatever the reason for Ward's non-service, no public blame ever seems to have been attached to him.

From New Orleans Artemus proceeded across Mississippi, Alabama, Georgia, and South Carolina, lecturing in Mobile, Montgomery, Columbus, Macon, Augusta, Savannah, and Charleston. This tour through the deep South was something of a phenomenon. He was a Northerner who, as an editor on *Vanity Fair,* had been a conspicuous foe of the Rebellion, once the issue of the 1860 election had been decided. Yet he was greeted warmly and with enthusiasm. Writing to a Southern correspondent later, Artemus said, "The sun usually shines brightly on my head. It never shone more brightly than it did in your generous land, and I never grasped hands that I would be more glad to get hold of again than I did there."[10] Inescapably, he must have often thought of the contrast between this tour and one he had created for his fictional Artemus Ward in 1861 in which the Southerners had shouted, "Hang the bald-headed aberlitionist, and bust up his immoral exhibition!"[11] and had then seized the Old Showman and tied him to a stump, while boys threw stones and beer bottles at him and other rebels smashed his wax works "to attums" and let his animals loose. The contrast must have been particularly thought-provoking in Montgomery, where in fancy his *alter ego* had been placed in "durans vial." Of his lecture in that city the Montgomery *Daily Mail* reported, "So great was the anxiety to see the 'showman' that a large crowd collected near the building before the doors were opened. And what a glorious time everybody had with Artemus. We don't think we ever saw an audience so tickled and pleased."[12] Ward wrote to Horace Maxfield that his expenses were terrible but he was doing well. On his last night in Montgomery he took in $970.

It was the same everywhere: people standing in line and jamming the halls for an evening of that hard-to-come-by commodity, laughter and forgetfulness. The review of the Columbus *Daily Enquirer,* appearing beneath one story about a proposed monument for the Columbus war dead and another about the inflated prices of corn and wheat, said: "Our people turned out as they were wont to do, in days of yore, and as they have not done since before the war closed. Old Temperance Hall was full, and . . . Artemus was frequently interrupted by the unrestrainable laughter of the audience. We think he drew out some *old laughs* that have been subjugated by morose brows, and rusting in unshaken sides, since last April. We trust all of us will feel better for the shaking he gave us."[13]

Many people of the South remembered a letter that their own Georgia humorist, Bill Arp (pseudonym of Charles Henry Smith), had addressed to "Mr. Artemus Ward, Showman" in 1865. It went in part: "we made a bully fite . . . and the whole American nation ought to feel proud of it. It shows what Americans can do when they think they are imposed upon. . . . We had good men, great men, Christian men who thought we was right, and many of 'em have gone to the undiscovered country. . . . When I die I am mighty willing to risk myself under the shadow of their wings, whether the climate be hot or cold."[14]

In reporting on the enthusiastic reception of Ward's lecture in the South, the *Daily Constitutionalist* of Augusta said that Artemus Ward and Bill Arp could do more toward reconstructing the Union and harmonizing its people than all the reconstruction bureaus and committees appointed or ever to be appointed by Congress. There was more to this opinion than extravagant kindness. Certainly, in the mid-1860s there were few men compared with Ward who had attained a better grasp of what America looked like, felt, and thought, simply because of his travels. Within the span of a relatively few years he had known the forests of Maine, walked up Beacon Hill and down Broadway, worked beside the shores of Lake Erie, toured the gold fields, seen terrain as disparate as the Sierras and savannas, crossed the Rockies and the grassy, wind-waved plains, and traveled by ship up and down the coasts and along the Ohio and Mississippi. With the exception of the Southwest he had, in fact, been practically everywhere—by steamboat, train, canal boat, and stagecoach, and on foot. He'd been in big towns and little ones, heard big talk and small talk. He'd known the greats like Mark Twain and Whitman; the near-greats like Stoddard and Stedman; the might-have-beens like George Arnold and Fitz-James O'Brien; and thousands of never-heard-ofs—farmers, lumbermen, miners, boarding-house landladies, bartenders, cavalrymen, boatmen, railway conductors, show people, gamblers, storekeepers, Yankees, Indians, Negroes, Swedes, Germans, Irishmen, all kinds of people, all going by the name *"American."*

Meanwhile, something had happened to Charlie Brown / Charles Farrar Browne / Artemus Ward. Even in the ordinary course of events it is impossible for a celebrity to avoid becoming something of a charlatan; always he must produce the expected mannerisms, the expected words, the expected image, until finally the image threatens to mould the man and the celebrity begins to resemble a waxen effigy of himself. In the case of Artemus, with his different names, his different characters, and his rather fantastic platform personality, the removal from reality was particularly extreme.

But there was always one way he could bring himself back to earth:

he could visit a printshop, and perhaps that is why he did this so often. Once in among the type cases and the aproned compositors who greeted him (as one of them) so cordially, once smelling the ink and touching the familiar tools of the trade, he could feel that he was again a real person: Charles F. Brown, printer—a man who knew a good, honest craft and who, when the honest and worthwhile day's work was done, could go out and have a beer with his fellows.

After Ward delivered his final lecture in Augusta, on January 27, the next day's *Constitutionalist* bade him an affectionate farewell, implying that about the only fault to be found with Artemus was that he drank gin cocktails (he had evidently abandoned bourbon for some current version of the martini). It also reported, with a tantalizing lack of detail, what seems to have been a common incident with a rather uncommon outcome: Ward's dropping into the newspaper's printing shop and giving the printers a little talk which "brought tears to the eyes of all, and amid much weeping, and wishes of God-speed, Mr. Ward took his departure."[15]

The report touched only lightly on the subject of Ward's talk: something about his going away to England, something about his hope that the people of the North and South would be reunited. We are therefore left with only an outline of the situation.

Yet sketchy as it may appear to us, this was an extraordinary scene. Here was Ward speaking informally to a group of printers, not the most impressionable class of men generally and likely to be less so as far as a Northerner was concerned. Yet they had responded to Artemus with a tearful display of fraternal emotion. This indicated that along with Ward's skillful press-agentry, and along with his undoubted yearning for personal popularity, something more genuine was also at work; and part of this may well have been his sense of the "mystic chords of memory" still binding together a nation that few men had seen as he had seen it.

Ward's Southern tour concluded with an engagement on February 13 and 14 at Richmond, Virginia. This, as previously related, had been the scene of one of the Old Showman's fictional visits, ("I cum here a few days arter the city catterpillertulated"),[16] when his "hart" had softened with respect to the South and he had mourned for the vast devastation of death the war had left. Now the real author of the letter could see for himself physical evidence of the war's destruction: the roofless walls of gutted factories and mills fired by the departing garrison, ghostly ruins standing mournfully against the sky as symbols of the economic disaster the South had suffered.

As Artemus headed up the East Coast, completing the border-to-border and coast-to-coast peregrinations, he had this memory with him, and he could add to it his awareness of other great changes the war had made in speeding the industrialization of the North. Artemus had never been impressed much by the leadership in the vanguard of this progress, if progress it could be called. He had once remarked upon "'the particular gigantic evil of the age, Money Getting.'"[17] He once had the Old Showman say, "I have allers sustained a good moral character. I was never a Railroad director in my life."[18] And it was no accident that sometimes, in shifting heads among his waxwork bodies, the Showman would place the head of a pirate on a figure intended to represent one of the current captains of industry. Of Western bankers he had once had the Showman say he would like to own as good a house as some of them would break into.

Traveling north in the winter of 1865–66, Ward wandered through New York and Boston like a ghost, picking up the threads of old associations. One he visited in Boston was Benjamin Penhallow Shillaber, whom he described as "getting a little frosty about the head, but his heart is as young and warm as ever."[19] Friendship was important to Artemus Ward, and it was something he was always attentive to, with a letter or a note now and then, a call here and there, a few words from time to time serving to freshen or renew valued ties. But old friends were disappearing. Many had been killed in the war, many had died. Moreover, his kind of people was becoming a rarity. Men were driving, pushing, grasping for money as their lives became more and more dependent on moneyed activities. The Bohemian group which Ward had known at Pfaff's had dissolved. His brother, Cyrus, was gone. The gentle people were passing out of style. Even Waterford would not be what it had been in past summers; the fun-loving Dan Setchell had also disappeared. In the fall of the previous year, 1865, while on a West Coast tour, Setchell had boarded a steamboat called the *Yosemite*, and it had exploded on the river near Sacramento. As though to confirm his premonition that he was going to die of apoplexy, Setchell had escaped without injury. Then, early in January 1866, he had embarked on the sailing-ship *Trieste*, bound for New Zealand, and that vessel was never heard of again.

As Ward walked past Tremont Temple, in Boston, scene of his first big-city triumph with "The Children in the Wood," he was apparently in a weary daze when his hand was grasped by that of a young man whose face was alight with enthusiastic recognition. Strangers were always stopping him on the street, and almost automatically Artemus gave the fellow his usual hearty but impersonal "How do you do? How are you?"

and so on. Suddenly the face snapped into focus. It was William Dean Howells. "Then," Howells remembered, "he seized my hand and wrung it all over again, and repeated his friendly demands with an intonation that was now, 'Why, *how* are you,—how *are* you?' for me alone."[20]

Howells had just come to Boston to take a new job as assistant editor of the *Atlantic.* Compared with the older New England writers of the class which was so much admired by Howells, Artemus Ward was something of a freak; he was, but he wasn't, a New Englander. Howells considered him a westernized Yankee. But Howells liked Ward, and if affairs had turned out differently he might have become as valuable a counselor to him as he was a few years later, to another freakish friend, Mark Twain, for he considered Artemus a much better writer than anyone might suspect in examining the scrambled syntax and odd spelling in the letters of the Old Showman. As for Ward, he admired Howells and he also admired the *Atlantic,* judging by some words he once put into the mouth of the Showman: "I like it because it has got sense. It don't print stories with piruts and honist young men into 'em, makin' the piruts splendid fellers and honist young men dis'agree'ble idiots—so that our darters very nat'rally prefer the piruts to the honist young idiots; but it gives us good square American literatoor."[21] This was not a bad appraisal. The magazine had an inclination toward realism which Howells, of course, would enhance; and in contrast to certain New York periodicals that borrowed extensively from England, it was devoted largely to American authors. It may have been on a plane somewhat above the writing that made Artemus Ward famous, but the essence of Americanism that pervaded his work was in tune with the *Atlantic;* further, there were a couple of indications, about this time, that Artemus was becoming dissatisfied with his literary typecasting as an author of hick writing and that he intended to shift into a higher gear. A note to an editor, written soon afterward from Waterford, offered a series of letters to be written on a planned tour of Europe, "to be humorous, of course, but to be distinguished by no bad spelling. I have done so much in that way that I really feel I shall overdo it."[22]

And another letter, to the editor of the Boston *Saturday Evening Gazette,* gave evidence of considerable anguish at being associated with a book of pseudo-Wardisms that had just appeared. This was *Betsey Jane Ward (Better Half to Artemus) Hur Book of Goaks,* written by some obscure author who was not identified in it. Like most imitations of Artemus Ward's style, it was simply a mangling of the English lanuage without sublety or wit. Ward sent the editor a protesting paragraph and with it this appeal: "Can you find room for something like the enclosed in your next *Gazette?* This Betsey Jane book is a hideous fraud, and is fast driving me to the brink of madness. Editors notice it and gloomily say that it is 'unworthy' of me. I should think so!"[23]

Concerning their chance meeting in Boston, Howells further remembered that Ward looked terrible: his mouth was drawn; his profile, which "burlesqued an eagle's,"[24] was now that of a drooping eagle; and he was so thin that his tall, spare figure seemed to tremble in Howell's field of vision and waver away into the distance as they parted. A few days later he received a letter from Waterford that began: "My Dear Howells,—The extremely cordial manner in which I did not remember who you were, the other day, has preyed upon my mind somewhat, I hope it did not strike you, even for a moment, that, because I didn't recognize your form and face, I was unfamiliar with the many fine things you had done, in a literary way, since we parted in Ohio." The letter then went on in a gracious and congratulatory vein, referring to their newspaper days in Ohio and to Howell's subsequent accomplishments. It concluded, "In a stupid, quiet way, I am resting here in the little village where I was born, for a few weeks. I was really worn out, and the quiet and country fare are doing me good."[25]

Of all the scenes in Ward's life, this meeting with Howells is one of the most poignant. It marked the possible beginnings of an association with Howells, then rising toward the editorship of the *Atlantic,* that might have turned Ward's maturing talent into one capable of making a more substantial contribution to American literature. But all this was now virtually in the past for Artemus Ward. America's burlesque eagle was about to leave its shores.

13

"A. Ward Has Hit 'Em Hard"

The rest in Waterford improved Ward's health and spirits. On April 10 he wrote lightheartedly to a friend in Portland, saying he would soon be sailing for England, and that he had intended sailing from that port. However, he added, "I am told your steamers leave punctually but seldom reach the other side. This will deter me from patronizing them. I would not die in Spring time, unless it was strictly necessary."[1]

His precautions were, nevertheless, sensible. One day his old friend Horace Maxfield was with Ward in his room in the Waterford house, and he recalled that Artemus was busy counting his money, sorting his papers, and otherwise putting his affairs in order so that, as he explained to Maxfield, his mother would be all right if anything happened to him. Ward had a pile of notes on the table, according to Maxfield, that must have amounted to $8,000 or $10,000 in cash.

Having made his preparations and said his farewells, he journeyed to New York and left there June 2, 1866, on *The City of Boston* bound for Liverpool. He and George Stephens reached London on June 15.

Hingston, who met Ward at Euston Square Terminus, was shocked at his appearance. On the way to the station he'd been talking with a friend and describing the American humorist as a genial, lively, hilarious person, but, as he later wrote, "When Artemus and I shook hands on the platform, I was grieved to see that I had been describing some one whom I had known a year previously, and that the description did not tally with the worn, wasted, and more grave than merry man who stepped out of the railway carriage."[2]

Artemus Ward had always longed to visit London. Now that he was in the city of his dreams, he was eager to go everywhere, see everything. After only a few hours rest he had Hingston taking him around on a sight-seeing tour. Between sights, they talked over plans for the lecture. Hingston advised him to go slow; there were no good lecture halls available just then, and besides, Artemus was obviously in need of rest. Hingston suggested a few weeks at the seashore, then a period of getting acquainted, and a careful build-up toward a fall opening. Soon afterward, he persuaded Ward to move from London to Broadstairs, on the coast of Kent, where, it was hoped, the invigorating air would soon have him back in shape.

It was a sound idea with respect to Artemus Ward's body but a poor one considering his temperament and frame of mind. He couldn't stand the quiet and inactivity of the seashore, and he was soon back in London, exploring its attractions and carrying letters of introduction to editors, critics, reporters, theatrical people, and others whose backing, he knew from experience in America, would be important to the success of his venture. He knew also that in many quarters he had a generally unfavorable impression of Americans to overcome. Even since the end of the Revolution, British travel writers had been returning from tours of the United States to write derogatory accounts of their cousins across the ocean. Americans were often portrayed as uncouth, tobacco-chewing, arrogant, materialistic, boastful bores; as intolerably dull; and as hypocrites—they were not the free individuals they bragged of being but lived in constant dread of "public opinion." The matching word for American was vulgar. As the Old Showman once said of an Englishman, "He had fallen into a few triflin errers in regard to America—he was under the impression, for instance, that we et hay."[3]

The Civil War had not helped much. On one occasion, when Capt. Charles Wilkes of the U. S. S. *San Jacinto* had stopped the British ship *Trent* and seized two of its passengers, Mason and Slidell, Confederate commissioners to Great Britain and France, war had almost erupted between the United States and Britain. The London *Times* had characterized Wilkes as the typical American: swaggering, vulgar, seemingly ferocious but cowardly. It was true that Artemus Ward was arriving in England at a time when its attitude toward the United States was improving somewhat. The strength of democracy as demonstrated by the preservation of the Union had led England to regard America with new respect and a more serious interest in its culture. The great human anguish of the war and the martyrdom of Lincoln had awakened a new sympathy. But there was still a large and strong residuum of disapproval which was not to be quickly swept away after a build-up through so many decades.

Further, there was the question as to whether a humorist of what was understood to be the rather rough cut of Artemus Ward as exemplified by his published work would be accepted in London. Much of his writing had reflected the more unusual aspects of America: the California mining camps, the Mormons, the Rocky Mountains, the great plains where the Indians roamed, and so on. The total impression of Ward must have been that he was colorful, different, interesting—one of the odd new Western humorists. But—and here was the catch—when Charles Farrar Browne stood forth on the platform as Artemus Ward there would be nothing about him to live up to the billing. No rough mannerism or garish dress. No peculiar accent. Nothing particularly "Western." He would only be himself. Of course, he had initially been up against a somewhat similar situation when he first started lecturing in America. But when faced with a person so different from the bizarre character which had stirred their interest and curiosity, would the British be satisfied with the pale substitute?

Artemus believed that whatever the outcome, his best chance lay in getting to know the people who could help him publicize and promote his show. Fortunately, one of the first homes in which he was entertained was that of Charles Millward, at 9 Malden Crescent, Prince of Wales Road.

Millward was neither famous nor rich; in fact, he seems to have been a man of modest or middle means. His nominal business was that of a "monumental mason," a commercial euphemism for being in the gravestone business. But this seems to have been merely a rather solid but unobtrusive foundation for his other activities. Millward's bent was toward literature and the arts. Before coming to London he had helped found the *Porcupine,* a bright little journal published in Liverpool, and had continued to contribute a "London letter" to it, as well as articles to other publications. He was also active in private theatricals, and wrote plays and pantomimes for both the amateur and professional stages.

However, Millward's true gift seems to have been friendship. Literature and the arts, at the level on which Millward worked at them (if he had been more successful, the story of his friendships might have been less fortunate), were peopled by strugglers of the most desperate sort, and the presence among them of one who had any money at all was rare. With whatever means he had, Millward seems to have befriended so many impecunious and unknown young writers, actors, and artists that some of them were bound to become well-known, and in rising they cherished their associations with him and carried him along into higher circles of acquaintance.

Millward family photographs show Charles wearing a stovepipe hat; this, in combination with a heavy beard which extends downward about as far as the hat extends upward, gives the initial appearance of a long face, but the first impression of solemnity is quickly corrected by humorous eyebrows and clear, cheerful eyes. Through another photograph the otherwise confirmed personality of his wife, Mary Ann, glows unmistakably; she was a plump little woman of that sort of plainness which is so irradiated from within by decency and kindliness that it becomes something akin to beauty. A more genuine beauty—she would turn out to be a stunner—was one of the children, Jessie Millward, who was destined to grace the stages of England and America as a popular actress until the time of World War I.

With Jessie, Artemus immediately formed one of those friendships with little girls that had always been so characteristic of him. His visits to 9 Malden Crescent left her with a vivid memory that was to survive and keep its place among the impressions of more than half a century of theatrical life, finally to be recorded in her reminiscences, published in 1923. In the same book Jessie described an incident, equally unforgettable, that had happened in the Millward home not long before the arrival of Ward and that serves to introduce a man with whom Artemus became closely and warmly associated, possibly after meeting him at the Millwards'. As Jessie remembered the incident, one day a gentle, nervous fellow with brown eyes and a reddish beard called at the home about noon. Charles Millward was out, but Mary Ann asked the visitor to stay and share the children's lunch, which was very substantial and included a huge rice pudding. After sitting at the table a while, motionless and in silence, the man broke into tears, and when Mrs. Millward wanted to know what the trouble was, he sobbed, "'My children are starving.'"[4]

The Millward children Jessie recalled, had very little to eat for the rest of the day, for their mother ransacked the larder and sent most of the food to the home of their visitor, Thomas William Robertson, then struggling for existence as a playwright. Shortly afterward, the dramatist's first wife died, and Jessie always thought that malnutrition had something to do with it. Then, ironically enough, an overwhelming success had burst upon Robertson, and this was his situation when Artemus Ward first met him, when he was about thirty-seven. Only the year before, in 1865, his hit play *Society* had made Robertson popular and well-to-do while revolutionizing the English stage with its breakaway from stylized classical patterns in favor of a new realism in the writing and production of plays.

In some ways the red-bearded playwright was like Artemus Ward personally. He was high-strung, restless, prone to poor health, and affectionate in his personal relationships. Yet it seems to have been not so much this similarity that attracted Robertson to Ward but his predilection for "the real thing" so evident in his stagecraft. He remembered the surprise of his first meeting with Ward, who was, Robertson said, the least like a showman of any man he had ever encountered. "No man could see him without liking him at once. His manner was straightforward and genial, and had in it the dignity of a gentleman, tempered, as it were, by the fun of the humorist. When you heard his talk you wanted to make much of him, not because he was 'Artemus Ward', but because he was himself."[5]

Ward's initial impact on his new acquaintances lay in the fact that he was not only the antithesis of all the bad things Englishmen had thought about Americans, but antithetical in a spectacular degree in terms of grooming, speech, modesty, a positive otherworldliness as far as money went, independence, originality, lightheartedness, gaiety, and charm. His effect on most people he met in England, as on Robertson, was a quick process of fascination and endearment. In London he was in a condition of euphoria comparable to the one that had seized him in Virginia City when, as noted by Joe Goodman, he was "as if strung on wires, virbrating to every impulse of its tumultuous life," even though the vibrations in London were not those emanating from pistol shots in a barroom. The excitement here was generated by literature, the stage, the arts, club life, the culture and customs of the mother-country–storybook-land Artemus had dreamed about for years. For this experience he had worked himself up to a high flame which, in his much less than robust state of health, gave him a somewhat incorporeal aspect. One writer who met him recorded his thinness, his "singularly brilliant eyes," his "pearly white teeth" and his long, shapely hands with blue veins showing through the white skin and nails "of a shape usually associated with a delicate constitution." Yet this slightly diaphanous creature was full of energy. One English friend wrote that "he had the vivacity of a schoolboy, and he considered no jest too extravagant or absurd . . . one wonders still at a frivolity so intense."[6] When this chap was around, things brightened up a bit; what a pleasure it was to see him come into a room! And it was the expression of this happiness—manifested by social companions or an audience—that had come to be almost an addictive drug to Artemus Ward. It was as though he had brought them something intensely delightful that they very much desired, something that also returned to him a lift of the spirits, a heightening of all his faculties and perceptions. It was by far the best thing in life, this glow of affection, this lighting up of faces that at one moment might seem weary or wistful or wanting something they did not have, and in the next instant be transfigured as if by a sudden passage back to childhood.

A writer for one of the English periodicals recalled, "'I do not think our literary, dramatic or artistic world ever took to a stranger with more hearty cordiality than they did to Browne.'"[7] In London, Ward's gift for friendship bloomed into a phenomenal flowering of new associations and activities. One of the most important of these was the London equivalent of Bohemia, the Savage Club, where, owing to the good offices of Millward and Robertson, Artemus became a member on August 4, 1866. Like the Pfaffians of New York, the Savages had begun their meetings in a tavern, but unlike the Pfaffians they had gone on to establish a cohesive organization then meeting in Ashley's Hotel, on Henrietta Street, Covent Garden. There seems to have been confusion as to where the name "Savage" had come from; some members thought the club had been named for Richard Savage, the somewhat disreputable eighteenth-century poet, and others held that the name was meant to be taken literally. This latter view was supported by the motif of the club room, whose walls were decorated with tomahawks, boomerangs, assegais, and other weapons of aboriginal warfare. Further, according to one account, the Savages "sedulously practiced a shrill shriek or war-whoop which was given in unison at stated intervals." The qualifications for joining this literary Lion's Club were simple; they were "to be a working man in literature or art, and a good fellow."[8] In the group were several staff members of or contributors to *Punch*, and this led to Ward's meeting at a dinner party Mark Lemon, who was the editor and one of the founders of the magazine. It was Lemon more than anyone else who had given *Punch* its consistent and recognizable character. In this process (taking Mark Lemon's view of it), he suffered untold agonies in bringing together and keeping productive a staff of writers and artists who may have been witty and brilliant but who had no common sense whatever and couldn't be depended on. After the dinner party where they met, Lemon asked Ward to become a contributor to *Punch*, an invitation that was accepted with delight, Artemus writing to a friend at home. "'This is the proudest moment of my life.'"[9] Lemon found him no more reliable than the English contributors whose dilatoriness he bore as a permanent cross. "'You want discipline!'" he barked at Ward one day.[10] But eight letters, later collected with other sketches in *Artemus Ward In London*, appeared in *Punch*.

The second of these gently satirized certain British impressions of Americans.

> You'll be glad to learn that I've made a good impression onto the mind of the lan'lord of the Greenlion tavern. He made a speech about me last night. Risin' in the bar he spoke as follers, there bein over 20 individooals present: "This North American has been a inmate of my 'ouse over two weeks, yit he hasn't made no attempt to scalp any member of my fam'ly. He hasn't broke no cups or sassers, or furnitur of any kind. *(Hear, hear.)* I find I can trust him with lited candles. He eats his wittles with a knive and a fork. Peple of this kind should be encurridged. I purpose 'is 'elth!" *(Loud'plaws.)*[11]

Others dealt with standard tourist attractions. One gave a showman's appraisal of Shakespeare's tomb—"It is a success"—and went on, in part,

> William Shakspeare was born in Stratford in 1564. All the commentaters, Shaksperian scholars, etsetry, are agreed on this, which is about the only thing they are agreed on in regard to him, except that his mantle hasn't fallen onto any poet or dramatist hard enough to hurt said poet or dramatist *much*. And there is no doubt if these commentaters and persons continner investigatin Shakspeare's career, we shall not, in doo time, know anything about it at all.[12]

At the Tower of London, Artemus observed that the Traitor's Gate is "wide enuff to admit about twenty traters abrest," which moved him to a bit of philosophy.

> Traters, I will here remark, are a onfortnit class of peple. If they wasn't, they wouldn't be traters. They conspire to bust up a country—they fail, and they're traters. They bust her, and they become statesmen and heroes.[13]

One of Ward's new-found friends in London was W. S. Gilbert, who was just starting to write and illustrate articles for the weekly papers. Many of his contributions were rejected by the editors, but when this happened Gilbert simply redirected his contributions to the proprietors of the papers, evidently supposing that the man who owned the enterprise had to be more intelligent than the people who only worked for it. In a surprising number of cases this tactic had worked, and the front office had instructed editors to publish Gilbert's work. This, of course, had made him enormously unpopular with editors all over London, and he was, significantly, not a member of the Savage Club, to which writers and editors for both *Punch* and its rival, *Fun,* belonged. In order to provide himself with a club of his own, Gilbert had assembled a small group of dramatists, critics, journalists, and other writers who met weekly in his quarters in South Square, Gray's Inn, calling itself "the Serious Family." Artemus Ward was taken into this group, probably introduced by Tom Robertson, who was a member of it and who, with characteristic kindness, had also taken Gilbert under his wing to teach him some of the principles of stagecraft—useful knowledge when he became the Gilbert of Gilbert and Sullivan ten years later. Other members of the *Fun* circle who became Ward's friends included Clement Scott, the drama critic; Tom Hood, the editor of *Fun* and son of the elder humorist of the same name; and Arthur Sketchley, the comic writer and monologist. Ward joined some of the *Fun* writers that year in contributing to *Wärne's Christmas Annual,* a handsome publication of ninety-six pages, with the result that his story "Pyrotechny" appears in this annual side-by-side with three contributions by W. S. Gilbert. The story is about a young New England rustic who decided he could made fireworks "just as good as them in Boston." At the local Fourth of July celebration at which his handiwork was set off, however, the rockets went sideways instead of up, "causing the masses to jump around in a very insane manner." The writing is not in the Old Showman's manner but in Browne's own, and it had a subtle charm that the British found attractive, as illustrated when one of the inept pyrotechnist's more successful qualities was commented on.

> He was an extraordinarily skilful young man in the use of a common clasp-knife.
> With that simple weapon he could make, from soft wood, horses, dogs, cats, &c. He carved excellent soldiers also.
> I remember his masterpiece.
> It was "Napoleon crossing the Alps."
> Looking at it critically, I should say it was rather short of Alps.
> An Alp or two more would have improved it: but, as a whole, it was a wonderful piece of work; and what a wonderful piece of work is a wooden man, when his legs and arms are all right.[14]

Other associations that Artemus Ward formed in England were less important but no less interesting. There was a cordial acquaintance with Charles Reade, then on the crest of his fame as a novelist, who saddled him with the phrase "Artemus the delicious" in much the same way that Shaw attached "the incomparable Max" to Beerbohm years later.[15] And there was Swinburne, who may not have been close to Artemus socially but who appeared among the invited guests for the first night of Ward's lecture. The hand that wrote Ward's introductory letter to Reade was probably that of Adah Menken, who on a previous trip to London had added the novelist to her list of conquests. The link with Swinburne may have been Hotten. Artemus had arrived in London just in time to witness a violent outburst of Victorian morality—the storm of censure that descended on Swinburne's head with the issuance of his *Poems and Ballads,* in which the little poet was publicly attacked as a sort of literary rapist, one anonymous letter writer even going so far as to threaten to cut off his testicles and a reputable reviewer calling him "'the libidinous laureate of a pack of satyrs.'"[16] When Swinburne's affrighted publisher withdrew his work from sale, Hotten stepped forward to take it on and keep it in print.

Artemus worked hard through the summer and early fall of 1866 in laying the groundwork for acceptance of his show, getting acquainted with the people who might help make it a success. Charles Leland had once oberved that Ward had found out everything about New York in three weeks after his arrival; he was all over London with comparable speed, and the same old pattern repeated itself: friendships, invitations, parties, dinners, Londoners fascinated by this quaint young gentleman from America. There was a great deal of drinking to be done and a great deal of impromptu entertainment to be provided; both of these activities were welcomed by Artemus, but their effects began to be noticed. Mary Ann Millward kept telling Ward that he'd better learn to say no. One night just after midnight the Millwards heard a knock on their door, and it was Artemus in evening dress, sober. He wanted Mrs. Millward to know that he'd been at the Savage Club all evening and had said no. The Millwards invited him in, and the three of them talked until dawn. Even sober, Ward was under the spell of an intense, continuing excitement.

The great Joseph Jefferson also gave Ward a talking-to. Jefferson was in London to open with his immortal "Rip Van Winkle" on September 5, and Ward had gone to him with a letter of introduction from a famous Boston actor, William Warren. Jefferson hadn't seen "Artemus Ward Among the Mormons," but from all he had heard of it he felt quite confident that it would be a successful show. What Artemus ought to worry about, Joe Jefferson told him after looking him over, was his health. Once his show started, he ought to give his friends Sunday evenings only and on no account expose himself to "the pernicious effects of the London fog." Watch out, Jefferson emphasized, or your friends will kill you. It was one of his pet peeves, which he expressed in a little tirade to an imaginary group of hearers: "See how unfair you gentlemen are who fancy you are friends of the actor. You sit quietly among the audience during the whole evening, enjoying an actor's performance and resting yourself at the expense of his labor. When this is over you are thoroughly recuperated and he is weary; yet you ask him now, when he needs the rest that he has given you, to sit up till daylight—for what? To amuse you again."[17] It was significant that

An ailing Artemus Ward in London, fall, 1866. Of the photo he wrote a lady friend "I send you my *carte de visite*. It represents me in a studious attitude, and for those who admire my style of beauty it is doubtless just that style of beauty which people who admire my style of beauty admire." Author's collection.

Jefferson talked to Ward not as to a lecturer but a fellow *actor*. Whether he had expected this or ever really wanted it, Artemus was one no longer of the "men and women" but of the "people on the stage."

For his performance Artemus engaged one of the chambers of Egyptian Hall. Located on the south side of Piccadilly, opposite a point about midway between the Burlington Arcade and the entrance of Old Bond Street, Egyptian Hall was one of the oddest structures in London. It had been built in 1812 in partial imitation of an Egyptian temple, and besides serving as a museum from time to time, it had housed a number of very odd entertainments including Tom Thumb, the Siamese Twins, an exhibition of Laplanders and Reindeer, Prof. Faber's Euphonium or speaking automaton, a group of African bushmen, panoramas, and many other curiosities. Londoners expected something equally odd from Artemus Ward. The lecture, they supposed, would be funny, but something crude, eccentric, and "American."

Fortunately, the way had been made easy by Artemus Ward's diligent and astute preparation. On opening night, November 13, he had the house well papered with free passes and full of distinguished people—members of the press and celebrities who included many literary figures. A boyhood friend of Ward's then living in London, Albion Chadbourn, came with a group of people whom he had organized to bulk up the audience and add to the applause. But Chadbourn and his claque found the hall so crowded that they could hardly get in.

Artemus had mounted his show expertly and at some cost. The panorama appeared within a giant gilt frame, being covered by a crimson curtain when not displayed. The "crankist" who worked the panorama, the "moonist" who handled lighting effects, and the pianist were concealed behind curtains, but there was a little opening behind the rostrum through which Artemus could disappear at selected points to give these people instructions. (A lack of coordination among them was one of the charms of the show—the haphazardness, of course, carefully planned and rehearsed.)

Once in their seats, members of the audience began to read the outrageous program. This was the old Dodworth Hall program after many months of refinement and improvement. It began with a note saying that Artemus Ward would call on the citizens of London at their residences and explain any jokes that they did not understand; that a person of integrity would take care of their bonnets and cloaks during the entertainment, but the audience had better leave its money with Mr. Ward—he would return it to them in a day or two, or invest it for them in America, as they thought best; that "nobody must say that he likes the

Lecture unless he wishes to be thought eccentric, and nobody must say that he doesn't like it unless he really *is* eccentric"; and that Mr. Ward would not be responsible for any debts of his own contracting.

There were also notes describing the scenes for the panorama, such as the one pertaining to Virginia City: "There are instances on record of young men going to this place without a shilling—poor and friendless—yet by energy, intelligence, and a careful disregard to business they have been enabled to leave there, owing hundreds of pounds."

The program concluded with a burlesque puff, an imagined excerpt from a review in a Yorkshire paper: "It was a grand scene, Mr. Artemus Ward standing on the platform, talking; many of the audience sleeping tranquilly in their seats; others leaving the room and not returning; others crying like a child at some of his jokes—all, all formed a most impressive scene, and showed the powers of this remarkable orator. And when he announced that he should never lecture in that town again, the applause was absolutely deafening."[18]

At eight o'clock the footlights were turned up, and Artemus Ward faced his first London audience. As always, his appearance was a shock to those who had read his works but had never seen him; many people were entirely unprepared for this slim, scholarly-looking young man in evening dress whose intent, utterly solemn face—had it not been for a suspicious brightness of the eye—seemed to predict an impassioned discourse on the salvation of souls.

J. E. Preston Muddock, who was present in Egyptian Hall on this evening, indicated that Ward used his delayed-fuse opening, that he "came down to the footlights and stood silent, casting his deep-set, brilliant eyes over the vast audience, and twiddling his thumbs in the most unconcerned way," and then, after the audience had grown restive and loudly audible, told it that he would continue when the inconsiderate and unseemly interruption subsided, whereupon the people "almost raised the roof with their applause, and it was fully five minutes before he could proceed."[19]

With the curtain still closed on the panorama, Artemus launched into a prologue consisting of his time-tested jokes adapted, when necessary, for his London audience (as, "I don't want to live in vain—I'd rather live in Margate"). They all worked: the cartload of turnips joke; the "Oh my Maria!" bit; the one about the toothless man who could, in spite of that, play the bass drum superbly; and the celebrated living skeleton tale—a ridiculous story about a living skeleton Ward said he had once taken on a tour to Australia, only to have the long sea voyage stimulate the skeleton's appetite and consequent voracious eating so much that he was ruined as an exhibit by the time they got to Melbourne, so they turned back and sailed to San Francisco, where Ward recouped by showing his charge as a celebrated fat man. And there were solemnly perpetrated atrocities such as, "She played the accordion divinely—accordionly I praised her."[20]

The Londoners laughed immoderately, and it was, of course, not so much the material they laughed at as the performance—the owl-eyed gravity, the abstraction, the intellectual pratfalls, the way in which Ward reacted to their laughter with sad indignation, his seeming to be laboring under a depressing sense of failure, his effort to conciliate the audience, inspire pity, claim indulgence. Ward was so sad, so serious, so earnest that people somehow felt they really shouldn't be laughing, but as he kept unmercifully piling one ridiculous image on top of another, mirth bubbled up until it could no longer be suppressed. The *Spectator* described his "bust" routine—Ward's discussion of his refusal to allow the services of a sculptor: "... when he mentions that he would not allow a bust of himself to be taken because he could not bear the idea of people carrying him about everywhere, making him common, and hugging him in plaster of Paris, and his audience (rather prematurely) laugh, he assumes the laugh to be skeptical, and says with a sharp, half snappish air of innocent, argumentative irritation, 'Yes, they *would,*'—and then those who saw nothing humorous before are fully carried away now, and join in the universal chorus."[21]

When the curtain opened on the panorama, the lecture became more informative, but the solemn foolishness relieved it at intervals, often based on the studied crudity of the paintings. At one point, gloomily indicating a few brown splotches with his riding whip (the pointer he used in London), Artemus announced, "Those animals are horses. I know they are, because my artist says so. I had the picture two years before I discovered the fact. The artist came to me about six months ago and said, 'It is useless to disguise it from you any longer—they are horses.'"[22] He also went through the business of the malfunctioning moon and the misbehaving prairie fire. As in the performances in America, the pianist played music that always had some absurd relationship to the scene being displayed, and Artemus was delighted with the way the English pianist took to this assignment. Back in America he had always had to argue and struggle with "artists" whose sense of propriety was invariably outraged when they were called upon to play such inappropriate music. This was symbolic of the way in which the English were falling in with the spirit of the lecture, or it with *their* spirit—more likely the latter. In fact, one episode in the performance would have even been called Gilbert-and -Sullivanish if there had been, at the time, any Gilbert and Sullivan. This had to do with a fictitious and lugubrious incident of Ward's visit to Salt Lake City. It was presumably related with much sad rolling of the eyes heavenward, passionate sighing, and wringing of hands. "It was leap year when I was there—and seventeen young widows—the wives of a deceased Mormon—offered me their hands and hearts. I called on them one day and taking their soft white hands in mine, which made eighteen hands altogether, I found them in tears. And I said, 'Why is this thus? What is the reason for this thusness?' They hove a sigh—seventeen sighs of different size. They said 'Oh—soon thou wilt be gonest away! . . . Doth not like us?' I said, 'I doth—I doth! I also said, 'I hope your intentions are honorable, as I am a lone child, my parents being far, far away.' Then they said, 'Wilt not marry us?' I said, 'Oh no—no. . . .' Again they asked me to marry them, and again I declined. When they cried, 'Oh—cruel man! This is too much—oh! too much!' I told them that it was on account of the muchness that I declined."[23]

By the time the curtain closed, to the sound of applause and cheering, on Artemus Ward's first London performance, Albion Chadbourn wondered why he had ever bothered to organize and bring a claque. "I found I need not have done so," he wrote to Ward's cousin in Waterford, "for never has anyone come over here and met with such reception."[24] Artemus had struck a chord with the English that would go on vibrating enthusiastically. Ward waited to see how the next couple of audiences would behave and what the papers would have to say; then he wrote a friend in America a letter that, though triumphant, lacked his usual playfulness and had undertones of weariness. "It is a very large success. I had a reception that was absolutely tremendous, and everything went off like fireworks. The papers, without an exception, and even the heavy Saturday papers, are enthusiastically complimentary." He continued almost automatically with a bit of his habitual press-agentry. "I send a few notices. Can't one or two be smuggled into the *Tribune?*"[25]

Lloyd's Weekly London Newspaper, in its review on November 18, said, "A great many people, who knowing nothing of the entertainment, were able to give impartial opinion, had said that it 'wouldn't do.' They were wrong. It did do, and will do very well in all probability for some time to come."[26]

Speaking of Ward's initial appearance on the platform, one critic wrote, "Between the rough showman of his book and the refined-looking, intellectual master of wit, without a touch of personal vulgarity, the chasm seemed immense, and yet on his appearance it was instantly bridged."[27]

The reviewer for the *Observer* confessed to a certain bewilderment as to just what had happened. "There is a curious directness and simplicity in the lecturer's manner of saying even some common place remark, accepted truism, or well-known fact that produces a laugh—one does not know why or how. . . . Everybody must certainly ask himself when the lecture is over why he has been so greatly amused, and will probably find himself unable to answer the question."[28]

The man for the *Spectator* was more successful in coming to grips with the elusive quality of Ward's performance. He pointed to the surrealistic, intellectual quality of the humor as seeming to come from some native, unpretending innocence of the slender performer himself. "All his best points are made by producing this impression,—that his mind is floating inevitably along a natural current of ideas where his audience sees the most absurd combinations. . . . A general effect of having to grope for his language before he can explain himself, always hovers about his manner. . . . He seems like a man who, having taken a good run, cannot stop himself at the right point, but must run beyond it. . . . The humour of all this is the humour of helplessness, the humour of letting your thoughts drift idly with the most absurd association that crosses them, and never rescuing yourself by any insurrection of common sense."[29]

The *News* said the whole thing was a terrific surprise. "Those who go to the Egyptian Hall with the impression that they are about to hear a two hours' narrative crammed full of those exaggerated stories which the popular weekly journals have been serving for many years as samples of American humour, will be agreeably disappointed."[30]

Punch used its appreciation of Ward as a stick with which to lambaste the 1866 equivalent of the lower-grade nightclub comedians and other contemporary funnymen who were allowed "to outrage good taste, good sense, and good breeding, and to minister, unreproved, to coarseness, imbecility and vulgarity. . . . Unlike them, Artemus Ward has brains."[31]

The American journalist Henry Watterson, later to be known as "Marse Henry," was in London at the time. He had met Ward in Cincinnati in the spring of 1865 when, just out of a Confederate colonel's uniform he had come north looking for a newspaper job and Artemus had introduced him to editors, helping him to overcome an initial hostility to ex-rebels. The two had become fast friends, sharing literary interests and also an affinity for what Artemus once described as "that superior star-spangled Bourbon Whiskey—the only beverage the American eagle ever permits himself to indulge in." Watterson was impressed by Ward's performance. He remembered that seats for the show were being purchased for seven or eight days in advance and that "up and down Piccadilly . . . carriages bearing the first arms in the kingdom were parked night after night. . . The success was complete. As to an American, London had never seen the like."[32]

Nearly seventy years afterward one Londoner could still vividly recall going to the lecture as a boy with a party of his schoolmates one afternoon in the Christmas holidays. He remembered Egyptian Hall being mobbed by ticket seekers, with the excitement heightened by what was apparently a repetition of the stunt that Ward and Hingston had staged on Broadway in 1864: men dressed as Indians, flourishing daggers, horse pistols, and bows and arrows as they war-danced along Piccadilly distributing leaflets advertising the show. He remembered a large poster, several feet square, blank except for the "Artemus Ward Will Speak a Piece" announcement in very small block letters in one bottom corner, and that always there was a crowd in front of this poster looking at it. He described Artemus Ward's famous "silent opening," when he approached to the front of the rostrum and stood there, owl-like, saying nothing. "He looked fixedly at the sea of faces before him and, for no apparent reason, the whole house burst into a roar. . . . Even now I can call up a vision of the slim lecturer with curls and a ferocious moustache, and a big nose, and pale woebegone cheeks."[33]

On their way home, going westward along Piccadilly toward Hyde Park, the boys passed the shop of John Camden Hotten, where boxes of Artemus Ward's published works were stacked upon the pavement and attendants were selling them as fast as they could give people change for their money.

Even the *New York Clipper,* which had long been Ward's admirer and booster, confessed that it had openly predicted that Artemus would not make the grade with the English, but "We find we have erred, and A. Ward has hit 'em hard."[34]

14

An Unfading Recollection

With Artemus Ward's smashing success in London came lioniza-
tion by the social and literary community and a flood of invitations. This
was the danger Joe Jefferson had warned him against, but with Ward's
liking for the English and his love of London life, he found all too many
of the invitations impossible to resist. George Stephens remembered
that time and time again Artemus would be out until two o'clock or so in
the morning and would come home "all fagged out." Soon the effects
were so obviously deleterious as to warrant a suspicion of willful self-
destruction. Stephens begged him to take care of himself, later recalling
"'he would just turn us off with a joke and keep on as before. He was just
killing himself and we knew it.'"[1] The same idea occurred to Henry
Watterson. Ward's tour de force in London, he thought, was turning into
a kind of suicide.

As winter approached, the fog on some nights drifted up from the
Thames, across St. James's and Green parks, along Piccadilly, and even
into Egyptian Hall, and Artemus discovered that Joe Jefferson hadn't
been fooling about London fog, either. He seemed to be having respira-
tory trouble, and the fog bothered him. The lecture was a taxing exercise.
Delivered every weekday evening from 8:00 to 9:30 and at 3:00 on
Saturday afternoons, it was a seemingly quiet, casual, almost unconscious
performance, but nevertheless it called for careful voice effects, great
mental effort, and instant alertness to audience reactions. Sometimes the
densely packed hall was uncomfortably hot and close. Sweating under the

gas lights, Artemus would mop his brow and say, "I wish when the Egyptians built this hall they had given it a little more ventilation."[2]

One night before the show Tom Robertson saw Ward sink into a chair and almost faint from the simple exertion of dressing, but he insisted on being up and on the platform at eight o'clock. Ward's guise of solemnity during the lecture aided in the concealment of his illness, and his increasing gauntness only served to accentuate the incongruous qualities that added so much to the humor of the performance. He began using make-up to hide his pallor and contrived some business which allowed him to sit down and continue talking from a chair when weakness overcame him on the platform. As far as the people in the audience knew, the young man who stepped so lightly out in front of the footlights and kept them laughing for an hour and a half was in perfect health; he was simply thin and a little shaky by nature.

As the year wore on and the weather worsened, Ward began to suffer more and more from depression. This was partly due to his declining health and partly, it seems, to a growing dissatisfaction with his role in life—a feeling, which had been creeping up on him for a year or so, that he should have achieved something more distinguished as a literary man. Now, by the very fact of his stunning flash of fame in the capital of the English-speaking world, his image had been fixed as upon a photographic plate, and the permanent portrait was likely to be that of a clown. Ironically, Ward never came to see what his English contemporaries would make plain in pages of commentary and analysis later on— that he had done much to elevate the intellectual status of humor.

Much of Ward's frame of mind was revealed in conversations he had with the Henry Wattersons shortly before Christmas. Ward was living in quarters over an apothecary shop across the street from Egyptian Hall, on Piccadilly. Watterson and his wife had lodgings on Jermyn Street, practically around the corner. According to Watterson, Artemus had received numerous invitations from distinguished people including "nobility and gentry" to spend the weekend before Christmas with them, but his health was now such that he had to decline. Early on the evening of Friday, December 21, Ward had dinner with the Wattersons, who were leaving London next morning. Over the holidays, he told them, he intended only to rest. He realized that he had overworked and that he'd have to be careful or he'd have a breakdown. But he had been through these spells before; by spring he'd almost surely be all right. He was making $300 a night on the show and intended to remain in London until the audience began to fall off—then he'd go over to the Continent. By the time he got back to the United States, he would have set enough aside from his earnings to make himself independent; then he'd give up this "mountebank business," this "damnable iteration" of the lecture, and do some real writing.[3]

In recalling the conversation, Watterson wrote, "He had a great respect for scholarly culture and personal respectability and thought if he could get time and health he might do something in the 'high comedy line.'" Among the projects discussed with the Southern journalist were a humorous novel, a series of essays of a more ambitious nature than any he had attempted before, and the possible origination of a new American magazine. Watterson's impression was that "his mind was beginning to soar above the showman and merrymaker."[4] In common with many other people, he was beginning to recognize that Artemus Ward was much more than a laugh-maker, that underneath his humor was *intelligence* in the deepest sense of the word—an ability to see things exactly as they are—and that this ability, whether manifested in seriousness or humor, could be of some value to a society now grown attentive to his thoughts and observations.

The dinner in London was remembered sadly by the American couple. Particularly painful to the future "Marse Henry" was that Ward was drinking only water. He didn't eat much, either, and seemed to be having trouble breathing and walking. It was no accident that Arthur Sketchley dropped in after dinner and that Artemus Ward left hanging onto Sketchley's arm, on his way to his nightly appearance at Egyptian Hall.

On Tuesday, New Year's Day 1867, a heavy storm broke over London, filling the streets with snow. The thermometer dropped to three degrees on Friday, and the bad weather—snow, rain, and wind, with temperatures often in the twenties—continued for the next three weeks. The *Spectator* noted that bronchial diseases were increasing. Braving this weather, Ward was still struggling back and forth between his quarters over the apothecary shop and Egyptian Hall, but on three nights he broke down and the audience had to be released and its money refunded. While in his rooms he was often so weak that George Stephens had to lift him from place to place in his arms. At Egyptian Hall, a doctor stood behind the panorama, ready with stimulants to keep the lecturer going, if need be.

Winter's final thrust at Artemus Ward had a particular cruelty, faced as he was with his short but difficult walk each evening. An hour before the show on Tuesday, January 22, a light rain began to fall and freeze, covering the streets with a sheet of ice, so that even well-shod horses could hardly move and pedestrians were tumbling, rolling, and crawling. Artemus somehow made it to the hall and delivered his lecture that night, but on the following evening, when he was part of the way through his performance, he found himself unable to continue and retired behind the scenes. Hingston went out front and explained that Artemus Ward was ill; the audience quietly dispersed. The stricken man was carried back to his quarters, and in taking care of him George Stephens remembered that he got scarcely a wink of sleep for three days and nights. On Thursday his doctor issued a statement saying that Ward was too ill to continue and that he was being urged to suspend his lectures for a few weeks so that he could recover his health and resume them.

What Artemus Ward apparently had was pulmonary tuberculosis, of which almost nothing was known at the time. What he needed immediately was good nourishment and complete rest in bed. What he got was a prescription for some irrelevant medicines, "sea air," and a sea voyage which took him to the island of Jersey. It was a bad move in almost every possible way. The trip was tiring. The climate offered no tremendous improvement, Jersey being only a hundred and fifty miles or so south of London and exposed to mid-winter Atlantic gales. And what was worst of all about Jersey was that Artemus Ward was removed from all familiar human companionship except that of young George Stephens. His loneliness and the remorseless roaring of the wind oppressed him. On February 5 he wrote Hingston from St. Helier to say that now the excitement of the lecture campaign was over, he seemed to be having a reaction; he was extremely weak and "gone" and probably couldn't begin lecturing for another month. In the meantime, he thought he'd be better off in London.

He and Stephens started for England shortly afterward, but when they reached Southampton, Ward could go no farther. The boy got him to Radley's Hotel, a rather elegant establishment on Terminus Terrace, close to the docks. Doctors were summoned. Hingston arrived from London. Charles Millward, Tom Robertson, Arthur Sketchley, and other members of the Savage Club began coming down from London on a regular schedule of visits. The company of friends revived Artemus somewhat, and there were occasional flashes of the old Wardian humor. One day Robertson poured out some medicine in a glass and offered it to the invalid. Ward said, "'My dear Tom, I can't take that dreadful stuff.'" Urging him to swallow the unpleasant dose, Robertson coaxed, "'Come, come . . . do it for my sake; you know I would do anything for you.'" Artemus feebly reached out his hand to grasp that of his friend. "'Would you?'" Robertson replied, "'I would indeed.'" And Ward said, "'Then you take it.'"[5]

Artemus told Hingston that he ought to have some of the raw dogmeat that they had once seen the Sioux eating to renew their inner strength and spirits. During his illness he had often thought about the trip they had made across the mountains and plains. Someday he wanted to go back in summertime—he and a good friend or two, with a team and a rig of their own, just taking it easy, loafing along. "We will do that ride yet, Artemus," one of the Savages said. "Short stages at first, and longer ones as we go along." Ward held up his hands to the light of the winter sun, hanging low over the Southampton water, and then against the glow of the coal fire in his room. His hands had become so translucent and attenuated that the light shone through them. Ward tried to make a joke. "'Do you think these would do to hold a rein with? Why, the horses would laugh at them.'"[6]

Late in February he decided to make his will. John Neat Pocock, a young Southampton lawyer, came to the room, and the will was completed on February 24. Charles Millward was present that day, and he was sure Ward's mind was still clear, but he saw signs of approaching unconsciousness. Millward, caught in a life-and death-situation, so to speak—his wife was expecting a baby—hurried back to London, but next day he was writing anxiously, instructing Hingston to telegraph if he was needed; he'd be down on the next train. The letter contained messages of affection from the Millwards to be given to Artemus if he was still able to hear them. It was a sunny, spring-like day in London, Millward wrote, but he was dreading its passage, lest evening bring bad news from Southampton. If the worst did happen, Hingston was asked to cut off a small lock of Ward's hair for Caroline and also one for him and his wife. They planned to name their child Charles Artemus, if it proved to be a boy. (It would be a girl.)

Ward was unconscious for about ten days. During this period he was like one of his remembered Sioux on the platform of a "mid-air tomb," high above the medicine men and their incantations, beyond the reach of everyone, blowing away in the wind. He died at four o'clock on the afternoon of Ash Wednesday, March 6, 1867, at the age of thirty-three.

Late on the following evening, at the home of Charles Millward, in London, little Jessie Millward heard a noise downstairs. She got out of bed, left the nursery, peeped over the banister, and saw a coffin being carried through the hall and into the drawing room below. The Millwards were performing an Arimathaean act of hospitality, taking into their home Ward's body, which Hingston had brought to London on the evening train from Southampton. Next morning Jessie and her father went out and bought a large bunch of violets. Millward lifted the little girl up level with the top of the closed coffin and told her to place the flowers on it. Jessie hesitated, looked at her father, and asked, "Where is Mr. Ward's heart?"[7] She then carefully laid the bouquet on the spot Millward indicated.

That day they read in the *Times,* to which the death of a comedian was not ordinarily an event worthy of much notice, an obituary of nearly two hundred and fifty words, concluding with "The respect in which Mr. Browne was held, and the anxiety entertained as to his ultimate recovery, has been manifested by the constant inquiries at the hotel by all classes of the community, and the intelligence of his early death will be received with sorrow by thousands of people in England and America."[8]

On March 9 a funeral service, arranged by the Savage Club, was held at Kensal Green Cemetery, where Ward's body was temporarily interred in a vault. The service was singular, the *Illustrated London News* said, "for the large crowd of English writers and artists who ... had been called together by a well-known literary club, and came willingly, if sorrowfully, to prove their friendship and respect."[9] The route to Kensal Green was long, and the weather was terrible, with temperatures near freezing, snow flurries, and occasional rattlings of hail. The cortege left the Millward house on Malden Crescent at 1:30: a hearse drawn by four black horses; behind it four carriages bearing close friends and the pallbearers; next the carriages of the American Legation in London, containing a delegation headed by the first secretary, Benjamin Moran; and following these, fifteen or so broughams and other vehicles. At the entrance of the cemetery some sixty members of the Savage Club fell into line, and one observer noted that in all about two thousand people thronged into the cemetery, many more than the chapel could accommodate. At the end of the Church of England service, there was a poignant touch produced by mechanical engineering: at the words "earth to earth, ashes to ashes" the coffin began to sink from view; a contrivance was lowering it through the floor of the chapel to the level of the vaults underneath. Artemus had once spoken of humor "thingified"; this was just the opposite, grief thingified; a physical departure that symbolized the passing from the world of a beloved presence who was never to be seen again.

Late in May 1867, Hingston had Ward's coffin removed from the vault and placed aboard the steamer *Deutschland* at Southampton, accompanied by George Stephens, for whose education at North

Bridgton College, in Maine, Ward had made provisions in his will. The ship arrived in New York on May 31, and Ward's old friends Horace Maxfield and Livingston Robinson (now his trustees) were waiting on the dock. They took the boy and the coffin to Waterford, and on June 6 there was a brief service at the old homestead, followed by burial in Elm Vale Cemetery. The children of the village gathered wildflowers from the woods and placed them on the grave. Sometime later a stonecutter carved these two lines at the bottom of Ward's marble headstone:

His memory will live as a sweet
and unfading recollection

The English kept the memory of Artemus Ward green for a remarkably long time. Astonishingly, Radley's, the fashionable hotel in Southampton, attached to the door of his old room a plaque that said "Artemus Ward died in this room," and kept it there for decades in spite of the discouraging effect it must have had on guests assigned those accommodations. Around the turn of the century Radley's ceased to exist as a hotel and eventually became the Royal Mail House. In 1930 the Master Mariner's Club moved into a section of the second floor that includes Ward's old quarters. "I can remember the plaque on the door when the club took over," the secretary once said. He recalled that it stayed there until the middle thirties, when it was judged to be inappropriate and was discarded. "'A bit gloomy for a club, don't you know.'"[10]

On the centenary of Ward's birth, in 1934, the *Times Literary Supplement* gave Artemus its entire front page with a long runover on page two and commented, " . . . to most English people Artemus Ward is now only a name, yet the name persists."[11]

In 1967, as the one hundredth anniversary of Ward's death was approaching, Jeffrey Harwood, a young Englishman, noticed that there was no longer any marker commemorating the event in Southampton. He had a plaque made and attached, with proper ceremony, to a building across the street from the former Radley's Hotel, and paid for it out of his own pocket.

Artemus Ward's influence—as pervasive, though as incorporeal, as sunlight in the summer air—was summarized by his old friend Joe Goodman: "His life was a constant sparkle, and it was that more than the work he did which left such an impression upon those who knew him and upon his time."[12]

The deep and lasting impression Artemus Ward made in England had a very curious effect on the American literary community—an effect that, as Goodman suggested, could not have resulted from the works Ward left behind or his reputation in America prior to 1866. His reception overseas was a surprising phenomenon to Americans. Soon after the American Revolution, America had declared its intention to produce a national literature of its own, and had ever since been nervously glancing over its shoulder at England, waiting for an admission that it had succeeded. This ambition had been the subject of insulting comments, such as those of Sydney Smith, who wondered why anyone would read an American book or why an American should write one. Why, indeed, when "a six-weeks' passage brings them, in their own tongue, our sense, science and genius, in bales and hogsheads? Prairies, steamboats, gristmills, are their natural objects for centuries to come."[13] As if in refutation of those snide remarks, America had produced, mostly in the more cultured centers of the East, writers of the caliber of Emerson, Hawthorne, Thoreau, Longfellow, and others who rivaled England's best; yet there had been only polite nods of approbation—no great enthusiasm. James Russell Lowell was sadly remarking about this time, "It will take England a great while to get over her airs of patronage about us."[14]

And now, after all that, here was England idolizing an *Artemus Ward!*

It appeared that what England considered admirable and distinctive was not coming from the halls of learning in the East, whence it should have come, but from the land beyond, of prairies, steamboats, and gristmills. Then—and later—the English have seemed inclined to patronize American writers who write like Englishmen, as though saying, "Why should we admire them for what we do better?" Hence, perhaps, their admiration for Artemus.

The reflection of this regard was seen by Americans in the mourning for Ward and the scholarly analyses of his work that went on for days in the public prints of England immediately following his death. Dr. James Rhoades, translator of Latin classics, scholar, and educator, wrote for the *Spectator* a poem about Artemus that concluded:

> He came with a heart full of gladness
>   From the glad-hearted world of the West—
> Won our laughter, but not with mere madness,
>   Spake and joked with us, not in mere jest;
> For the Man in our heart lingered after,
>   When the merriment died from our ears,
> And those that were loudest in laughter
>   Are silent in tears.[15]

The *London Review* said that Ward's genius "was like our church service, in one respect, that is, made 'to be understanded of the common people.'" The article closed on an unabashedly sentimental note, referring to one of Ward's bogus reviews that had appeared in the Egyptian Hall program notes: "And when he announced that he should never lecture in that town again, the applause was absolutely deafening." As a proffered footnote to this the *Review* declared, "We must, as we think sadly of him, give his gentle spirit the pleasure of hearing a hearty contradiction. . . . Truly, when he rose to go, and turned his steps to the silent shore where we all are travelling, there were many hearts that were sad, and many eyes that were wet with tears."[16]

In America many people had thought of Artemus as only a clown. But in England there were analyses of his work that seemed to raise American humor, and perhaps all humor, to a new level.

An article in the *Spectator* about Artemus Ward a week after the funeral raised the philosophical question of what place humor has in the life of man. The author had chosen the most difficult aspect of his question, calling his article "Humour and Faith," and going on to point out that we know God only through the gravest and most reverential side of human nature; therefore it is extremely hard to recognize or imagine a place for laughter in that knowledge, "for the same reason for which we should not be able to speculate calmly on the interior constitution of the Sun, if we were falling rapidly into it. . . ." Continuing, the writer said that although there appears to be a splendid rationality in the universe as revealed or explained by religion, logic, or aesthetics, it might be advisable to develop an awareness of a certain irrationality in man's affairs. This awareness would help explain life; it would be comforting, and appropriate. "Why should there be anything more inconsistent between the growth of the divine life in us and a keen sense of moral and intellectual disproportions—which gives humor—than between the growth of the divine life in us and a keen sense of moral and intellectual proportions—which gives science and art? The scientific and the artistic minds naturally bring together the facts and forms which tend to explain, to complete, to set off each other in the most striking light. The mind of the humourist has the same sense of proportion—only in the inverted form of an intense appreciation of the disproportion between those facts and forms which render each other mutually inexplicable, or somewhat incredible."

And the author concluded; "We do not see why humour should not have its place in a fuller life, in which it would not displace the moral and spiritual nature, but serve as its framework and its foil."[17]

The lesson of Ward's great success was not lost upon Mark Twain. Indeed, there was something symbolic of a passing of torches in the fact that when the *Deutschland,* bearing the body of Artemus Ward, sailed into New York Harbor on May 31, 1867, there was another vessel in the harbor about to depart and advertised as

Excursion
to Paris, Italy, Greece, Crimea, Holy Land, Egypt, etc.
THE MAGNIFICENT SIDE-WHEEL OCEAN STEAMSHIP
QUAKER CITY[18]

This was the ship on which Mark Twain was outward bound, heading for *The Innocents Abroad* and the real beginning of his own reputation. A few years afterward Mark Twain, Bret Harte, and others of similar distinction were journeying to England to enjoy a welcome that Ward had to some degree prepared for them. Even the older and more traditional humorists, Lowell and Holmes, shared in this enhanced regard; they were, in the words of Clarence Gohdes, "swept along on a veritable avalanche of enthusiasn for fun from the West which developed rapidly in the late sixties and the years immediately following."[19]

That Artemus Ward and the other humorists who crossed the Atlantic at this time had an important ambassadorial as well as a literary role can hardly be doubted. They arrived in England at a time when much animosity still lingered between Great Britain and the United States following the American Civil War. There were many citizens of the North who thought that Britain's neutrality in the war had been insincere and the attitudes of its aristocracy hostile, while many British considered that the United States had been arrogant in its interference with British shipping, in its claims for damages caused by British-built Confederate ships, and in other ways. Within a decade or so these disputes had been amicably settled, and within fifty years the two countries had been bound together by what Winston Churchill referred to as "ties of honour and fraternal loyalty" that remained firm through and beyond two world conflicts. It is not unreasonable to suppose that humorists, on both sides, had at least some part of all this; that they did something to convince the British that not all Americans are beetle-browed barbarians, and to convince the Americans that not all English people are sneering snobs. From his own diplomatic experiences in England and Spain, Washington Irving had once written, " 'I have always had an opinion that much good might be done by keeping mankind in good humor with one another.' "[20] The *Times* of London, in commenting on Artemus Ward's lectures, predicted in them a foundation for what is called an entente cordiale between England and America and said, "When two persons laugh together, they cannot hate each other much as long as the laugh continues."[21]

The American Legation's attendance at Ward's funeral in London and its attention to him during his last days were significant. In response to a message from the legation in London, when it became known that Artemus Ward was ill in Southampton, John Britton, the United States consul at Southampton, went to Ward's bedside in Radley's Hotel immediately, visited him daily and was with him when he died. When it was over he sent a dispatch to Secretary of State William H. Seward in Washington which said in part, "The death of Mr. Brown has caused universal regret among the literary men of this country."[22]

Reading the message, Seward could not have failed to remember the day when he was present in the cabinet room where the Emancipation Proclamation and *Artemus Ward, His Book* had lain on the table side by side and Lincoln had observed that a good laugh is good medicine for everyone.

Appendix

Lecturing Itineraries, October 17, 1864, to January 23, 1867,
with "Artemus Ward Among the Mormons"

During the seven years in which he lectured, Artemus Ward traveled to large and small communities all over the country, from Maine to California, from Montreal to New Orleans. His early tours reflect no particular plan or progression, but by the time he went on the road with "Artemus Ward Among the Mormons," his itineraries were professionally planned and managed. The schedule of 1865 is particularly strenuous. There are a few gaps in the entries that follow, but these may be due to the author's inability to find records of appearances that Ward actually made. Some of the sources supporting the entries, described in more detail in the Bibliography, are abbreviated as follows:

Hingston *GS*	Hingston, Edward P., *The Genial Showman.*
NY Clip.	*New York Clipper, The.*
OD	Odell, George C. D., *Annals of the New York Stage.*
SM	*New York Sunday Mercury, The*

Dates and Places of Appearances
with Names and Dates of Documenting Sources

1864

OCTOBER 17

–DECEMBER 23 New York, Dodworth Hall, Hingston *GS,* p. 512; *NY Clip.,* Dec. 31 and Jan. 12.

DECEMBER 26, 1864

–JANUARY 7, 1865 Boston, Melodeon, *NY Clip.,* Dec. 31 and Jan. 12.

1865

JANUARY

9–14	Providence, R. I., New City Hall, *Providence Daily Journal,* Jan. 9.
17	Salem, Mass., *NY Clip.,* Jan. 21.
18	Haverhill, Mass., ibid.
19	Lowell, Mass., ibid.
20, 21	Worcester, Mass., ibid.
23, 24	Hartford, Conn., Allyn Hall, *Hartford Daily Courant,* Jan. 21.
25, 26	New Haven, Conn., Music Hall, *New Haven Daily Register,* Jan. 26.
27, 28	Brooklyn, N. Y., Academy of Music, *SM,* Jan. 22.
30–Feb. 4	Philadelphia, Concert Hall, *NY Clip.,* Jan. 28, Feb. 4.

FEBRUARY

6, 7	Wilmington, Del., *NY Clip.,* Jan. 28.
8–11	Baltimore, Maryland Institute, *SM,* Jan. 22.
13, 14	Harrisburg, Pa., *NY Clip.,* Feb. 25.
15–18	Pittsburgh, Masonic Hall, *NY Clip.,* Feb. 18 and 25.
23	Zanesville, Ohio, *NY Clip.,* Feb. 18.
24, 25	Newark, Ohio, ibid.
27, 28, Mar. 1	Columbus, Ohio, Athenaeum, *NY Clip.,* Feb. 18 and Mar. 11.

MARCH

2, 3	Dayton, Ohio, *NY Clip.,* Feb. 18.
4	Hamilton, Ohio, *Cincinnati Daily Commercial,* Mar. 4.
6, 7	Cincinnati, Ohio, Mozart Hall, *NY Clip.,* March 11.

8, 9	Covington, Ky., *NY Clip.*, March 18.
13–18	Louisville, Ky., Masonic Temple, *Louisville Daily Journal,* Mar. 11.
20, 21	Indianapolis, Ind., Masonic Hall, *Indianapolis Journal,* Mar. 20.
(Exact date not given)	Terre Haute, Ind., *NY Clip.*, Mar. 18.
23, 24	Evansville, Ind., Crescent City Hall, *Evansville Daily Journal,* Mar. 24.
(Exact date not given)	Vincennes, Ind., *NY Clip.*, Mar. 18.
27–30	St. Louis, Mo., *Daily Missouri Republican,* Mar. 27.
31	Alton, Ill., *NY Clip.*, Mar. 25.

APRIL

1	Springfield, Ill., *NY Clip.*, Mar. 25.
2	Bloomington, Ill., ibid.
3	Peoria, Ill., ibid.
5	Galesburg, Ill., ibid.
6	Burlington, Iowa, ibid.
20–29	Chicago, Smith & Nixon's Music Hall, *NY Clip.*, May 6.

MAY

1	Fort Wayne, Ind., *NY Clip.*, May 6.
2, 3	Toledo, Ohio, ibid.
4	Jackson, Mich., ibid.
5	Ann Arbor, Mich., ibid.
6	Detroit, Mich., ibid.
8	Sandusky, Ohio, ibid.
9, 10	Cleveland, Ohio, ibid.
11	Warren, Ohio, ibid.
12	Meadville, Pa., ibid.
13	Erie, Pa., ibid.
15–18	Buffalo, N. Y., St. James Hall, *SM,* May 21.
19	Lockport, N. Y., *NY Clip.*, May 13.
20	Albion, N. Y., ibid.
22, 23	Rochester, N. Y., Washington Hall, *SM,* May 28.
24	Canandaigua, N. Y., *NY Clip.*, May 13.
25, 26	Syracuse, N. Y., ibid.
27	Oswego, N. Y., ibid.
29	Utica, N. Y., ibid.

30	Schenectady, N. Y., ibid.
31	Poughkeepsie, N. Y., ibid.

JUNE

1	Newburgh, N. Y., ibid.
2, 3	Albany, N. Y., ibid.
5, 6	Troy, N. Y., ibid.
7	Hudson, N. Y., ibid.
8	Pittsfield, Mass., *NY Clip.*, June 3.
9, 10	Springfield, Mass., ibid.
12	Norwich, Conn., ibid.
13	New London, Conn., ibid.
14	Providence, R. I., ibid.
15	Newport, R. I., ibid.
16	Fall River, Mass., ibid.
17	New Bedford, Mass., ibid.
19	Boston, ibid.
20	Roxbury, Mass., *NY Clip.*, June 24.
21	South Boston, Mass., ibid.
22	East Boston, Mass., ibid.
23	Charlestown, Mass., ibid.
24	Nashua, N. H., ibid.
26	Manchester, N. H., ibid.
27	Concord, N. H., ibid.
28	Portsmouth, N. H., ibid.
29	Biddeford, Me., ibid.
30	Portland, Me., ibid.

JULY

1	Lewiston, Me., ibid.

AUGUST

28–Sept. 9	New York, Irving Hall, OD, Vol. 8, p. 91.

SEPTEMBER

12–19	Washington, D.C., Carusi's Theatre, *NY Clip.*, Sept. 16 and 30, and Oct. 7.
20	Alexandria, Va., *NY Clip.*, Sept. 30.
25–27	Philadelphia, Pa., *NY Clip.*, Sept. 30 and Oct. 7.

OCTOBER

24–27	Montreal, Que., Mechanics' Hall, *Montreal Gazette,* Oct. 21.

31   Kingston, Ontario, City Hall, *Daily Globe,* Toronto, Nov. 4.

NOVEMBER

4–6   Toronto, Ont., Music Hall, ibid., Nov. 3.
(Exact date   Hamilton, Ont., ibid., Nov. 4.
not given)
9, 10   Detroit, Mich., Athenaeum, *Detroit Free Press,* Nov. 10.
20   Painesville, Ohio, *SM,* Nov. 26.
21   Ashtabula, Ohio, ibid.
22   Erie, Pa., ibid.
23   Corry, Pa., ibid.
24, 25   Titusville, Pa., Bliss Opera House, *Titusville Morning Herald,* Nov. 24.

DECEMBER

1, 2   Pittsburgh, Pa., Masonic Hall, *NY Clip.,* Dec. 2.
11–14   Cincinnati, Ohio, Mozart Hall, *NY Clip.,* Dec. 16.
18, 19   Louisville, Ky., Masonic Temple, *Louisville Daily Journal,* Dec. 18.
21–23   Nashville, Tenn., Masonic Hall, *Nashville Republican Banner,* Dec. 19.

1866

JANUARY

2   Vicksburg, Miss., Vicksburg Theater, *Vicksburg Journal,* Dec. 29, 1865.
(Exact dates   Memphis, Tenn., and Natchez, Miss., Melville D.
not given)   Landon, "Traveling With Artemus Ward" *Galaxy,* Sept. 1871, pp. 442–3.
8–12   New Orleans, Miss., Masonic Hall, *Daily Picayune,* Jan. 7.
13   New Orleans, Miss., St. Charles St. Opera House, ibid., Jan. 13.
16, 17   Mobile, Ala., Temperance Hall, *Mobile Register and Advertiser,* Jan. 17.
19, 20   Montgomery, Ala., *Daily Advertiser,* Jan. 17.
22   Columbus, Ga., Temperance Hall, *Columbus Daily Enquirer,* Jan. 21.

(Exact date not given)	Macon, Ga., *NY Clip.*, Feb. 17.
26, 27	Augusta, Ga., Masonic Hall, *Daily Constitutionalist,* Jan. 25.
29–Feb. 1	Savannah, Ga., *Savannah Daily Herald,* Jan. 30.

FEBRUARY

3, 5	Charleston, S. C., *Charleston Daily Courier,* Feb. 3, 5.
(Exact date not given)	Petersburg, Va., *SM*, Feb. 18.
13, 14	Richmond, Va., Richmond Theater, *Richmond Daily Dispatch,* Feb. 13 and 14; 1 *SM*, Feb. 18.

After resting through the spring at his home in Maine, Ward went to London and spent the summer and early autumn preparing for the opening of his show there.

NOVEMBER

Nov. 13, 1866 –Jan. 23, 1867	London, England, Egyptian Hall, Hingston *GS*, p. 518.

Notes

In citing works in these notes, short titles have generally been used after an initial reference to the full title. Full particulars of the sources will be found in the selected bibliography. Further, persons and works frequently referred to are identified by the following abbreviations.

AW	Artemus Ward, pseudonym for Charles Farrar Brown or Browne.
AW Lect.	*Artemus Ward's Lecture,* Ed. T. W. Robertson and E. P. Hingston (London: John Camden Hotten; New York: G. W. Carleton & Co., 1869).
CFB	Charles Farrar Brown(e).
Cle. PD	*Cleveland Daily Plain Dealer.*
Compl. Wks. AW	*The Complete Works of Artemus Ward,* with biographical sketch by Melville D. Landon, rev. ed. (New York: G. W. Dillingham Co., Publishers, 1901).
Hingston *GS*	Edward P. Hingston, *The Genial Showman,* new illus. ed. (London: John Camden Hotten, [1872]).
NY Clip.	*The New York Clipper.*
Seitz, *AW*	Don. C. Seitz, *Artemus Ward, a Biography and Bibliography* (New York: Harper & Brothers Publishers, 1919).

1. *The Man Who Made Lincoln Laugh*

1. Seitz, *AW*, pp. 113–15; *Compl. Wks. AW*, pp. 36–37.

2. Paul M. Angle, ed., *The Lincoln Reader*, p. 275.

3. *Compl. Wks. AW*, pp. 98–99.

4. "The Early Life of Abe Lincoln," *Cle. PD*, 19 July 1860.

5. "Captain Lincoln," *Campaign Plain Dealer and Popular Sovereignty Advocate* (Cleveland, Ohio), 14 July 1860.

6. *Compl. Wks. AW*, pp. 100–104.

7. W. D. Howells, *Literary Friends and Acquaintance*, p. 127.

8. "Amusements," *NY Clip.*, 21 November 1863.

9. Seitz, *AW*, p. 238.

10. Editorial (under p. 2 masthead), *Nashville Republican Banner*, (Tenn.), 22 December 1865.

11. Seitz, *AW*, p. 233.

12. *Compl. Wks. AW*, pp. 27–28.

13. "Letter from Artemus Ward," *Cle. PD*, 9 March 1858.

14. "Letter from Artemus Ward," *Cle. PD*, 17 April 1858.

15. *Compl. Wks. AW* (in order of quotations), pp. 412, 55, 412, 175.

16. Ibid. (in order), pp. 61, 169, 210, 59, 198.

17. Ibid., p. 36.

18. Ibid., p. 177; Hesketh Pearson, *Oscar Wilde, His Life and Wit* (New York: Harper & Brothers, 1946), pp. 280–81.

19. Matthew Freke Turner, "Artemus Ward and the Humorists of America," p. 205.

2. *"I Should Think We Came from Jerusalem."*

1. Hingston *GS*, p. 86.

2. Melville D. Landon, biographical sketch in *Compl. Wks. AW*, p. 16.

3. Seitz *AW*, p. 21.

4. William Winter, *Old Friends* (New York: Moffat, Yard and Company, 1909), p. 285.

5. C. C. Ruthrauff, "Artemus Ward at Cleveland;" p. 790.

6. Hingston *GS*, p. 63.

7. *Compl. Wks. AW*, p. 327.

8. Nathaniel Hawthorne, *The Scarlet Letter*, pp. 9–10.

9. CFB to a Charles Brown, reproduced in Seitz *AW*, p. 233.

10. James F. Ryder, *Voigtlander and I in Pursuit of Shadow Catching*, pp. 177–78; also Ryder's "Recollections of Artemus Ward," pp. 151–52.

11. AW to an unidentified friend, AW Collection, Waterford Historical Society, Waterford, Maine.

3. The Years in Boston and Ohio

1. Elizabeth Akers Allan, "Benjamin Penhallow Shillaber," *New England Magazine*, n.s. 4 (June 1891): 431.

2. "To the Reader," *Carpet-Bag* 1 (29 March 1891): 5.

3. Edward P. Hingston, preface to *AW Lect.*, p. 27.

4. Hingston *GS*, pp. 81–82.

5. Enoch Knight, "Artemus Ward, a Biographical Sketch," clipping in file M-837, Maine Historical Society, Portland, Maine, publication unrecorded.

6. W. D. Howells, *Years of My Youth*, pp. 17, 90.

7. Howells, *Literary Friends*, p. 127.

8. W. D. Howells, intro. to *Artemus Ward's Best Stories*, p. viii.

9. Charles C. Cole, Jr., *The Social Ideas of the Northern Evangelists, 1826-1860*, p. 113.

10. Hingston *GS*, p. 117.

11. *AW Lect.*, n., p. 64.

12. Edward Everett Hale, intro, to *Famous Lectures*, pp. ix–xxii.

13. George Hoyt, "Personal Recollections of Artemus Ward," *Daily Graphic* (New York), 23 March 1889; "Our Speech," *Cle. PD*, 18 January 1859.

14. *Compl. Wks. AW*, pp. 28–30.

15. Ibid., pp. 100–104.

16. Archer H. Shaw, *The Plain Dealer—One Hundred Years in Cleveland*, p. 40.

17. "Charles F. Brown, Alias Artemus Ward," *Cle. PD*, 19 November 1860.

18. *The Letters of Artemus Ward to Charles E. Wilson, 1858-1861*, pp. 81, 86.

4. Man About Manhattan

1. Charles Godfrey Leland, *Memoirs*, 2:21.

2. Winter, *Old Friends*, p. 56.

3. Albert Parry, *Garrets and Pretenders*, p. 43.

4. "Howard's Letter," *Boston Sunday Globe*, 13 September 1896.

5. Winter, *Old Friends*, pp. 57–64.

6. Emory Holloway, ed., *The Uncollected Poetry and Prose of Walt Whitman*, 2:92–93.

7. Parry, *Garrets*, p. 32.

8. Laura Stedman and George M. Gould, *Life and Letters of Edmund Clarence Stedman*, 1:207–9.

9. *The Letters of Artemus Ward to Charles E. Wilson, 1858–1861*, pp. 61–65.

10. Hingston *GS*, p. 108.

11. Ibid., p. 140.

12. CFB to R. H. Stoddard, 5 October 1861, Gratz Collection, Historical Society of Pennsylvania, Philadelphia.

13. CFB to an unidentified correspondent, 16 November 1861, Dreer Collection, Historical Society of Pennsylvania, Philadelphia.

14. *Compl. Wks. AW*, pp. 75–76.

15. "Puss-in-Boots," *Nashville Republican Banner* (Tenn.), 24 December 1865.

5. The Children in the Wood

1. "'Artemas [sic] Ward' on the Rostrum," *Boston Post*, 7 December 1861.

2. "Artemus Ward in Boston," *Boston Daily Evening Transcript*, 7 December 1861.

3. "Artemus Ward—Mr. Charles F. Browne's Lecture," *Boston Daily Advertiser*, 7 December 1861.

4. "Artemus Ward," *Boston Daily Journal*, 7 December 1861.

5. M. A. DeWolfe Howe, *Memories of a Hostess*, p. 7.

6. M. A. DeWolfe Howe, *American Bookmen*, p. 273; Oliver Wendell Holmes, *The Autocrat of the Breakfast Table* (Boston: Phillips, Sampson and Company, 1858), p. 13.

7. Howe, *Memories*, p. 21.

8. Howe, *Bookmen*, p. 168.

9. J. E. Preston Muddock, *Pages from an Adventurous Life*, p. 96.

10. Charles J. Woodbury, "Artemus Ward at Springfield, Massachusetts," pp. 636–37.

11. Charles O. Stickney, "Maine Stories of Artemus Ward."

12. Melville D. Landon, *Thirty Years of Wit*, p. 176.

13. "Artemus Ward in London," *Spectator* (London) 39 (24 November 1866):1306.

14. *AW Lect.*, p. 70.

15. Carolyn Wells, ed., *An Outline of Humor*, p. 13.

16. *AW Lect.*, pp.105–6.

17. Ibid., p. 112 and n. p. 112.

18. Ibid., pp. 63, 70.

19. Ryder, *Voigtlander and I*, p. 199.

20. *AW Lect.*, p. 62.

21. "Foreign Dramatic and Show News," *NY Clip.*, 8 December 1866.

22. "Humorous Lectures," *Cincinnati Daily Commercial*, 2 March 1865.

23. *AW Lect.*, p. 65 and n., p. 65.

24. H. R. Haweis, *American Humorists*, p. 128.

25. Charles Godfrey Leland, *Hans Breitmann's Ballads*, p. 233.

6. Lecturing, Literary, and Other Affairs

1. "Artemus Ward Tonight," *Lewiston Daily Evening Journal* (Maine), 15 March 1862.

2. Reprinted in "Artemus Ward's Lecture," *Semi-Weekly Sentinel* (Bath, Maine), 15 March 1862.

3. "Artemus Ward in a Boarding School," *New York Times,* 5 November 1882.

4. Adah Isaacs Menken to "Dear Daly" (probably John Augustin Daly), 18 July 1862, Adah Isaacs Menken Papers, by permission of the Harvard Libraries, Cambridge, Mass.

5. *Compl. Wks. AW*, p. 188.

6. "Artemus Ward," *Providence Sunday Journal* (R.I.), 21 September 1890.

7. Clifton Johnson, "Recollections of Artemus Ward," pp. 30–31.

8. *Compl. Wks. AW*, pp. 105–6.

9. Ibid., p. 429.

10. AW to James R. Osgood, 29 July 1862, Typographic Library Manuscripts, Rare Book and Manuscript Library, Columbia University, New York.

11. AW to James R. Osgood, 6 September 1864, Anthony Collection, Rare Books and Manuscript Division, The New York Public Library, Astor, Lenox and Tilden Foundations.

7. Forty Nights in California

1. "The City—Artemus Ward at Bryan Hall," *Chicago Times,* 18 December 1862.

2. "Artemus Ward's 'Piece,'" *Louisville Daily Democrat* (Ky.), 4 January 1863.

3. Thomas Hobbes, *Humane Nature, or Fundamental Elements of Policy* (London: T. Newcomb, 1654), p. 103.

4. *Compl. Wks. AW,*p. 104.

5. "Miscellaneous," *NY Clip.,* 25 April 1863.

6. "Miscellaneous," *NY Clip.,* 14 February 1863.

7. "Miscellaneous," *NY Clip.,* 10 January 1863.

8. "Miscellaneous," *NY Clip.,* 27 December 1862.

9. "Miscellaneous," *NY Clip.,* 26 June 1863.

10. David Mead, *Yankee Eloquence in the Middle West: The Ohio Lyceum, 1850-1870,* p. 215.

11. "Miscellaneous," *NY Clip.,* 21 February 1863.

12. Hingston *GS,* pp. 150-52.

13. Ibid., pp. 162-63.

14. *Compl. Wks. AW,* p. 50.

15. Hingston, *GS,* pp. 1-11.

16. G. L. M. Strauss, *Reminiscences of an Old Bohemian,* 2:150.

17. Hingston *GS,* p. 10.

18. Ibid., p. 60.

19. Ibid., pp. 164-66.

20. Ibid., p. 300.

21. Ibid., p. 369.

22. Eugene F. Ware, *The Indian War of 1864,* p. 81.

23. Hingston *GS,* p. 382.

24. Bret Harte, "Artemus Ward," *Golden Era* (San Francisco), 27 December 1863.

8. *Virginia City.*

1. Hingston *GS,* pp. 401-5.

2. Jared B. Graham, *Handset Reminiscences,* p. 138.

3. Joseph T. Goodman, "Artemus Ward: His Visit to the Comstock Lode."

4. Graham, *Reminiscences,* pp. 140-42.

5. Ibid., p. 143.

6. Goodman, "Artemus Ward."

7. Ibid.

8. Dan de Quille [pseud.], "Artemus Ward in Nevada," *Californian Illustrated Magazine* 4 (August 1893): 404-5.

9. Mark Twain, *Sketches New and Old,* pp. 368-69.

10. Goodman, "Artemus Ward."

11. *Mark Twain's Letters,* 2:773.

9. *Mark Ward and Artemus Twain.*

1. AW to Mark Twain, 1 January 1864, courtesy of the Mark Twain Project, Bancroft Library, University of California, Berkeley.

2. Ibid.

3. Henry Nash Smith, ed., *Mark Twain of the Enterprise,* pp. 129–30.

4. Howells, intro. to *Artemus Ward's Best Stories,* pp. xiv, xv.

5. *Compl. Wks. AW,* p. 240.

6. Seitz *AW,* pp. 172–73.

7. "The City—Artemus Ward at Bryan Hall," *Chicago Times,* 18 December 1862.

8. *Compl. Wks. AW,* p. 186; Mark Twain, *Roughing It,* p. 132.

9. Ryder, *Voigtlander and I,* p. 199; Mark Twain, *Literary Essays,* pp. 182–92.

10. "Scene at a Restaurant," *Campaign Plain Dealer and Popular Sovereignty Advocate* (Cleveland), 20 October 1860; Twain, *Sketches New and Old,* p. 204.

11. Twain, *Literary Essays,* p. 126–27.

12. *Mark Twain's Autobiography,* 1:xii.

13. James C. Austin, *Artemus Ward,* p. 114.

14. Twain, *Literary Essays,* p. 8.

15. Moncure D. Conway, *Autobiography,* 2:142–43.

16. W. D. Howells, *My Mark Twain,* p. 51.

17. Twain, *Sketches New and Old,* p. 369.

18. *Mark Twain's Letters,* 1:101.

19. Ibid., 1:124, 276–78.

20. Paul Fatout, *Mark Twain on the Lecture Circuit,* p. 152.

21. "Mark Twain's Lecture," *Portland Daily Press* (Maine), 17 November 1871.

22. Goodman, "Artemus Ward."

23. "Mark Twain," *Spectator* 45 (18 October 1873):1302–3.

24. Muddock, *Pages,* p. 106.

25. Albert Bigelow Paine, *Mark Twain, a Biography,* 1:464.

26. Edward P. Hingston, intro. to *The Innocents Abroad* (London: John Camden Hotten, [1870]), p. 8.

27. "Foreign Dramatic and Show News," *NY Clip.,* 17 November 1866.

28. Paine, *Biography,* 1:464.

29. *Mark Twain's Speeches,* p. 421.

30. Justin Kaplan, *Mr. Clemens and Mark Twain,* p. 381.

10. The Wild Humorist of the Plains

1. Edward P. Hingston, "Artemus Ward Among the Shoshones," p. 127.

2. *Artemus Ward (His Travels) Among the Mormons,* p. xiv.

3. Hingston *GS,* p. 440.

4. Ibid., p. 435.

5. Ibid., p. 426. The quotation in this edition is actually, "The better stand we shall make against the sons of———[lady-dogs]."

6. Ibid., p. 443.

7. Ibid., p. 439.

8. Ibid., p. 450.

9. *Artemus Ward Among the Mormons,* p. 40.

10. Hingston *GS,* p. 452.

11. Ibid., p. 485–86.

12. Ibid., p. 490.

13. Ibid., p. 490.

14. Ibid., p. 493.

15. AW to Mark Twain, 21 January 1864, courtesy of the Mark Twain Project, Bancroft Library, University of California, Berkeley.

16. *Compl. Wks. AW,* p. 289.

17. *Artemus Ward Among the Mormons,* p. 68.

18. Ibid., p. 70.

19. "Local—Artemus Ward," *Daily Miners' Register,* (Central City, Colorado), 24 February 1864.

20. Frank A. Root and William E. Connelley, *The Overland Stage Line to California,* pp. 233, 245.

21. Ware, *Indian War,* p. 59.

22. *AW Lect.,* p. 166; illus., pp. 167,183.

23. Ware, *Indian War,* pp. 129–30.

24. *Artemus Ward Among the Mormons,* p. 75.

25. Hingston *GS,* p. 440.

26. George Augustus Sala, *My Diary in America in the Midst of War,* 1:62–63.

27. George Augustus Sala, intro. to *Artemus Ward His Travels,* unpaginated.

28. Hingston, preface to *AW Lect.,* p. 46.

11. Adoo! Adoo!

1. Seitz, *AW,* p. 234.

2. CFB, "Wallace Thaxter," *Saturday Evening Gazette* (Boston), 18 June 1864.

3. George C. D. Odell, *Annals of the New York Stage*, 7:89, 199, 370.

4. Hingston *GS*, pp. 510–11. The printed flyer is one of the four recently discovered pieces of AW material referred to under Seitz, "Artemus Ward Letters," in the Bibliography.

5. Hingston *GS*, p. 511.

6. Program reproduced in *AW Lect.*, pp. 209–13.

7. Ibid., and program for lecture at Masonic Hall, Pittsburgh, 15–18 February, 1865, in possession of Toledo Public Library (Ohio).

8. *AW Lect.*, p. 68.

9. Ibid., p. 100.

10. Ibid., p. 130.

11. Miscellaneous," *NY Clip.*, 31 December 1864.

12. *AW Lect.*, p. 159.

13. Ibid., pp. 180–85.

14. Melville D. Landon, "Travelling With Artemus Ward," p. 443.

15. "Anecdotes of Artemus Ward," *New York Times*, 29 May 1881.

16. Program for Pittsburgh.

17. "Miscellaneous," *NY Clip.*, 25 February 1865.

18. "Artemus Ward," *Louisville Daily Journal*, 13 and 16 March, 1865.

19. Frederick T. Wallace, *Men and Events of Half a Century*, p. 185.

20. "Miscellaneous," *NY Clip.*, 1 April 1865.

21. Josiah G. Holland, "Triflers on the Platform," *Scribner's Monthly* 3 (February 1872): 489.

22. Kaplan, *Mr. Clemens and Mark Twain*, p. 147.

23. *Compl. Wks. AW*, pp. 210–12.

12. And Again, Adoo

1. Pisanus Fraxi [pseud.], *Bibliography of Prohibited Books*, 1:253–56.

2. *Compl. Wks. AW*, pp. 80–82.

3. Ibid., pp. 216–17.

4. Seitz *AW*, p. 237.

5. Robert Morris, "Artemus Ward, Reminiscences of a Friend," *New York Times*, 28 August 1885.

6. "Miscellaneous," *NY Clip.*, 17 February 1866.

7. Henry Watterson, *"Marse Henry" An Autobiography*, 1:114; "Miscellaneous," *New York Sunday Mercury*, 25 March 1866.

8. *Compl. Wks. AW,* p. 177.

9. "Artemus Ward in New Orleans," *Manhattan* 2 (December 1883): 585–86.

10. AW to an unidentified correspondent in Lynchburg, Va., 12 March 1866, in "Artemus Ward Letters," p. 196.

11. *Compl. Wks. AW,* p. 168.

12. "Local Matters—A. Ward at the Theatre," *Montgomery Daily Mail* (Ala.), 20 January 1866.

13. "Artemus Ward," *Daily Enquirer,* (Columbus, Ga.), 24 January 1866.

14. Charles Henry Smith, *Bill Arp's Scrap Book,* p. 58.

15. "Artemus Ward," *Daily Constitutionalist* (Augusta, Ga.), 28 January 1866.

16. *Compl. Wks. AW,* p. 208.

17. Austin, *Artemus Ward,* p. 65.

18. *Compl. Wks. AW,* p. 412.

19. AW to a Mr. Pickard, 10 April 1866, in "Artemus Ward Letters" p. 197.

20. Howells, *Literary Friends,* pp. 127–28.

21. *Compl. Wks. AW,* p. 96.

22. AW to Mr. Childs, editor of *"Ledger,"* 8 April 1866, Historical Society of Pennsylvania, Philadelphia.

23. AW to W. W. Clapp, 1 May 1866, by permission of the Houghton Library, Harvard University, Cambridge, Mass.

24. Howells, *Literary Friends,* pp. 127–28.

25. AW to W. D. Howells, 12 March 1866, by permission of the Houghton Library, Harvard University, Cambridge, Mass.

13. "A. Ward Has Hit 'Em Hard."

1. AW to Mr. Pickard, 10 April 1866, in "Artemus Ward Letters," pp. 196–97.

2. Hingston *GS,* p. 515.

3. *Compl. Wks. AW,* p. 311.

4. Jessie Millward, with J. B. Booth, *Myself and Others,* p. 36.

5. T. W. Robertson, intro. to *AW Lect.,* pp. 11–12.

6. Muddock, *Pages,* p. 94; Aaron Watson, *The Savage Club,* pp. 119–20.

7. "Artemus Ward in London 'from the Round Table, London,'" *New York Times,* 18 March 1867.

8. Watson, *Savage Club*, pp. 21, 33.

9. Landon, *Thirty Years of Wit*, p. 182.

10. Hingston *GS*, p. 75.

11. *Compl. Wks. AW*, p. 312.

12. Ibid, pp. 321,325.

13. Ibid., p. 332.

14. Ibid., p. 241.

15. Conway, *Autobiography*, 2:136.

16. Edmund Gosse, *The Life of Algernon Charles Swinburne* (New York: The Macmillan Company, 1917), p. 152.

17. Joseph Jefferson, *The Autobiography of Joseph Jefferson*, pp. 310, 320–21.

18. Program reproduced in *AW Lect., pp. 203-8.*

19. *Muddock, Pages*, pp. 95–96.

20. *AW Lect.*, pp. 65–68, 70.

21. "Artemus Ward in London," *Spectator* 39 (24 November 1866), 1306.

22. *AW Lect.*, pp. 166–69.

23. Ibid., pp. 137–41.

24. A. Chadbourn to Daniel Brown, 15 March 1867, possession of Ruth E. Rounds, of Waterford, Maine.

25. AW to "Dear Ned," 17 November 1866, Charles Farrar Browne Collection (#7476), Clifton Waller Barrett Library, University of Virginia Library, Charlottesville.

26. "Artemus Ward at the Egyptian Hall," *Lloyd's Weekly London Newspaper*, 18 November 1866.

27. Haweis, *American Humorists*, p. 135.

28. "Mr. Artemus Ward at Egyptian Hall," *Observer* (London), 18 November 1866.

29. "Artemus Ward in London," *Spectator* 39 (24 November 1866): 1306.

30. "Foreign Dramatic and Show News" (reprint of *News* article), *NY Clip.*, 24 December 1866.

31. "A Ward That Deserves Watching," *Punch* 51 (1 December 1866): 228.

32. Watterson, *"Marse Henry,"* 1:108.

33. E. A. Wallis Budge, "Artemus Ward in London," *Times* (London), 30 April 1934.

34. "Foreign Dramatic and Show News," *NY Clip.*, 29 December 1866.

14. An Unfading Recollection

1. Charles O. Stickney, "It Was a Memorable Scene," *Boston Sunday Herald,* 17 February 1901.

2. *AW Lect.,* p. 61.

3. Watterson, "Marse Henry," 1:108, 112.

4. Ibid., p. 113.

5. Jefferson, *Autobiography,* p. 321.

6. Hingston, preface to *AW Lect.,* pp. 25–26.

7. Millward, *Myself and Others,* p. 36.

8. "Death of Artemus Ward," *Times* (London), 7 March 1867.

9. "Echoes of the Week," *Illustrated London News* 50 (16 March 1867), 255.

10. "Too Gloomy," *Southern Evening Echo* (Southampton, England), 4 March 1967.

11. "Artemus Ward," *Times Literary Supplement* (London), 26 April 1934.

12. Goodman, "Artemus Ward."

13. Sydney Smith, *The Wit and Wisdom of the Rev. Sydney Smith,* p. 187.

14. James Russell Lowell, "On a Certain Condescension in Foreigners," in vol. 3 of *Literary Essays* (Boston: Houghton, Mifflin and Company; Cambridge, Mass.: Riverside Press, 1890), p. 252.

15. James Rhoades, "Artemus Ward," Spectator 40 (16 March 1867):299.

16. "Artemus Ward," *London Review* article, reprinted in *Every Saturday* (Boston), 13 April 1867.

17. "Humour and Faith," *Spectator* 40 (16 March 1867):295–96.

18. Advertisement, p. 7., col. 1, *New York Times,* 1 June 1867.

19. Clarence Gohdes, *American Literature in Nineteenth Century,* p. 85.

20. Howe, *American Bookmen,* p. 17.

21. "Egyptian Hall," *Times* (London), 16 November 1866.

22. John Britton, Consul Southampton, to Secretary of State William H. Seward, 8 March 1867. Despatch No. 64 of Despatches from U. S. Consuls in Southampton, U.K., General Records of the Department of State, Record Group 59, Legislative and Diplomatic Branch of the National Archives.

Selected Bibliography

This list includes only the works that have been of basic use in the writing of *Comic Relief*. Daily newspapers, unless they contain articles of unusual importance, are not listed, although a great many of them, published in the cities where Artemus Ward lectured, were consulted. A few entries in the Notes bear upon minor quotations only and so are not listed here again. Standard reference works such as *Dictionary of American Biography* and Boase's *Modern English Biography* are not detailed. Documents and information concerning Artemus Ward's death and distribution of property as well as transfers of property within his family, obtained from depositories of official records in England, Maine, and New York, are not listed.

Angle, Paul M., ed. *The Lincoln Reader.* New Brunswick, N. J.: Rutgers University Press, 1947.
"Artemus Ward in New Orleans." In *Manhattan* 2 (December 1883):585–86.
Austin, James C. *Artemus Ward.* New York: Twayne Publishers, 1964. Part of Twayne's United States Author Series, and a scholarly work on Ward by a professor of American literature. Austin supports the view that in several ways Artemus prepared the way for Mark Twain's literary and lecturing achievements and had a considerable influence on Mark Twain himself.

Bates, David H. *Lincoln in the Telegraph Office*. New York: Century Company, 1907. Lincoln quotes "from memory" an Artemus Ward story on p. 187.

Berger, Max. *The British Traveller in America*. New York: Columbia University Press, 1943. Reflects many of the British attitudes toward their "boorish and uncouth" American cousins which Artemus Ward had to overcome in his first appearance in London and which made his stunning success there such an overwhelming surprise. This comment also applies to entries for Trollope and Nevins.

Blanck, Jacob, compiler. "Charles Farrar Browne (Artemus Ward)," pp. 312–24. In vol. 1 of his *Bibliography of American Literature*. New Haven: Yale University Press, 1955.

Branch, E. Douglas. *The Sentimental Years, 1836–1860*. New York: D. Appleton-Century Company, 1934. Years in which books, stories, poems, entertainments, etc., were expected to teach moral lessons. Presents the social background against which Artemus Ward portrayed himself as the "Moral Showman" and gently satirized the more intense moralistic efforts of the times. The same comment applies to entries for Cole, Griffin, and Winsor.

Briggs, William. *The Law of International Copyright*. London: Stevens & Haynes., 1906. Gives some of the history of the years during which there was no Anglo-American copyright agreement, when Artemus Ward's works were extensively pirated in England, so extensively that a complete list of the British publications has yet to be compiled, according to Jacob Blanck. Other entries bearing on the copyright situation are Carey, Hotten, and U. S. Congress.

Brooks, Van Wyck. *The Times of Melville and Whitman*. New York: E. P. Dutton, 1947. Brooks wrote that Artemus Ward was "largely effective in changing the tone of thought and speech in more than one respect during these decades." His deflation of the pompous, the pretentious, and the trite, Brooks thought, helped produce the more natural style that followed in literature and on the stage.

Byington, Ezra Hoyt. *The Puritan in England and New England*. Boston: Roberts Bros., 1896. Discusses the extent to which the Puritan influence pervaded the population in Artemus Ward's day.

Campaign Plain Dealer and Popular Sovereignty Advocate. Cleveland: published by the *Cleveland Daily Plain Dealer*, 30 June 1860 to 17 November 1860. Supported the candidacy of Stephen A. Douglas. Charles F. Brown was associate editor.

Carey, H. C. *The International Copyright Question Considered, With*

Special Reference to the Interests of American Authors, American Printers and Publishers, and American Readers. Philadelphia: H. C. Baird, 1882. (See comment under Briggs.)

Carpet-Bag, The: A Literary Journal. Boston: 29 March 1851 to 26 March 1853. Charles F. Brown a compositor and contributor.

Cleveland Daily Plain Dealer. Issues of 31 July 1857 to 31 December 1860.

Cole, Charles C., Jr. *The Social Ideas of the Northern Evangelists, 1826-1860.* New York: Columbia University Press, 1954. (See comment under Branch.)

Conway, Moncure D. *Autobiography.* 2 vols. Boston: Houghton, Mifflin and Company, 1904. Descriptions of both Artemus Ward and Mark Twain in London. Conway conducted Ward's funeral service there.

De Quille, Dan [William Wright]. "Artemus Ward in Nevada." *Californian Illustrated Magazine* 4 (August, 1893):403-06.

————. "Salad Days of Mark Twain." *San Francisco Examiner,* 19 March 1893.

Falk, Bernard. *The Naked Lady, or Storm Over Adah.* London: Hutchinson & Co., 1934.

Fatout, Paul. *Mark Twain on the Lecture Circuit.* Bloomington: Indiana University Press, 1960.

————. *Mark Twain in Virginia City.* Bloomington: Indiana University Press, 1964.

Fraxi, Pisanus, [pseud.]. *Bibliography of Prohibited Books.* 3 vols. New York: Jack Brussel, Publisher, 1962. Includes information about Ward's publisher in England, John Camden Hotten.

Gage, Thomas H., Jr., ed. *Notes on the History of Waterford, Maine.* Worcester, Mass., 1913. Information about Artemus Ward's hometown and his family. (See also *History of Waterford.*)

Gohdes, Clarence. *American Literature in Nineteenth Century England.* New York: Columbia University Press, 1944. Speaks of the influence of Artemus Ward in the acceptance of American works in England.

Goodman, Joseph T. "Artemus Ward: His Visit to the Comstock Lode." *San Francisco Chronicle,* 10 January 1892.

Graham, Jared B. *Handset Reminiscences.* Salt Lake City, Utah: Century Printing Company, 1915. Firsthand accounts of Artemus Ward and Mark Twain in Virginia City, Nevada.

Griffin, Clifford S. *Their Brothers' Keepers. Moral Stewardship in the United States, 1800-1865.* New Brunswick, N. J.: Rutgers University Press, 1960. (See comment under Branch.)

Hafen, Le Roy R. *The Overland Mail, 1849-1869.* Cleveland: Arthur H. Clark Company, 1926. Describes conditions under which Artemus Ward made his journey on the Overland Stage in the winter of 1863–64, as do the entries for Root and Connelley, and Ware.

Hale, Edward Everett. Introduction to *Famous Lectures,* vol. 8 of *Modern Eloquence.* New York: Modern Eloquence Corporation, 1923. Explains why the lecture, which Artemus Ward converted to a comic performance, was so acceptable to the Puritan element of the population.

Harte, Bret. "Artemus Ward." *Golden Era* (San Francisco), 27 December 1863.

Haweis, H. R. *American Humorists.* New York: Funk and Wagnalls, [1882]. First-class criticism and comment on Artemus Ward and other humorists of his time.

Hawthorne, Nathaniel. *The Scarlet Letter.* Boston: Ticknor, Reed, and Fields, 1850. In his introduction, Hawthorne reveals some of the Puritan attitudes toward entertainers.

Heilbron, Bertha L. *Making a Motion Picture in 1848.* St. Paul: Minnesota Historical Society, 1936. The "motion pictures" of that day were the panoramas which Artemus Ward burlesqued. Detailed information about them is scarce, and none seems to have survived.

Hingston, Edward P. "Artemus Ward Among the Shoshones." In *Savage Club Papers for 1868,* edited by Andrew Halliday, 2d ser., pp. 124–39. London: Tinsley Brothers, 1868.

———. *The Genial Showman.* New illus. ed. London: John Camden Hotten, n.d. (back matter includes a list of new books headed 1872).

———. Introduction to *Artemus Ward (His Travels) Among the Mormons.* (See under Ward, Artemus.)

———. Preface and notes in *Artemus Ward's Lecture.* (See under Ward, Artemus.) Hingston was Ward's agent and manager during his tour of the far West in 1863–64, including the hazardous journey back East on the Overland Stage in that winter. He was also Ward's agent in England in 1866–67, and when Ward died there he became his literary co-executor along with playwright T. W. Robertson. In view of his close association with Artemus Ward in England, his accounts of Ward's experiences there are disappointingly brief.

History of Waterford, Oxford County, Maine, The. Portland, Maine: Hoyt, Fogg & Donham, 1879. (See comment under Gage.)

Holloway, Emory, ed. *The Uncollected Poetry and Prose of Walt Whitman.* Garden City, L. I.: Doubleday Page & Company, 1921.

Hotten, John Camden. *Seven Letters Addressed by Permission to the*

Right Hon. the Earl Stanhope. London: John Camden Hotten, 1871. (Has to do with international copyright. See comment under Briggs.)

Howe, M. A. DeWolfe. *American Bookmen*. New York: Dodd, Mead and Company, 1898.

———. *Memories of a Hostess*. Boston: The Atlantic Monthly Press, 1922.

Howells, William Dean. Introduction to *Artemus Ward's Best Stories*. (See under Ward. Artemus.)

———. *Literary Friends and Acquaintance*. New York: Harper & Brothers Publishers, 1900.

———. *My Mark Twain*. New York: Harper & Brothers Publishers, 1910.

———. *Years of My Youth*. New York: Harper & Brothers Publishers, 1916.

Jefferson, Joseph. *The Autobiography of Joseph Jefferson*. New York: The Century Company, 1897.

Johnson, Clifton. Biographical notes in *Artemus Ward's Best Stories*. (See under Ward, Artemus.)

———. "Recollections of Artemus Ward." *Overland Monthly* 67 (January 1916):28–33.

Kaplan, Justin. *Mr. Clemens and Mark Twain*. New York: Simon and Schuster, 1966.

London, Melville D. "A Biographical Sketch." In *Complete Works of Artemus Ward*. (See under Ward, Artemus.)

———. *Kings of the Platform and Pulpit*. New York: The Werner Company, 1896.

———. *Thirty Years of Wit*. New York: Cassell Publishing Company, 1891.

———. *"Travelling With Artemus Ward."* In *Galaxy* 12 (September 1871):442–45. Landon was a friend and traveling companion of Artemus Ward. Some years after Wards's death he obtained his manuscripts and took them home, around 1875. When Landon died in Yonkers, in 1910, his wife and daughter moved out of their big house and into a smaller one, throwing out in the process bundles of old papers for which there would no longer be room. It seems likely that the bulk of Ward's manscripts were thus disposed of, with the exception of a package that was stolen from Landon on the elevated in New York and never recovered from what, it is to be feared, was a non-literary thief.

Leavitt, M. B. *Fifty Years in Theatrical Management*. New York:

Broadway Publishing Co., 1912. Discusses social attitudes toward the theater and other entertainments and contains information on panoramas.

Leland, Charles Godfrey. *Hans Breitmann's Ballads*. New York: Dover Publications, 1965.

———. *Memoirs*. 2 vols. London: William Heinemann, 1893.

Lesser, Allen. *Enchanting Rebel (The Secret of Adah Isaacs Menken)* New York: The Beechhurst Press, 1947.

Lorch, Fred W. "Mark Twain's 'Artemus Ward' Lecture on the Tour of 1871–1872." *New England Quarterly* 25 (September 1952):327–44.

Lyman, George D. *The Saga of the Comstock Lode*. New York: Charles Scribner's Sons, 1934.

Mack, Effie Mona. *Mark Twain in Nevada*. New York: Charles Scribner's Sons, 1947.

McKee, Irving. "Artemus Ward in California and Nevada, 1863–1864."In *Pacific Historical Review* 20 (February 1951):11–23.

Mead, David. *Yankee Eloquence in the Middle West: The Ohio Lyceum, 1850–1870*. East Lansing: Michigan State College Press, 1951.

Meine, Franklin J. "American Comic Periodicals." *Collector's Journal* 4 "No. 1, The Carpet Bag" (issue of October–December, 1933); "No. 2, Vanity Fair" (issue of January–March, 1934).

Millward, Jessie, with Booth, J. B. *Myself and Others*. London: Hutchinson & Co., 1923.

Moran, Benjamin. *Proceedings of the Massachusetts Historical Society* (Boston) 48 (October 1914–June 1915). Contains extracts from the diary of Benjamin Moran for the years 1860–68. The entry for March 9, 1867, records Moran's attendance, in his official capacity as first secretary of the U. S. Legation in London, at Artemus Ward's funeral.

Muddock, J. E. Preston. *Pages From an Adventurous Life*. 2d ed. London: T. Werner Laurie, n.d. Descriptions of Artemus Ward in London.

Nevins, Allan, comp. and ed. *America Through British Eyes*. New York: Oxford University Press, 1948. (See comment under Berger.)

New York Clipper, The. Issues of 1861–1867. American sporting and theatrical journal with much news about Artemus Ward on his lecture tours.

New York Sunday Mercury, The. Issues of 1862–66. Another prolific source of news about Artemus Ward.

Nock, Albert Jay. Preface (pp. 7–26) to *Selected Works of Artemus*

Ward. (See under Ward, Artemus.) An appreciation of Artemus Ward's intellectual qualities by a perceptive essayist, editor, and educator.

Odell, George C. D. *Annals of the New York Stage.* 15 vols. New York: Columbia University Press, 1927–1949. Artemus Ward's lectures were considered theatrical performances; they are chronicled in this and in the "show-business" journals of the day.

Paine, Albert Bigelow. *Mark Twain, a Biography.* 3 vols. New York: Harper & Brothers Publishers, 1912.

Parry, Albert. *Garrets and Pretenders.* New York: Dover Publications, 1960. A prime source of information on the group that gathered in Pfaff's restaurant, New York, in the early 1860s.

Pearson, Hesketh. *Gilbert, His Life and Strife.* London: Methuen & Co., 1957.

———. *Gilbert and Sullivan, a Biography.* London: Hamish Hamilton, 1935. Although the association between W. S. Gilbert and Artemus Ward, touched upon in these books, was brief, one likes to think that traces of the Ward style of nonsense found their way into the great comic operas that began appearing a few years after Ward's death.

Perkins, J. R. *Trails, Rails and War; the Life of General G. M. Dodge.* Indianapolis: Bobbs-Merrill Company, 1929. President Lincoln enjoys an Artemus Ward story on p. 154.

Quinn, Arthur Hobson. *Edgar Allan Poe, a Critical Biography.* New York: D. Appleton-Century Company, 1941. Artemus Ward's defense of Poe found ample justification in this work about the poet, published eighty-three years later.

Reed, John Q. *"Artemus Ward, A Critical Study."* Ph.D. dissertation, State University of Ohio, 1955. Publication no. 12,120 (bound reprint) in Doctoral Dissertation Series. Ann Arbor, Mich: University Microfilms, 1967. A comprehensive study of Artemus Ward as an observer and critic of his age, a humorous writer, and a comic lecturer. Dr. Reed concludes that the quality of Ward's humor assures him a secure place in the annals of American humor and at least a minor place in American literature. Contains a good checklist of Ward's writings.

Robertson, Thomas William. Introduction to *Artemus Ward's Lecture.* (See under Ward, Artemus.)

Root, Frank A., and Connelley, William E. *The Overland Stage Line to California.* Topeka, Kans.: published by the authors, 1901. (See comment under Hafen.)

Ruthrauff, C. C. "Artemus Ward at Cleveland." *Scribner's Monthly* 16 (October 1878):785–91.

Ryder, James F. "Recollections of Artemus Ward." *Century Illustrated Monthly Magazine* 63 (November 1901):151–55.

———. *Voigtlander and I in Pursuit of Shadow Catching.* Cleveland: Cleveland Printing and Publishing Co., 1902.

Sala, George Augustus. Introduction to *Artemus Ward His Travels.* London: George Routledge and Sons, n.d.

———. *My Diary in America in the Midst of War.* 2 vols. London: Tinsley Brothers, 1865.

Sandburg, Carl. *Abraham Lincoln.* 4 vols. New York: Harcourt, Brace & Company, 1939. Many anecdotes of Lincoln's enjoying Artemus Ward's stories.

Seitz, Don C. *Artemus Ward, A Biography and Bibliography.* New York: Harper & Brothers Publishers, 1919.

———. "Artemus Ward, His Home and Family." *Scribner's Monthly* 22 (May 1881):46–53.

———. "Artemus Ward Letters." (See under Ward, Artemus.)

Don C. Seitz was collecting material on Artemus Ward for more than thirty-five years. His 1919 book, although journalistic in style and jumbled in its extensive bibliography, has undoubtedly been the basis and beginning point for all subsequent writers about Artemus Ward. In the foreword to this book, Mr. Seitz said he delayed his biography for many years in the hope of securing "several hundred" letters supposedly written by Artemus Ward to one of his early managers, Charles A. Shaw, who had given them to his wife. Mrs. Shaw intended to make a book out of them, but after her death, no trace of the letters could be found. The present author reviewed the correspondence related to this matter in the Seitz papers at Princeton, reinstituted the search, and found four pieces of Artemus Ward material that had appeared in the estate of a deceased nephew of Mrs. Shaw. I am hoping to arrange their transfer to a public depository, where they will be available for reference. The rest of the "several hundred" letters, which Charles Shaw told Seitz contained much that was funnier than any of Ward's published material, remains undiscovered, if it still exists.

Shaw, Archer H. *The Plain Dealer—One Hundred Years in Cleveland.* New York: Alfred A. Knopf, 1942.

Smith, Charles Henry. *Bill Arp's Scrap Book.* Atlanta: J. P. Harrison & Co., 1884.

Smith, Henry Nash, ed. *Mark Twain of the Enterprise*. Berkeley and Los Angeles: University of California Press, 1957.

Smith J. Eugene. *One Hundred Years of Hartford's Courant*. New Haven: Yale University Press, 1949. Information on lyceums, lectures, and attitudes toward actors and acting.

Smith, Sydney. *The Wit and Wisdom of the Rev. Sydney Smith*. New York: A. C. Armstrong & Son, 1880.

Spielman, M. H. *The History of Punch*. New York: Cassell Publishing Company, 1895.

Stedman, Laura, and Gould, George M. *Life and Letters of Edmund Clarence Stedman*. 2 vols. New York: Moffat, Yard and Company, 1910.

Stern, Madeleine B. *Imprints on History*. Bloomington: Indiana University Press, 1956. Information on Ward's first book publisher, George W. Carleton.

Stickney, Charles O. "It Was a Memorable Scene." *Boston Sunday Herald*. 17 February 1901.

———. "Maine Stories of Artemus Ward." *Lewiston Journal Magazine*, (Maine), 4–8 April, 1908.

Strauss, G. L. M. *Reminiscences of an Old Bohemian*. 2 vols. London: Tinsley Brothers, 1882.

Trent, W. P. "A Retrospect of American Humor." *Century Illustrated Monthly Magazine* 63 (November 1901):45–64.

Trollope, Frances. *Domestic Manners of the Americans*. Ed. Donald Smalley. New York: Alfred A. Knopf, 1949. (See comment under Berger.)

Trowbridge, John Townsend. *My Own Story, With Recollections of Noted Persons*. Boston: Houghton, Mifflin & Company; Cambridge: The Riverside Press, 1903. Glimpses of Artemus Ward as a young printer in Boston.

Turner, Matthew Freke. "Artemus Ward and the Humorists of America." *New Quarterly Magazine* 6 (April–July, 1876):198–220.

Twain, Mark [Samuel Clemens]. Author's National Edition, The Writings of Mark Twain. New York: Harper & Brothers Publishers. Vols. 7 and 8, *Roughing It*, 1913; vol. 19, *Sketches New and Old*, 1917; vol. 22, *Literary Essays*, 1899.

———. *Mark Twain's Autobiography*. With introduction by Albert Bigelow Paine. 2 vols. New York: Harper & Brothers Publishers, 1924.

———. *Mark Twain's Letters*. Arranged with comment by Albert

Bigelow Paine. 2 vols. New York: Harper & Brothers Publishers, 1917.

——. *Mark Twain's Notebook*. With comments by Albert Bigelow Paine. New York: Harper & Brothers, 1935.

——. *Mark Twain's Speeches*. With introduction by W. D. Howells. New York: Harper & Brothers Publishers, 1910.

U. S. Congress, Senate. *A Report on the Effect of International Copyright Law in the United States*. 56th Cong. 2d sess. Document no. 87. Washington: GPO, 1901. (See comment under Briggs.)

Vanity Fair. New York. Issues of 31 December 1859 to 4 July 1863.

Walker, Franklin. *San Francisco's Literary Frontier*. New York: Alfred A. Knopf, 1939.

Wallace, Frederick T. *Men and Events of Half a Century*. Cleveland: Cleveland Evangelical Association, 1882.

Ward, Artemus [Charles Farrar Brown(e)]. *Artemus Ward's Best Stories*. With introduction by W. D. Howells, editing and biographical notes by Clifton Johnson, New York: Harper & Brothers Publishers, 1912.

——. *Artemus Ward, His Book*. New York: G. W. Carleton & Co., 1862.

——. *Artemus Ward (His Travels) Among the Mormons*. Edited by Edward P. Hingston. London: John Camden Hotten, 1865.

——. *Artemus Ward's Lecture*. Edited by T. W. Robertson and Edward P. Hingston. London: John Camden Hotten; New York: G. W. Carleton & Co., 1869.

——. "Artemus Ward Letters." Complied by Don C. Seitz. *American Collector* (February 1927):195–98.

——. *Artemus Ward in London*. New York: G. W. Carleton & Co: London: S. Low, Son & Co., 1867.

——. *Complete Works of Artemus Ward*. With biographical sketch by Melville D. Landon. Rev. ed. New York: G. W. Dillingham Co., Publishers, 1901.

——. *The Letters of Artemus Ward to Charles E. Wilson, 1858–1861*. Cleveland: The Rowfant Club, 1900.

——. Letters at Buffalo and Erie County Public Library, Buffalo; University of California, Berkeley (The Bancroft Library, courtesy of the Mark Twain Project); Columbia University, New York (Typographic Library Manuscripts, Rare Book and Manuscript Library); Harvard University, by permission of the Houghton Library; Historical Society of Pennsylvania (Dreer, Gratz, and other collections), Philadelphia; Illinois State Historical Library, Springfield; Anthony Collection, Rare Book and Manuscript Division, The New York Public Library, Astor, Lenox and Tilden Foundation; University of Virginia Library (Charles Farrar Browne Collection [#7476], Clifton Waller Barrett Library), Charlottesville; Waterford Historical Society, Waterford, Maine; and, in private possession, Ruth E. Rounds, Waterford, Maine.

————. *Selected Works of Artemus Ward.* Edited with introduction by Albert J. Nock. New York: Albert & Charles Boni, 1924. Nock saw Artemus Ward as a "first-class critic of society," and said "he has lived . . . by precisely the same power that gave a more robust longevity to Cervantes and Rebelais."

Ware, Eugene F. *The Indian War of 1864.* Topeka, Kans.: Crane & Company, 1911. (See comment under Hafen.)

Watson, Aaron. *The Savage Club.* London: T. Fisher Unwin, 1907.

Watterson, Henry. *"Marse Henry" An Autobiography.* 2 vols. New York: George H. Doran Company, 1919.

Wells, Carolyn, ed. *An Outline of Humor.* New York: G. P. Putnam's Sons, 1923.

Werner, M. R. *Barnum.* New York: Harcourt, Brace and Company, 1923. Artemus Ward, the "Old Showman" of the printed page, had marked similarities to Barnum. When Ward's creator himself became a showman, he sometimes sought Barnum's advice.

Wheatley, Henry B. *Round About Piccadilly and Pall Mall.* 4 vols. London: Smith, Elder & Co., 1870. Information about Egyptian Hall, where Artemus Ward lectured in London.

Williams, Stanley T. "Artemus the Delicious." *Virginia Quarterly Review* 28 (Spring, 1952):214–27.

Winsor, Justin, ed. *The Memorial History of Boston.* 4 vols. Boston: James R. Osgood and Company, 1881. (See comment under Branch.)

Woodbury, Charles J. "Artemus Ward at Springfield, Massachusetts." *Century Illustrated Monthly Magazine,* n.s. 41 (February 1902):636–37.

Index

Canada tour, 130
Carleton, George W., 57, 93, 95, 113, 126
Carncross & Dixey, 67, 69
Carpet-Bag, 21, 22, 23
Carson City (Nevada), 79
Chadbourn, Albion, 151, 154
Chaucer, Geoffrey, 22
Chicago, 10, 64
Christy, George, 69
Churchill, Winston, 166
Cincinnati, 23, 70, 71
Civil War, the, 13, 37, 75, 113, 142, 166
Clapp, Henry, 35, 36, 92
Clare, Ada, 37
Clemens, Samuel, 22, 26, 41, 80–81. *See also* Twain, Mark
Cleveland, 14, 15, 24
Cleveland Daily Plain Dealer, 1, 3, 4, 8, 14, 24, 27, 32, 33, 81
Clewline, Charley, 22
Colton, "Dr." Gardner Q., 67
Comic writing, 22–23
Copyright laws, 127
Cottonwood Springs station, 110

Daily Territorial Enterprise, 79, 80, 81, 83, 84, 85, 89
Daly, John Augustin, 129–30
Davis, Jefferson, 132, 133
Davis, Jerome, 106
Denver, 108
Derby, George H. (John Phoenix and John P. Squibob), 22, 23
Deutschland, the, 162, 166
Dickens, Charles, 12, 21, 37
Dodge, Ossian E., 33
Douglas, Stephen A., 3, 4
Downing, Jack (pseud. of Seba Smith), 22, 23
Dug Way station, 104
Dumas, the elder, 37, 63

Eastman, C. J. F., 60–61
Editors' and Publishers' Association, 24
Emancipation Proclamation, 3
Emerson, Ralph Waldo, 39, 45

Farrar, Calvin (grandfather), 15, 17
Farrar, Calvin (uncle), 19
Fatout, Paul, 93
Fields, Annie, 45–46
Fields, James T., 45, 46
Fitzwhistle, Enoch, 22
Franklin Festival, the, 29

Fredericksburg, battle of, 3, 64, 65
Freequill, Fred, 22

Gilbert, W. S., 147, 148, 154
Gohdes, Clarence, 166
Golden Era, 73, 74, 76
Goodman, Joseph T., 80, 81, 83, 84, 85, 86, 97, 163, 164
Gough, John B., 29
Graham, Jared, 81, 82
Gray, J. W., 24, 27, 33
Greeley, Horace, 35, 39
Griswold, Rev. Rufus W., 6

Hale, Edward Everett, 28
Halpine, Charles G., 22
Hanks, Charles, 4
Harte, Bret, 26, 73, 74, 76, 77, 96, 166
Harwood, Jeffrey, 163
Hawthorne, Nathaniel, 16, 45
Heenan, John C., 38, 82
Hingston, E. P., 68–80, 85, 89, 98–111, 113, 114, 115, 121, 127, 141, 142, 156, 160, 161, 162
Hobbes, Thomas, 65
Holland, Josiah Gilbert, 123
Holmes, Oliver Wendell, 45, 46, 96, 166
Hood, Tom, 148
Hotten, John Camden, 98, 126–28, 149, 156
Howells, W. D., 5, 26, 90, 94, 139–40
Humor (American) 21–22, 26, 51, 126
Humor (English) 126, 143, 165

Indian "mid-air tomb," 110, 161
Indian War of 1864, 110
Irving, Washington, 166

Jackson, Andrew, 23
James, Henry, 45
Jefferson, Joseph, 149–51, 157

Kant, Immanuel, 50

Landon, Melville D., 132
Lectures, 28–29, 39, 51, 67, 123
Leland, Charles G., 33, 35, 54, 149
Lemon, Mark, 146
Lincoln, Abraham, 1, 2, 3, 4, 5, 30–33, 65, 124, 167
Lind, Jenny, 67
London, 99, 142, 145–48, 157, 159
London reviews, 153–55, 166–67
Longfellow, Henry Wadsworth, 45, 71, 111

Strauss, G. L. M., 71
Swinburne, Algernon, 37, 63, 149

Taylor, Bayard, 26
Theater, 27, 28
Ticknor & Fields, 45, 63
Tiffin (Ohio), 23
Toledo (Ohio), 10, 23, 29
Tom Pond, 61, 63
Trowbridge, John T., 22
Twain, Mark, 22, 35, 41, 81, 83, 84, 85, 86, 106, 123, 136, 139, 166; career, 90–91; "The Celebrated Jumping Frog of Calaveras County," 35, 92, 93, 95, 98; childhood, 87; as a lecturer, 93–95, 96–97; in London, 97, 98–99; nature, 89; writing, 91–92, 94; youth, 87–88. See also Clemens, Samuel

Vanity Fair, 1, 29, 32, 33, 34, 35, 42, 56, 57, 62, 88, 135
Virginia City (Nevada), 79–86, 88, 89, 100, 101, 152

Walker, Franklin, 77
Ward, Artemas, 8
Ward, Artemas, (as Old Showman), 1; in Augusta, 136–37; in Boston, 43–46; in Canada, 130; character, 87, 122, 123–24; childhood, 11, 87; in Columbus, 135; creation, 7, 8, 24; death, 161; in Denver, 108; at the Egyptian Hall (London), 151–54, 155, 156; fictional family, 11; fictional home, 26; final illness, 160–61; fondness for children, 59–60; friendship with Mark Twain, 89–90; funeral, 162, 167; health, 105–6, 121, 130, 141–42, 150–51, 157–59; humor, 50–53, 76–77, 87–88, 97, 113, 119–20, 159; imitators, 139–40; influence on Mark Twain, 90, 92, 94–95; lectures, 29–32, 39, 40, 46, 52–53, 55–58, 67, 72–73, 82–83, 101–2, 106, 113, 121–22; letters, 5, 8–11, 62; in Louisville, 122; on marriage, 59; misspelling, 11–12, 77, 139; in Montgomery, 135; in New Orleans, 132–34; obituaries, 162–65; panoramas, 112–13, 114, 116, 118–20, 130–32; in Philadelphia, 67–68; physical appearance, 68, 70, 108, 111, 115, 140, 145; popularity, 26–27, 57, 65–66; quality of voice, 52; reputation in England, 12, 126, 142–43, 145, 146, 154–56, 163–65; return to New York, 111; return to U.S., 166; in Richmond, 137; in Salt Lake City, 104–7, 113; in San Francisco, 73–74; spirit, 12–13; summers, 60–61; travels in America, 136; use of name "Artemus Ward," 41; in Virginia City, 88, 100; war service, 134; on the West, 111. Books: *Artemus Ward, His Book,* 2, 3, 8, 32, 56–57, 63, 65, 72, 104, 126, 127, 167; *Artemus Ward, His Travels,* 92, 107–8, 124, 126; *Artemus Ward (His Travels) Among the Mormons,* 126. Lectures: "The Children in the Wood" ("The Babes in the Wood"), 39, 43, 53, 56, 64, 72, 74, 91, 106, 138; "Sixty Minutes in Africa," 64, 65. Letters: "Artemus Ward on His Visit to Abe Lincoln," 30–32; "Forts," 29–30. Panorama: "Artemus Ward Among the Mormons," 114–17, 120, 149. Stories: "High Handed Outrage at Utica," 2, 32; "Sary Jane," 3.
Warhurst, Thomas, 121
Warner, Charles Dudley, 96
Warren, William, 149
Washington, D. C. 62–63
Waterford (Maine), 15, 59, 60–61, 63, 141, 163
Watterson, Henry, 155–56, 157, 158–59
Webb, C. H., 96
Western Orator, The, 29
Wheeling (West Virginia), 9
Whitman, Walt, 35, 36, 37, 136
Wilkes, Charles, 142
Winter, William, 36
Wood, Frank, 40, 56
Wright, William (pseud. Dan de Quille), 81, 83, 84, 85, 86, 88

Yonkers (New York), 121
Young, Brigham, 105, 106, 116